Two Japanese Villages

Matsunagi	Kurusu
A Japanese Mountain Community	A Japanese Agricultural Community
John B. Cornell	*Robert J. Smith*

GREENWOOD PRESS, PUBLISHERS
NEW YORK

EDITOR'S NOTE

With this the fifth issue of its Occasional Papers, the University of Michigan Center for Japanese Studies has embarked upon a new plan of publication. Instead of the former practice of including in each issue papers drawn from a variety of fields, this issue and those which follow will be devoted to one or more substantial monographs within a single field. The former biennial publication schedule has also been replaced by a more flexible one. Hereafter each issue will be announced separately.

Occasional Papers No. 5 contains two monographs representing the anthropological phase of the research undertaken at the Center's field station in Okayama, Japan. Special thanks for the preparation of the manuscripts for publication go to Dr. Robert P. Weeks of the College of Engineering and Dr. Richard K. Beardsley.

PREFACE

Since 1950 members of the University of Michigan Center for Japanese Studies, operating from the Center's field station in Okayama City on the Inland Sea in southwestern Japan, have undertaken the study of a number of Japanese communities, materials from which are now in the process of analysis. This work has focused, for the most part, on the elementary community unit in the social structure of rural Japan, the buraku. The two monographs presented here are based on field work done by the authors, Robert J. Smith and John B. Cornell, in two particular buraku, Kurusu and Matsunagi. Smith was in Kurusu from September, 1951 through August, 1952. Cornell was in Matsunagi from October, 1950 through August, 1951.

These two studies, written originally as doctoral dissertations and revised here for presentation in a combined volume, bring together essentially different approaches to the same kind of social unit. Cornell's main concern is with the social and kinship aspects of buraku life; Smith deals with the general picture of life in a buraku. Both the specialized and the more general approach, it is hoped, will contribute to an understanding of the rural scene. Each report, in its own way, examines a buraku against a background of anthropological and sociological theory about the life of common people, and in this respect the two studies are alike, diverging and becoming complementary only in respect to details of presentation.

An important element of the theoretical background referred to here is the concept of the "folk society." This concept, originating in Latin American studies and refined and brought to maturity through other field studies in various world areas, has become a useful tool for study of the way of life in rural Japan. The two community studies brought together in this volume have much of the flavor of Redfield's Yucatan studies or of various other descriptions of Central and South American folk community life. But because they are set in a Japanese cultural context, and because they examine peasant communities in a rapidly industrializing society, the present studies provide a further test of the usefulness of this concept.

These two projects were conducted in close sequence but not simultaneously, and neither author knew the other's buraku at first-hand. No systematic comparison of the "feel" of each community is possible. However, the joint publication of the two monographs gives the authors an opportunity to call attention to the similarity at large and in certain details between the two communities, and at the same time to underline differences of a sort which make Matsunagi closer to the "folk society" and Kurusu closer to the "urban society" archetype.

Both Kurusu and Matsunagi, however, are in part self-contained Japanese folk units. They are traditional communities that retain many features of a style of life a century or more old. Part of this folk conservatism is due to sheer isolation, and part to the retarded pace of industrialization in these Inland Sea provinces so remote from the modern industrial centers of Tokyo and Osaka. Yet each community has long been at least indirectly dependent on the commerce and manufacturing of the urban centers in their immediate areas.

Besides this fundamental similarity between the two datum communities, there are more detailed resemblances. Kurusu and Matsunagi are comparable because they may both be regarded as "mountain" or "upland" buraku. Their topography requires an emphasis on dry-field farming not found in the paddy buraku in the lowlands. In addition, the abundance and proximity of forests and of other untillable areas of natural vegetation that seem to

v

engulf the worked fields are a basis for other peculiarly "mountain" industries. They are further comparable because as mountain folk societies they represent the traditional Japanese peasant pattern today, as lowland communities do not. Even though the old extended family groups in the buraku are weaker than formerly, they and other time-hallowed social groupings of kin are better preserved in mountain buraku than elsewhere in Japanese peasant society. This fact indicates an additional value of studies of this sort: they provide a picture of the peasant society virtually as it was before the industrial revolution made the social and economic changes so striking in rural Japan today.

Kurusu is further along in this process of cultural change because, in the first place, it has a more productive setting; much of its income is derived from paddy cultivation and the resultant wealth has given rise to a number of landowners and even landlords. This is in marked contrast to the economic and social egalitarianism of Matsunagi. Kurusu's relations with the nearest city, Takamatsu, are closer than the relations of Matsunagi with its prefectural urban center, Okayama City. The people of Matsunagi continue to rely on the small town trading centers nearby. In gaining a livelihood the Kurusu farmer employs a greater variety of modern power-driven farm machinery than his counterpart in Matsunagi, yet both use the same native kit of tools with which generations of their forebears have tilled the same land. Some of the consequences of the introduction of modern technology can be seen by examining the economic and social contrasts between these two buraku.

Kurusu is a prosperous community by the standards of rural Japan, even though its farmers have had to turn to supplementary activities to maintain the well-being of the household. While the primary social and economic concern is this household unit, Kurusu displays a variety of cooperative groups on the buraku and other levels which indicate the strength of geographical bonds that largely transcend kinship groupings in importance. Conflict between households or individuals seldom is expressed overtly, but underneath the external manifestations of harmony, dissension and feuding are rife.

Matsunagi is not situated on particularly fertile land, but by dint of great effort its people are able to make their fields yield a simple but adequate level of subsistence and several reasonably profitable cash crops in addition. The average farmer tries to do more than just make ends meet; his motives are to benefit his own household and family, not usually any larger group. Individualism of the household groups dominates social relations and vitiates the buraku's sense of unity. This is expressed, too, in the existence of cliques of neighbor households and the presence of comparatively few forms of buraku cooperation; in the general irreverence toward traditional Japanese religious forms; and in the hard drinking and sometimes violent quarreling of these people.

However, the difference in emphasis between these studies is not so much due to the peculiarities of the two communities as to the special research interests of each author. Smith, because of previous experience with research on this topic, developed the problem of technological change and its effect on other parts of Kurusu's folk culture. Cornell had done earlier work on the social organization and social structure of rural Japan and applied this experience to his work in Matsunagi. Because their emphases are different but their content very much alike, it is hoped that these two reports will have a complementary value together that they lacked singly.

The data were collected with the following general requirements in mind: first, that it is essential to furnish detailed observations from which valid generalizations concerning Japanese rural life can be made; second, that these studies were to be made within the general framework of the program of the University of Michigan Center for Japanese Studies, whose emphasis has been the gathering of comparative materials from a variety of hamlet types in southwestern Japan.

The criteria for the selection of the communities studied were four in number:

1. The community should be from twenty-five to thirty-five households in number.

2. The community should be geographically distinguishable from other neighboring buraku but not necessarily isolated.

3. The community should be a sufficient distance from an urban center so as not to be part of an immediate urban social, occupational or service complex.

4. The community should be "typical" only in the sense that no outcaste (eta, hinin, sanka) community be chosen.

Techniques employed were entirely those of unstructured interviewing and observation; neither author was in a position to use the survey questionnaire technique which was subsequently utilized in the Center's program, nor did they feel themselves qualified to administer projective tests. Whenever it seemed appropriate or important to do so, each participated in activities of the villagers and attended weddings and funerals as well as other religious ceremonies. Each used a camera, and although initially both made it a rule to take no photographs without permission such cautions proved unnecessary after a short period of getting acquainted. Prints of these photographs proved to be very popular and were positive aids in maintaining good rapport.

In such small communities it is possible to talk to almost everyone, but as is invariably the case in this kind of work a few local people came to be friends and principal informants. Some of them are mentioned in the acknowledgments. First-hand observation was possible virtually everywhere, but possibilities for prolonged conversation and interviews were limited by a number of factors. Some individuals were busy at all seasons of the year, engaging in day labor when not otherwise employed, or working outside the buraku for most of the year. Others simply did not care to talk, either because of personal dislike or distrust of the researchers' motives. It was, of course, those with leisure time, either in slack seasons or throughout the year, who were most readily accessible and who provided much of the data. The authors were everywhere received with courtesy.

Methods of making initial and early contacts were somewhat different. Smith made a two-week general survey of Kagawa Prefecture on foot, by automobile, bus and electric interurban train, finally tentatively selecting Kurusu as one of a number of buraku which were suited to the study plan. Since lines of governmental authority extend fairly clearly from prefectural to village to hamlet level, he went first to the village office of the mura in which Kurusu is located. It was explained to the mayor and other officials that he was an American student interested in rural Japan, and that he wanted to find out about life in a buraku in their area. Smith's connection with the Center for Japanese Studies was made clear, and a Japanese-language newspaper clipping explaining some aspects of the Center's work proved useful. The mayor recommended several people who might be able to offer information about local history, customs and religious practices. One man, the agricultural affairs official in the village office, took an immediate interest in the study and continued to work closely with Smith in the collection of data on agricultural matters. All of the people mentioned by the mayor were contacted within a short time and the purpose of the study was explained to each of them. The sanction of approval from higher political quarters was never again needed, for acceptance was soon forthcoming from several people in Kurusu.

Cornell's initial contacts with Matsunagi were somewhat differently handled. Early in his stay in Okayama, he began to make a study of potentially suitable areas within reach of the city. After a month's survey of the upland and mountain settlements in the southern part of the prefecture, it became clear that the distinctively "mountain" type of community he sought could be found only in the northern, interior part of the prefecture. He was introduced by a Japanese friend in Okayama to Kusama Village, this man's ancestral seat, and to Matsunagi, where his relatives still lived. Kusama in general, and Matsunagi in particular, fitted the "mountain" pattern he had previously found only piecemeal.

After deciding on a place for work, Cornell enlisted the aid of three residents of Niiike, a buraku which was already under intensive study by the Center, and asked them to describe their experiences with Center field workers to a meeting of Matsunagi people. Meanwhile, Cornell was introduced to the village mayor and other local officials by his Japanese friend and obtained their official permission for his study. At the meeting of the buraku people, Cornell and another American colleague spoke, outlining the method of study and objectives. In reply, Matsunagi spokesmen made a formal speech of welcome to the researcher. Thereafter, there was general acceptance of the American stranger and rapport was slowly built up as the people's initial reaction of shyness and discomfiture at being interviewed wore off.

Each locality, thus, was chosen because it was a unit comparable to others under study by the Center and because it presented a situation of broad interest to the researcher. For many years Kurusu had enjoyed rail connections with the main city and thus was no longer the same isolated hill community it had been before the days of rapid transport. Matsunagi was a mountain community as inaccessible by modern transport as any that could be found in the region without abandoning contact with the field station altogether. Because of this difference, Smith emphasized the socio-economic situation as affected by closer contact with the city, while Cornell concentrated on traditional social groupings. But each in the last analysis was concerned with the life of the community as a specimen of folk society. The results are presented here as a contribution to the understanding of Japanese rural life, and as added material for the increased comprehension of world folk society.

Richard K. Beardsley

KURUSU

A JAPANESE AGRICULTURAL COMMUNITY

by

Robert J. Smith

ACKNOWLEDGMENTS

The services of Sato Tetsuo, of Takamatsu City, who acted as guide, translator, and occasional interpreter were particularly helpful during the course of this study.

For their unfailing courtesy and interest my special thanks are due the following residents of Kurusu: Takao Hoen, Tanimoto Hideko, Doi Yoshiko, Takao Kazuyoshi, Aoki Hideko and Matsuura Chizuko. Uehara Masao and Aoi Takashi, both of Yasuhara-mura, also contributed much to my work. The continuing support of Robert B. Hall, Allan R. Holmberg, Alexander H. Leighton and Morris Edward Opler is deeply appreciated.

Robert J. Smith

Ithaca, New York
September, 1955

CONTENTS

ILLUSTRATIONS

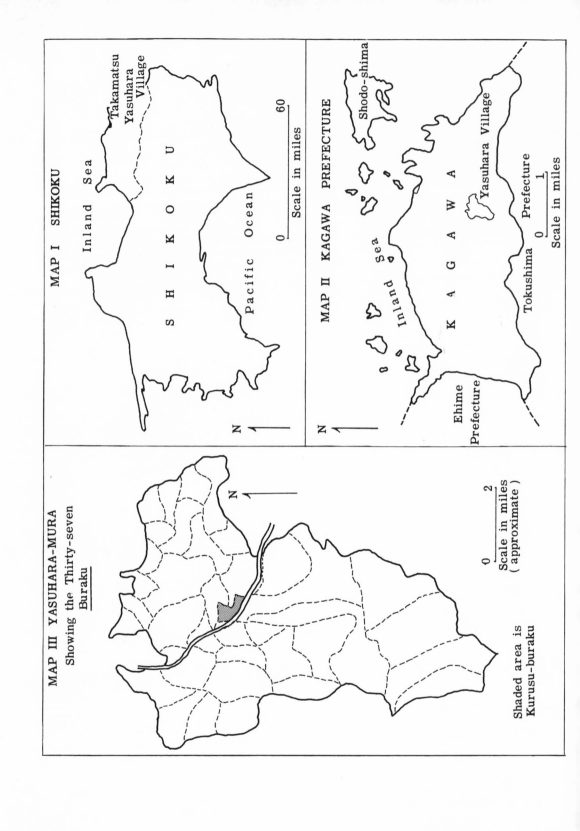

MAP I SHIKOKU

Inland Sea

Takamatsu
Yasuhara
Village

S H I K O K U

Pacific Ocean

0   60
Scale in miles

MAP II KAGAWA PREFECTURE

Shodo-shima

Inland Sea

K A G A W A

Yasuhara Village

Ehime
Prefecture

Tokushima
Prefecture

0   1
Scale in miles

MAP III YASUHARA-MURA
Showing the Thirty-seven
Buraku

N

0   2
Scale in miles
(approximate)

Shaded area is
Kurusu-buraku

Chapter I

KURUSU IN PROFILE

The plains of northern Shikoku offer the traveler from Tokyo a striking contrast to the rural areas of the northern and central regions of Honshu, for there is about them an air of prosperity and well-being not found in many areas in Japan. Even the trip from Taka-matsu to Kurusu on one of the little local buses on a hot July day fails to dim the impression of orderliness and beauty. All along the route row after row of bright green rice plants seem to float in the humid haze of the flooded paddy fields. There is an inflexibility about the greenness of rural Japan in summer which overwhelms those more accustomed to a variety of colors. As the highway lifts south into the foothills of the Shikoku mountains, it is closed in gradually by low, treeless hills which rise steeply on either side of the river along which the highway runs and to whose bank it clings, now on the east, now on the west. Negotiating the right-angle turns onto the narrow bridges is one of the major excitements of the trip from Takamatsu.

The hamlet, or buraku, of Kurusu has nothing to attract the attention of the casual observer; it looks very much like any one of the hundreds of such little communities backed up against the low-lying hills, with its fields spread out between it and the river like a lawn. The warm brown thatched roofs of its houses sit low in the pine and bamboo, and the paddies edge hard against the walls of the yard compounds.

If one's destination is Kurusu, the proper bus stop is that across from the village office. A few yards' walk down the dusty road leads to the large concrete bridge which spans the river bed at right angles to the road. A glance over from the cement railing reveals little more than dry, gray rocks worn by water conspicuously absent now; closer inspection will show that the thin, narrow strips of paddy step straight down the bank almost to the stony river bed, for this is an area hard-pressed for land.

At the far end of the bridge are cherry trees, which are green now like everything else in July, but which were an intense pink-white in their few days of spring flowering. Just beyond them on the right are the low, dark buildings of the sawmill, from which emerge the high whine of the big saw and the smell of newly sawn pine and cypress. For some yards beyond the mill, its sounds and smells dominate all else, but further down the path along which most of the Kurusu houses are strung, the stroller hears music from small radio sets, or conversational banter among women working near the houses. And one's progress past each uncovered night-soil cistern is clearly marked by the characteristic odor of all rural Japan in summer.

The country is quiet, and even the sawmill's complaints recede into the background almost at once. Standing high up behind the houses of Kurusu, one can look out to the south toward the high mountains of the interior of Shikoku, and although there are no considerable vistas, there is a sense of spaciousness. Man has done much to make his mark on the landscape, but his fields and his houses blend unobtrusively into what remains essentially a natural landscape.

From the gardens of the higher houses in the buraku, one can see most of the administrative center of the village, or mura, of Yasuhara: the school buildings, the village office and the commercial establishments which stretch in a line along the main road. Yasuhara-mura consists of much forest and farm land. It is comprised of thirty-seven scattered neighborhoods, or buraku, like Kurusu, all of them varying widely in size and most of them lying at some distance from the administrative heart of the village. These

buraku are social groupings based primarily on residence. They may or may not correspond to political sub-units of the mura called ko-aza. For official purposes, the buraku literally do not exist; they are, however, the major social grouping after the family
for most people in Yasuhara, and many activities are organized along buraku, not ko-aza,
lines.

Today Yasuhara is primarily an agricultural village, although both forestry and local
industry enter into the economic picture. In 1950, the latest date for which figures are
available, Yasuhara had a population of 4,215 comprising 848 households, of which 663
cultivated about 818 acres (3,340 tan) of land, most of which (about 62 percent) was
double-cropped, or made to yield two annual crops. The yield in paddy rice is about 1.8
koku per tan (about 36.8 bushels per acre); for naked barley and wheat it is 1.3 koku per
tan (about 26.7 bushels per acre). Other important crops are Irish potatoes, sweet potatoes, millet, tobacco and garden vegetables. The average amount of land cultivated by
one household in the village is 1.23 acres (slightly more than five tan).

Approximately 4,775 acres of Yasuhara's total area are taken up by forest lands, from
which a variety of products are obtained. During World War II, much of Japan's admira-
bly preserved forests were severely cut over, and Yasuhara suffered heavy damage. Thickly timbered hillsides are now bare slopes and peaks grown over with brush and saplings at
most. The cutting of the evergreen stands presents the most serious problem of reforestation, for with careful handling bamboo forests recover rapidly from depletion. In addition to lumber and bamboo, the forest lands yield bamboo shoots (take-no-ko) and mushrooms (matsu-take), both highly prized as delicacies.

Local industry is small-scale, the most important being the sawmills which produce
staves for boxes, construction materials for building purposes, and wood parts for agricultural machines. Tray manufacture, usually associated with a village sawmill, is of some
importance. Trays are turned on foot-powered lathes, polished by hand and lacquered by
artisans; most of the production goes to the urban centers to the northeast on the main
island of Honshu.

Home industries, like the manufacture of straw rope, mats and bags for fertilizer and
salt, are important sources of cash income for some families. Construction of a dam
about five miles to the south, work on a new prefectural road, and a variety of jobs with
government offices and private concerns in the village provide daily wages for a number of
people.

The commercial and governmental centers of the village are in two buraku along the
highway which runs through Yasuhara. They are Chūtoku and Ayutaki, and contain the village office, the primary and middle schools, the offices of the Agricultural Cooperative
Union, and a number of small business establishments—a hardware store, drug store,
textile shop, restaurant, tobacco shop, a barber shop and a variety of small concerns dealing in toys, fruits, candies, and notions. The owners of these small businesses and the
government employees and day laborers account for the twelve percent of Yasuhara households which derive less than half their income from agricultural pursuits.

From a point just north of the village boundary, the road parallels the Goto River,
running along its west bank. Kurusu lies on the east side of the river, and the small
buraku road is connected to the highway by a large ferro-concrete bridge, called the
Kangetsu Bridge, which spans the river near the Kurusu sawmill. It is a boon to the
area, for it serves the year round, unlike the small footbridges, which wash out in the
rainy season. Heavy animals and carts can move across it from the highway to the
buraku to the east of the river. A few hundred yards in both directions from the bridge
are located the village office, the primary school, middle school, the agricultural

cooperative offices and plant, several commercial establishments, and other less important offices. Kurusu people do not have far to go for goods and services not obtainable in
the buraku itself.

There is a bus line which operates on the main road through Yasuhara, running between Takamatsu, eleven miles to the north, and Shionoe-mura, the next village south
of Yasuhara. Buses run approximately once an hour (with an extra express for the morning and evening rush hours) from 6:45 a.m. to 7:45 p.m. (northbound) and from 8:00 a.m.
to 10:00 p.m. (southbound). The fare is about fifty yen to Takamatsu, and the round trip
takes just under one hour. Early morning and late afternoon buses are very crowded, and
village people complain that the ride is long and uncomfortable, especially if one has children or much luggage. Although most of the buses were built for thirty passengers, fifty
or more often are packed in for the long journey.

Transportation in Kagawa Prefecture was better before the war than it is at the present time. This is certainly the case in this area, for until 1941 there was a rail line con-
necting Shionoe with Takamatsu. Each of the six gasoline powered cars seated forty persons with standing room for many more. This kind of line is called gasorin-michi (gasoline road). Although the time required for the trip south was about that now needed by the
buses, people still speak wistfully of the greater comfort of the pre-war facilities.

Although there actually was a station and waiting area for the rail line in the buraku
itself, Kurusu people seem to have received almost no direct economic benefits from its
existence. This was not the case for the village as a whole, however, for the gasoline
cars made the area accessible to tourists and vacationers who came for the cherry blossoms and to the hot spring spa in Shionoe. Taxi companies flourished in the 1930's, and
business seems to have been very good for shops and restaurants, both of which have since
declined greatly in numbers.

The decision to abandon the line was made in 1941 when it became apparent that the
company could no longer obtain sufficient gasoline to keep the cars in operation. In addition, it was impossible to effect badly needed repairs on the line's equipment, most of
which had been placed in service late in 1929. Parts were not obtainable and new equipment was not being manufactured. As a result of these pressures, service was suspended
and the facilities of the line dismantled. The tracks were taken up and sold to the For-
mosa Sugar Company (Taiwan Seito); the cars themselves went to Mukden, capital of Manchuria, where they were electrified for use as city street cars. The twelve station buildings were leveled; all that is visible today at the site of the former Kurusu station are
some concrete foundations around which and within which are planted vegetables. Of the
ten bridges which carried the tracks across the winding Goto River, only the concrete pil-
ings still stand in the river bed.

Although the buraku seems to have derived little direct economic benefit from the existence of the line, the people of Kurusu did regain a substantial amount of farm land as a
result of its removal. The pattern of buraku fields (see Map VIII) shows clearly where
the right-of-way once cut across some of the community's best paddy lands. Apparently,
land which had been purchased for the right-of-way was in most cases resold to the households who had owned it originally. Other land on the right-of-way, but not in the cultiva-
ble area, has reverted to the village and serves as a good path from Kurusu to its neighbor buraku, Takabatake, replacing the older narrow trail.

By far the most important effect which the removal of the line has had on the people
of Kurusu, at least in their view, has been the decrease in contacts with other communities, especially Takamatsu. Travel, formerly undertaken with little difficulty, is now so
troublesome that trips are made much less often. This reduction in mobility is reflected

in the fact that young adults of Kurusu go to Takamatsu only seven or eight times a year on the average; many older people never go further than a two or three hour walk from their homes.

A partial compensation has been the great post-war increase in the number of bicycles owned in Kurusu. In 1950, seventeen individuals paid the 200 yen bicycle tax; only two households had two bicycles. In the warm seasons, the trip to Takamatsu can easily be made by bicycle, but since the return is uphill for most of the eleven miles, even the bus is considered more convenient. According to Kurusu people, only two households owned bicycles prior to 1945; that they are so common now is a good indication of the use to which the cash income of the post-war period of prosperity has been put.

Electricity came to Kurusu about thirty years ago. Today the power is weak and occasionally fails, but it is generally adequate to meet the ordinary needs of the community. Every house has electricity, which is paid for by the number of outlets rather than by the number of watt-hours consumed.

There are fifteen radios for Kurusu's eighteen dwellings, but the use to which they are put varies greatly from house to house. The program which probably is most generally listened to is the weather news, with musical programs a close second. Young people prefer Western or Western-style music, while older people listen chiefly to Japanese forms like naniwa-bushi. It is not unusual to play the radio very loudly, partly so that it can be heard by people working near the house, partly simply because high volume seems to be considered desirable.

Most of the trips which young people make to Takamatsu are for the purpose of attending the movies. Tastes in films tend toward Japanese-language productions, although every young adult has seen a number of foreign films as well. Movies also come through the countryside, brought by organizations which show them for a small fee at village schools or public halls. In Yasuhara, these itinerant film shows are usually presented at the middle school. The Youth Club (seinendan) of the village began sponsoring a monthly film in 1951, for which they planned to charge 40 yen a ticket in an effort to raise money for athletic and other equipment, but they seem to have met with indifferent success. About once a month a free film sponsored by the Shikoku Press is shown in the village. Most of these itinerant films are five or six years old, and usually are Japanese period pictures (jidai-geki) or American cowboy films (seibu-geki). Young people report that not many older people attend foreign films because they cannot read fast enough to follow the written sub-titles. A total of from three to four hundred people attend all the itinerant film programs given in Yasuhara in one month.

Mail is delivered to the house, or to a family's "mail box," a small cylinder of bamboo put up in a central place in Kurusu. Deliveries are twice a day during the week and once on Sunday, and are made by bicycle from the main post office in Seki, a buraku about a mile and a half north of Kurusu.

About 3:30 p.m. every day a man comes through Kurusu on a bicycle to deliver newspapers and magazines to subscribers. Subscription figures shift frequently, but about one-half of the Kurusu households ordinarily take a daily paper, and almost every adult in the buraku occasionally reads a paper. The most popular newspaper is the local Kagawa one, published in Takamatsu and carrying a high percentage of prefectural news. Since both the papers and the news they contain do circulate throughout the buraku, subscription figures give an incomplete indication of the extent to which current news is sought and obtained.

Only three or four families are on the magazine subscription lists at any one time, and then usually for home, women's or children's publications like Ie-no Hikari (Light of

the Home) and Fujin-no Tomo (The Woman's Companion). Occasionally an odd copy of
other magazines may be bought, usually by young people; these include the Japanese language edition of the Readers' Digest and the many general-interest farm periodicals. Children buy cheap, colored picture books, not unlike "comic books," which tell the stories of
ancient Japanese heroes, fairy tales or Western tales like "Snow White and the Seven
Dwarfs" and Aesop's Fables.

Telephones have been in the village for at least twenty-five years, but until 1950
Kurusu itself had none. In that year the owner of the sawmill had an instrument installed
in his home, but when it is necessary for someone from the buraku to make a call, he
still goes to use the telephone in the village office. Other government and business establishments in the village have telephones also, but these are seldom used for personal calls.
Actually, it is rare for anyone from Kurusu to use the telephone; sometimes in the event
of a death, distant relatives may be notified by telephone, but calls in other connections
are not common. Telegrams may be sent from the village post office, and incoming mes-
sages are delivered by bicycle from there. In the twelve months I was in the village, no
Kurusu resident sent or received a telegram.

The cliché that news travels fast describes the situation in the buraku rather well.
The best evidence of this rapid "grape-vining" was the rapidity with which word of my
doings traveled. Kurusu people were especially well-informed of things I had done in
other parts of the village, and usually not long after the event. The accuracy with which
my activities were reported was striking, and there was seldom a lapse of more than a
day or two. People would know to whom I had talked and about what subjects, a fact
which sometimes worked to my disadvantage, since if I had been talking with an unpopular
person, certain individuals in Kurusu would remonstrate with me, objecting that I would
not get the truth from him. Old feuds and jealousies sometimes came to the surface if I
was seen too frequently with the "wrong people," and I was often told unequivocally that I
was wasting my time in such company.

Very little happens in the realm of private affairs that does not find its way very
quickly into general conversation in the village. Gossip is rife and the power of waru-
kuchi (literally, "evil mouth," hence slander, abuse, calumny) is clearly recognized. Pre-
dilection for back-biting is regarded as a highly undesirable trait in an individual, but the
passing on of interesting gossip is a pleasant and all but universal occupation. The villager, for all his widening world, is still primarily concerned with his immediate surroundings.

Much of the religious activity in Kurusu centers on Yasuhara where there are three
major Shinto shrines, two served by the same priest. Today the largest and most important of these is the Nishitani Hachiman Jinja, dedicated to the "God of War," in which
since 1916 over thirty gods have been enshrined. In that year, the merger of a large
number of small buraku shrines with the Hachiman Shrine was effected by government
order, for it was felt that the small number of parishioners for each of the scattered
shrines made upkeep and proper observances difficult. The Hachiman Shrine, which was
established about seven hundred years ago during the Kamakura period, remained relatively unimportant in the village until its absorption of the smaller shrines. At that time it
was raised from the status of village shrine (son-sha) to the rank of county shrine (gō-sha).
These ranks did not indicate the nature of the area of jurisdiction of a shrine, but were
used rather for determining the amount of subsidy to be paid by the central government
towards its maintenance. Actually, government funds were never very important on this
level, for less than one-fifteenth of the expenses of the shrine were met by that source.
Dependence was chiefly on the donations of parishioners, which were collected with some
regularity until 1945, when shrine worship declined sharply with the end of World War II.
Hachiman, usually called the "God of War" in English, actually is regarded by the villagers
as the agricultural deity of the village and as such is responsible for the protection of crops.

There are four Buddhist temples in the village, two of which are of the Shinshu sect, one Shingon, and the fourth Tendai. The last of these is very small and seems virtually to have ceased to function. The population of Yasuhara is about equally divided between the Shingon and the Shinshu, but the largest and most important of the temples is Shingon. Shikoku is one of the strongholds of this sect, for its founder Kobo Daishi worked for many years on the island.

Only the very old go to the temple for prayers or services of any sort, the single exception being the occasion of the memorial services for the war dead of the village. At least one representative from each family which lost a member in the war attends this service. It is held at the Shingon temple, which is the only one large enough to accommodate the mourners. Although it has almost ceased to be a religious occasion, the Buddhist Bon Dance (performed during the so-called Festival of the Dead, or Festival of Lanterns) is held on a village-wide basis in the yard of the village primary school, the only uncultivated flat area large enough to accommodate the participants. Dancers from almost every buraku perform in the dancing circle, and recently a prize has been awarded to the most accomplished group.

As we have seen above, Kurusu is one of thirty-seven buraku which serve a variety of social functions, although they have no legal status. The manner in which these buraku are related socially to the village unit, and the ways in which the administration of the village uses the buraku deserve careful consideration.

Perhaps one of the best examples of these relationships is afforded by the village elections. Ordinarily a buraku tries to vote one of its own people into the village assembly, but if it is too small to do this effectively, an attempt will be made to reach an agreement with another small buraku whereby both will vote for a coalition candidate. People of a hamlet almost always vote for the approved candidate for office, unless very strong family ties indicate the necessity for voting for a relative who is running in another district. In pre-war days it was not uncommon for 100 percent of the voters to turn out. Voting percentages are still very high even since the franchise has been extended to all adults. Frequently there is no contest for the office of mayor, but if there is, buraku solidarity is less marked than in the voting for village assemblyman.[1]

Records of many sorts are maintained by the village office (yakuba), including vital statistics—registration of birth, marriage, adoption, divorce, change of residence, and death. The records of each ko-aza are kept in separate volumes in the office. There are also maps of each ko-aza, on which are recorded every piece of land in the community by number, official value, quality and type. In connection with the map, a large record-book is maintained, in which the name of the owner, the kind of land, tax assessments, official values, land transfers, and changes in use are recorded. This record is also maintained for individual ko-aza, and as in the case of the family register, only a single copy exists. Taxes are paid at the village office, except for the national income tax, which is sent directly to the government by the individual paying the tax. There are numerous other local taxes for which complete records of payment are kept at the yakuba.

For liaison with the village office, the buraku elects three officials, the head of the hamlet (now buraku-chō, but formerly sewa-gakari), the tax collector (zeikin-gakari) and the agricultural head (kairyō-kumiai-chō). The duties of this last official are few, and most of his contact is actually with the Agricultural Cooperative Union (nōgyō kyōdo kumiai). This organization is also very important in relations between the buraku and the mura, for it serves the entire mura. It handles the government crop requisition program, processes grains for farmer-members, performs credit and banking functions, gives advice on agricultural matters including services like soil testing, retails agricultural equipment, clothing and household utensils, and provides details of irrigation subsidies and insurance for farmers. Almost every farmer in Yasuhara is a member of this organization, which maintains separate records for each ko-aza.

Concerning the buraku's connections with both the yakuba and the agricultural cooperative, Ward says,

"These post-war years have been characterized by relative economic and social chaos in Japan and have (seen efforts) to put into effect nationwide economic and financial programs of the complexity and dimensions of the rationing and crop-requisitioning systems. The buraku have constituted the rural administrative termini of both these latter systems and have been most useful to the harassed village officials."[2]

Religious ties within the village are close, at least insofar as the people of every buraku are served by the three shrines and four temples, and by the priests from these institutions. All residents of the village are parishioners of one shrine and one temple, and although many people maintain contact with temples outside Yasuhara, all patronize shrines within the boundaries of the village. The annual Buddhist war-dead ceremony is a village affair, at which each buraku is officially represented by one individual. Although there are also separate buraku memorial services for their war dead, all who lost someone in the war ordinarily attend the big all-village service also. The major festivals at the Shinto shrines are village observances, sponsored by individual buraku in turn.

Another important unifying factor is public education; all village children must attend school for nine years, six at the primary level and three in middle school. No distinctions are made according to buraku membership, although children do tend to travel to and from school in buraku groups. The Parent Teachers Association is an all-village organization, again without buraku distinctions.

The mura has only one policeman. His duties are few, for if a crime is not too serious to be kept quiet, it will be settled without police aid. There is also a fire-fighting organization, but its equipment is so inadequate that it is commonly said that the houses of people who live any distance from the station would burn to the ground long before the firemen could reach the spot.

There are two village-wide organizations, the Youth Society (seinendan) and the Women's Club (fujin-kai), both of which have relatively minor functions at present. Both were very powerful during World War II, actively engaging in the promotion of the "war effort." Largely because of this past history, both groups came under a cloud of official disapproval in the Occupation period, and neither plays an important part in buraku life today. However, it should be noted that the formal organization of the groups provides for the appointment of a representative for each buraku in Yashuhara, thus further formalizing the ties among the various communities.

Of vital importance to every villager are the buraku in which commercial establishments are concentrated, clustered near the government buildings. Here the villager can obtain almost anything he needs—clothing, foods, drugs, bicycles, toys, household utensils, cosmetics, haircuts and permanent waves. There are very few items in general demand which cannot be purchased in this village center.

The study of a village of the size and complexity of Yasuhara offers special problems with which the lone anthropologist is not well equipped to deal. But to understand in detail the life of a buraku and its interrelations with surrounding communities is possible. In the pages that follow, I have attempted to go beyond the profile presented in this chapter by recording in detail those aspects of Kurusu life which seemed to me most important in terms of the changing Japanese rural community.

ROBERT J. SMITH

Notes

1. For an analysis of the socio-political role of the buraku in village affairs, see R. E. Ward, "The Socio-Political Role of the Buraku (Hamlet) in Japan," American Political Science Review, Vol. 45, No. 4 (1951), 1025-1040.

2. Ibid., 1033-1034.

Chapter II

NEIGHBORLY COOPERATION

An outstanding feature of life in Kurusu is the degree to which forms of cooperation still operate even with the development of a money economy. Cliques and friendship groups are definitely subordinated to buraku interests in the performance of community duties. Feuding families set aside their differences in order to carry out their obligations to the buraku as a whole.

While Kurusu does not now exhibit the great variety of these cooperative forms reported by Embree,[1] cooperative endeavor remains the key to buraku identity and functioning. In some instances, however, the presentation of cash has replaced contributions of labor and kind in community activities, whereas in other instances the activity has wholly disappeared.

The varieties of cooperative groups to which Kurusu residents belong may be divided for convenience into four categories: (1) Those limited to membership of the entire buraku, and only the buraku; (2) Those to which all buraku farmers and some outside farmers belong; (3) Those including some buraku households and some outside households; and (4) Those including only a few buraku households, and no outsiders. Each of these will be considered in detail.

1. Groups limited to membership of the entire buraku and only the buraku.

Every household at present within the geographical limits of ko-aza Kurusu, corresponding to the unit known locally and in this monograph as Kurusu-buraku, has membership in a group called the dōgyō. This word is written with the characters onaji and yuku, "together" and "to go," and is derived from the motto worn on the hats and backs of Buddhist pilgrims of Shingon. The dōgyō acts on seven major occasions: (1) Admitting a new household to membership; (2) Births; (3) Weddings; (4) Funerals; (5) Buraku festivals to Jichin-san; (6) Road repair; (7) Autumn festival to Hachiman.

The first five of these seven are organized and maintained within the buraku and have no necessary connection with the activities of other communities. The last two, however, are tied in with work and ceremonies in which many communities are involved. In this larger setting Kurusu remains a self-contained cooperating unit, but operates in relation to the other units of the system.

In theory, the buraku-chō serves as the head of the buraku, but his duties are light and the group frequently operates without supervision of any formal sort. The dōgyō owns equipment which may be used free of charge by any member of the group on certain occasions. The small hut where the funeral paraphernalia are kept, such as the palanquin on which the coffin is borne, belongs to the dōgyō. The dōgyō also owns twenty sets of dishes, trays and small tables which are used in serving guests at weddings, funerals and the festivals to Jichin-san. These are stored in the warehouse of one of the former buraku landowners, but there seems to be no particular honor attached to being the custodian of the equipment. Although no rent is charged for their use, damaged or broken pieces must be replaced by the house responsible for the breakage.

When a new family is admitted to the community, and since 1945 this has happened seven times, a simple ceremony is held, called dōgyō-iri (entering the dōgyō). If the new household is of the Shinshu sect, all members of the dōgyō gather at the newcomers' house and recite a Shinshu prayer. This affair is called shōshinge, a word whose origin is not

9

known to the people of the buraku. For families of the Shingon sect the entire dōgyō gathers, but only Shingon people pray, while Shinshū members stand by. The name for this ceremony is kanki.

At these welcoming parties, which are usually attended by a representative from each of the resident households rather than by all their members, no buraku person offers gifts of food or cash to the newcomers, but the latter are expected to provide food for everyone who attends. After paying the entrance fee of 50 yen to the head of the buraku, the new family becomes an active member of the community, accepting both the privileges and responsibilities falling to residents of the buraku.

Upon leaving the buraku, a family or individual usually is feted by close friends and neighbors, but the community as a whole does not participate in the farewell party. However, during the period of military conscription, which ended in 1945, all the dōgyō members accompanied the departing conscripts as far as the village office and met them there upon their return. The actual farewell and welcoming parties for the soldier were confined to his family and friends, however.

Not all people living in Kurusu at any given time are members of the dōgyō. In the fall of 1951 two women were staying at the house of a Kurusu family but they did not participate in any community functions.

News of the birth of a child is spread through the buraku by the buraku-chō. After this has been done, it is the duty of the local representative of the Women's Club of Yasuhara, of which there is one in every buraku, to make the rounds of the houses of Kurusu and collect 30 yen from each family. The cash is presented to the new parents as a gift from the community, but no party is held. Formerly, on the child's naming day, seven days after birth, the family distributed mochi (glutinous rice cakes) to all households as a reciprocal gift, but this custom is seldom observed today.

In Kurusu a funeral, like a wedding, is a buraku undertaking that calls for considerable labor, all of it provided by the dōgyō. Ordinarily, arrangements for the ceremony itself are supervised by an intimate friend (shinyū) of the bereaved family. It is this man who assumes responsibility for the funeral and directs the activities of the dōgyō during this period, not the buraku-chō. On the day of death, the dōgyō must do two important things. First, those relatives of the deceased who do not live in the buraku must be notified of his death. Often this means sending people out on foot or by bicycle, and it may sometimes require sending telegrams or making telephone calls if the person has relatives in the more distant cities. The second duty on the first day is the making of funeral clothing for the corpse. It must be made of white cotton without the use of scissors. Nor can there be knots in the thread with which these garments are sewn, for it is felt that knots interrupt the soul on its journey to paradise. The completed clothes are taken to the house of the deceased and the corpse dressed in them after the family has washed the body and the barber has shaved the face. The first night after the death the family sits up to watch the body, but no dōgyō members come.

Early on the morning of the second day, one woman from each household of the dōgyō begins the preparation of the funeral foods. One group of men goes to the hut where the funeral paraphernalia are kept and cleans and repairs them before bringing them to the house of the deceased. Another group of men goes to the crematory and cleans out the shallow depression in which the coffin will be burned. They also carry wood and straw to the place, and generally clean up the area around the crematory. If the house of the deceased is small, a neighbor will offer his house to accommodate the overflow of guests. Relatives and friends begin to arrive about noon of the day of the ceremony, which usually is held on the second day after death. The only duty of the bereaved family is to greet them, after which the dōgyō members take charge of them.   Each guest is fed while he waits for the ceremony to begin, the meal being served either in the house of the deceased or at the neighbor's house which has been lent for the occasion.   There is great emphasis on sparing the family any unnecessary worry or trouble on this day.

The first part of the funeral is held in the parlor (zashiki) and is attended only by the family and very close friends, while guests and dōgyō members sit about outside the house. Following this part of the service, the coffin and other paraphernalia are carried by men of the dōgyō in the funeral procession.   This procession goes to another spot, usually an open place where many people can gather, and the second part of the ceremony is held. This is called the farewell ceremony (kokubetsu-shiki); as a rule it is attended by almost everyone in the community, children included.   When this is over, the coffin is opened briefly for a last look at the deceased.   The men who previously have prepared for the cremation remove the coffin from its ornamental palanquin and carry it to the crematory.

Before cremation occurs the buraku people return to the house of the deceased to clean up the grounds and to wash the dishes and return them to the warehouse where they are stored.   The family changes from ceremonial black to regular clothing and hurries to the crematory.   There the coffin has been packed in wood and straw.   When the family has assembled, the dōgyō men light the pyre.   Cremation takes about twelve hours.   The same men of the dōgyō who prepared the cremation take turns checking through the night to see that the fire is kept burning properly.   In the morning these men clear away the wood and straw ashes, partly to cool the spot and partly to gather up the bones so that when the family comes once more, this time to collect the ashes, there will be only a small mound of bones and ashes in the center of the pit.   By the evening of the second day after death, all the equipment will have been returned to its proper place and all outward signs of the ceremony removed.   As far as the buraku is concerned, preparation for collection of the bones is the last duty to the deceased and his family, and it is only the family and a few friends of an individual who will later observe the long series of memorial services for him.

A few days before the autumn festival there is a mura-wide road repair project (michi-tsukuri) to which each buraku contributes labor for the repair of the roads and paths within its boundaries.   The repairs made on this day are usually minor, involving cutting the grass along the sides of roads, filling in small holes, and ditching the paths.   Each household in Kurusu sends one adult member of either sex for this work, and people begin to gather in mid-morning.   There is much joking and laughter, for this is the prelude to the biggest and gayest of the village festivals, and the work is not strenuous.   When they have finished in the late afternoon, the year's work on the roads is done, and although minor repairs may be made from time to time by individuals, any large-scale damage will be taken care of by hired labor paid for by the political unit responsible for the road.

Although the whole buraku cooperates in religious activity, money rather than labor constitutes the most important aid contributed by the households of Kurusu.   Kurusu is one of the twelve buraku whose members are parishioners (ujiko) of the Nishitani Hachiman Shrine, Yasuhara's largest Shinto shrine.   Before 1943, there were twelve sponsors for this shrine's annual autumn festival, among whom responsibility rotated.   Nine of these sponsors were buraku, and three were individuals—three of the biggest landlords in the mura.   In the years in which one of the nine buraku functioned as sponsor, one of its members was chosen sponsor (tōya) by lottery, and all members aided him in his duties.   When one of the three landlords was sponsor, however, he bore all costs of the festival himself, with no help from the other members of the buraku in which he lived.

From 1943 to 1945 this system was suspended, and the village office assumed the position of tōya.   Following the surrender and the abolition of state support of Shinto, the old

sponsoring group (tōgumi) system was revived in a slightly different form. The enforcement of the land reform program stripped the landlords of their holdings making it financially unfeasible for them to resume their former individual sponsorship. Consequently
the twelve buraku were organized into the present ten sponsoring groups and the responsibility for the festival preparations rotates among them. Kurusu has always functioned as
an independent group (kumi) in this system.

The autumn festival of Hachiman is held on October 13 and 14 in Yasuhara, but the
sponsor's duties actually begin on the tenth or eleventh. On the first day, called hanging-
the-sacred-rope (shime-age), the sponsor invites to his home the Shinto priest of the
shrine, and two representatives from the kumi which will sponsor the festival in the following year. These two representatives are elected and are in charge of shrine affairs
for their community. At the beginning of this party, the sponsor hangs the sacred straw
rope of Shinto (shime-nawa) above the entrance to his house as a symbol of his position.
He also erects a tall bamboo pole with three fans at the top, called hake-dake, near his
dwelling. This pole is used later by the priest to make charms to be placed on the banks
of the rice seed beds in the spring.

Many years ago the sponsor used to rent a horse on October 11 and install it in a
rough temporary stable erected in front of his house. On October 14, the main festival
day, the animal was used in the procession to carry a specially folded white paper figure
(gohei) in its capacity as the horse of the god. Nowadays the horse is rented on the morning of the fourteenth and taken directly to the shrine for this purpose.

On October 11 or 12, the sponsor and a few helpers from the tōgumi go to the shrine
to clean the grounds. They also get out the equipment to be used in the procession and
clean it, making necessary minor repairs. All the stone lanterns about the shrine must
have both new paper and candles, which are placed in each lantern to be lit on the eve of
the main festival.

With the other responsibilities, the sponsor must take charge of funds collected by the
buraku to be used for festival expenses. By far the most important help rendered him by
his community is financial aid. Since the rotation among the sponsoring groups is fixed,
although the individual sponsor himself is chosen by lot, it is possible to begin preparations far in advance. When Kurusu was last tōgumi, buraku people put aside cash for
three years to pay for the anticipated festival expenses. Each household contributed 30 yen
a month for three full years, and the total of about 20,000 yen proved adequate for the
cash outlay required. The amount of money spent in the preparations depends largely upon
the wishes of the community, and it is a matter of buraku pride to have given an especially noteworthy festival.

Certain members of the sponsoring group assume also the responsibility of performing
as lion (shishi) dancers on the two festival days of the thirteenth and fourteenth. The lion
costume consists of a large head of black, red and gold and a long strip of gaily patterned
cloth, wide enough to cover two crouching dancers, one of whom manipulates the head. The
dance is performed to the rhythm of gongs and a drum, and requires about a week of practice on the part of the musicians and young men who dance with the costume. In Kurusu
they are instructed by an old man who has much active interest in religious affairs, especially local Shinto customs. Since the practice is in the evening after work, the buraku
prepares a special evening meal for the performers each day they practice.

The lion is supposed to make the rounds of the twelve buraku during the festival, and
every house before which it stops to dance gives about 100 yen in cash for the luck thus
insured for the coming year. The dancers and musicians use this money to finance a
party, or for any other purpose which they may agree upon. On October 15, the day after

the festival, the tō-gumi uses the remaining funds and some of the money collected by the lion dancers to hold a final party to which only buraku people come.

The particular lion costume used by the sponsoring group is passed from kumi to kumi, and although there are three other buraku-owned costumes in the village, Kurusu does not have one of its own.

On the festival day, October 14, the sponsor attends the ceremony at the shrine, and is seated in the position of honor next to the priest. He gives a feast called kami-no zen (the god's table) to which are invited the priest, two representatives from each tō-gumi in the system, and a representative of each of the subordinate shrines (massha) under the jurisdiction of the Nishitani Hachiman Shrine. The total number of guests is about sixty-five, making this feast the major expense of the festival for the sponsor. On this occasion, he trades sake cups with the representatives of the next sponsoring group, marking the beginning of that group's responsibilities.

The procession begins, the young men of the tō-gumi carrying the ark of the god (mikoshi), but it is the representative of the next year's tō-gumi who directs them. In former years the procession went from the main shrine building down the long steps to the entrance of the shrine grounds, from where the god would survey the rice crop and then return. Recently, however, the god frequently is carried to the shopkeepers' buraku of Chūtoku, where he is placed before the houses of five or six wealthy merchants. This insures the best possible fortune for the house during the coming year, and it also earns for the bearers a shō of sake, for that is the appropriate gift. Often this is drunk on the spot, and by the time the god is carried back to the shrine, the progress is boisterous and somewhat unsteady.

The duties of the tōya end on October 15, when the buraku holds a final party at his house. He takes down the bamboo pole and the sacred straw rope, which gives the day the name shime-oroshi (removing the sacred rope).

An interesting parallel to the village autumn festival are Kurusu's own spring and autumn observances to Jichin-san, Shinto patron god of the buraku, to whom there is a small shrine in the community. The festivals are held on the middle days of the vernal and autumnal equinox. A tōya system operates within the buraku, the sponsor changing at every festival. Of the twenty-two households in Kurusu, two are excluded from this system, as they are considered to be only temporary residents in the community. By the buraku's reckoning, fifteen of the participating households are farming households, and five are non-farming. Before the surrender in 1945 brought an influx of permanent settlers, there were always twelve farming households and four non-farmers. The excluded families belong to this group of post-war immigrants. At present each of the farmers gives one shō of wheat and each non-farmer 50 yen in cash (roughly the price of the wheat) towards the festival meal served by the sponsor.

Sponsorship rotates from east to west in the community in fixed order. The tōya for a given festival is helped with the work of preparing the festival foods, not by the whole buraku, but by the four neighboring households, two on either side of his dwelling. This means, in effect, that the two previous and two succeeding sponsors extend aid. Since the community thinks of the rotation as circular, when the tōya is at the geographical end of the buraku (either east or west), two of the helping households are at the opposite end of the community.

No one works on these festival days. Throughout the afternoon almost everyone calls at the sponsor's house for a festival meal and sake. The old people sometimes stay all afternoon, and when the Shinto priest arrives about five o'clock there are usually some adults and a great number of children to go with him to the shrine. Here there is a very short ceremony, after which the offerings of cakes are taken from the altar and are distributed among the children; then everyone goes home.

Many people remember when this ceremony was far more elaborate, featuring amateur wrestling and other games, but interest has declined throughout the years. Although in the opinion of some Kurusu people the expense of sponsoring this festival is not great, the necessity for obtaining cash to pay for the sake and the cakes and other special foods sometimes forces a sponsor to find temporary day labor somewhere in the village.

2. Groups to which all buraku farmers and some outside farmers belong.
    The biggest formally organized cooperative, and the one which figures most prominently in agricultural life, is the Kurusu Irrigation Union (yōsui kumiai). It includes twenty-nine households, both resident and non-resident, that cultivate land in the buraku. The organization has an elected head whose term of office is one year, during which time he handles all finances and is the liaison man between the kumiai and the government agency in the village which handles funds subsidizing irrigation work. All members pay fixed dues, determined each year on the basis of the amount of land a man cultivates within the jurisdiction of the organization. These dues vary from year to year, depending on plans for a given year's work. Recently, for example, extensive repairs and improvements have been undertaken which have raised the dues considerably.

Dues may be paid in a combination of three ways, in labor, in equipment and in cash. If a man chooses to work for the kumiai to pay part of his dues, the daily wage of 150 yen is deducted from the total he owes the organization. He may sell the group a number of straw mats (komo) used in the construction of banks and channels. The way in which a household pays its dues varies greatly, but in general it is families with small amounts of land who submit the least cash. Only one household in the union pays more than half of its dues in cash.

One reason that the daily wages have not increased during the past five years to keep pace with other wages and rising costs is that they are in reality seldom paid out, but are simply a kind of "discount figure" allowed members of the cooperative when they work for it. Non-members are sometimes hired, but infrequently, so the wage paid is not primarily intended to appeal to prospective laborers.

In the event of flood, which sometimes seriously disrupts the irrigation system, each household is expected to send at least one member to work until the necessary repairs are made. This may sometimes require two full days of labor, and the wages paid on such occasions may account for almost half the annual expenditure. Actually, of course, no cash changes hands. The amount theoretically earned simply is deducted from the dues of the household.

All work of the cooperative is planned and discussed by the entire membership, and any extra expense incurred during the year must be approved by them. It should be noted that all the farming households in Kurusu cultivate some land outside the buraku, with the result that they belong to similar irrigation cooperatives in communities in which their land is located.

One of the most important functions of the group is the system of water use which it enforces in time of drought. Under this system, called hiki-mizu (drawing water), on a given day only two farmers are permitted to use irrigation water, and it is their duty to see that no one else tries to evade this restriction on that day. The turn of each member is fixed by discussion in the group. Because Kurusu lies along the river, it has none of the water disputes between individuals or buraku so typical of other areas of Kagawa.

At the end of the Japanese fiscal year (March 31) all members of the Kurusu Irrigation Union, and most of the outsiders who worked for the group during the preceding year
attend a party. It is usually the household heads who attend, but occasionally a wife may
come to help in the kitchen. The event, which is attended by as many as forty persons,
takes place at one of the larger houses in the buraku. Besides entertainment and modest
gifts for all, there is business to be attended to: a new head must be elected, the financial report must be read by the retiring chief, and a start must be made on planning work
for the coming year. The village official who handles mura irrigation affairs is given a
special place and special foods, but beyond having given some advice during the course of
the year he has played little part in the operation of the group.

The party itself is financed from the irrigation work fund supplied by the government,
a subsidy which amounts to from one-third to one-half the amount collected in dues from
members. According to several rough estimates, the cost of the party is usually only
slightly less than the total annual cost of the cooperative's undertakings. The estimated
outlay for the 1951 party was about 18,000 yen, whereas the total outlay for work done in
the fiscal year 1951 was 22,791 yen. There was some disagreement among informants
about the cost of the party, most claiming that it undoubtedly cost more. The pattern of
using official funds for entertainment is so prevalent in the Japanese government on all
levels that there is a popular derogatory term for it: enkai seiji or "party government."

One of the least active and most specialized cooperative groups is one that maintains
a lamp to attract and kill insects. During the summer months the rice fields on the plain
to the north of Yasuhara glow at night with the blue light of these fluorescent insect lamps.
They are of rather more limited occurrence in the mountain area, and Kurusu has only
one, which was bought in 1949. A group of farmers, including some Kurusu residents and
some non-residents farming land in the buraku, formed a cooperative and bought the lamp.
Kurusu people consider the cost of the lamp reasonable, but have delayed purchasing additional lamps because they question their effectiveness. The lamp is serviced by a Kurusu
man with some knowledge of electricity, but the group which owns the lamp has no official
head. The small dues, which are collected by this man, are figured according to the
proximity of the member's field to the light, with the nearest fields having the highest assessments. The group is called the Insect Lamp Cooperative (keikōtō kumiai), but the only
duty incumbent upon its members is the payment of dues for upkeep of the device. There
are no meetings or any other group activities. (For a full discussion of the controversy
surrounding the lamp itself, see Chapter III.)

3. Groups including some buraku households and some outside households.
To cross the river which separates it from the highway and the commercial center of
the village, Kurusu depends on bridges, not boats, as the waters of the Gōtō River are too
shallow and swift for the latter. All vehicular and animal traffic, and a great part of
human traffic, moves across the large ferro-concrete Kangetsu Bridge. There are, however, two small foot bridges within the jurisdiction of Kurusu to the east of the main
bridge. These are of such simple construction that they are either taken down or else
washed out every fall by the high waters. Occasionally summer rains wash them out. In
general they are used by people traveling between Kurusu and its nearest neighbor to the
east, Takabatake-buraku. Many of these people live in one buraku and farm land in the
other.

It is these people, then, who assume responsibility for the upkeep of the foot bridges.
The group is not a kumi, nor does it have a head or require dues. When a bridge must
be replaced, some individual makes the rounds of the responsible households to decide
upon a day when one member from each household will work on the bridge. The work is
not difficult. It is usually finished in a matter of a few hours after which the people simply return to their own work.

4. Groups including only a few buraku households and no outsiders.

Farmers in many different cultures depend upon cooperation to complete certain seasonal tasks. In Kurusu this cooperation takes the form of cooperative groups of a few households for setting out seed beds for rice, transplanting, cultivating and, finally, harvesting the rice. These groups, which are similar to the Suye kattari groups described by Embree,[2] use a system of exchange labor (tema-gae). Unlike the groups Embree describes, Kurusu's exchange labor groups change in composition from year to year and even from season to season. However, repayment for help is in exact equivalents, just as it was in Suye-mura. If two people from one house work a day for a neighbor, then the neighbor is obliged to send one person to work two days, or two people to work one day, or any other combination of man-days which makes an exact return. No record is kept of these exchanges, but people say that a man who fails to fulfill his obligations in the tema-gae system will never receive help from his neighbors again.

Tema-gae is found chiefly during rice transplanting, and to a lesser extent in harvesting, but Kurusu people admit that with the introduction of cash and machines the system is much less important than it was in the past.

An old kumi division which functioned during harvests seems to have disappeared since the surrender in 1945. Formerly the buraku was divided into a middle group (naka-gumi) and a far group (oku-gumi), each group renting a threshing machine and a huller from outside the buraku. The machines were used in rotation by member households in groups of three which worked together in order to get the crop in early. This was particularly true of the barley and wheat, for the rains begin shortly after harvest, and the drying of the grain and transplanting of rice should be finished as quickly as possible.

The major reason for the disappearance of these two groups, which apparently functioned only at harvest times, has been the purchase of five threshing machines by Kurusu residents within the past two years. In addition, in 1951, a buraku man bought a huller and selector. All of these machines are available for rental, and it is tema-gae groups which rent them as a group now, rather than the old middle and far kumi. One machine is even cooperatively owned. Three residents of Kurusu joined with two non-residents who cultivate land in the buraku to buy a threshing machine. One of the Kurusu men has already dropped out, having bought a machine of his own. Being of recent formation, this group has not yet resolved all the problems of maintenance and use-order, and other people feel that it is better to own a machine individually than to rent one.

This completes the survey of cooperative forms in Kurusu. It will be noted that there are no cooperative credit groups (kō) which are described at length by Embree.[3] People remember when they still existed some thirty or forty years ago, and they say that the increasing importance of cash and banking contributed largely to their disappearance. Formerly they were vital in the building of a new house, but today the family members do what work they can and hire skilled labor to do the rest. Also of great importance were the mutual financing associations (mujin-kō), commonly used before the introduction of banks and other credit and finance organizations in the area. Although the forms of cooperation are decreasing in number and although rituals and ceremonies tend to become simpler and less costly, it is evident that the community still places much value on the cooperative spirit, and that it regards itself as a distinctive social unit.

Only once in the memory of its residents has Kurusu ostracized a member, i.e., made him a village outcast (mura-hachibu). The expulsion occurred about thirty-five years ago and is of such importance in understanding the degree of solidarity of the buraku community that it is presented in some detail. The issue was a man's failure to fulfill his obligation in a two-household cooperative which maintained a small bridge across a stream between their houses. This bridge was also used by others, as it led to the buraku grist mill, but the responsibility for its upkeep was shared by the two households alone. One year the head of one household refused on the grounds of financial difficulty to make necessary repairs. When word of his refusal spread, several men urged him to reconsider, but he remained adamant. At last when it became evident that his decision was final, the buraku met and voted to expel his household.

For two years members of this household were outcasts. At length the village head (son-chō) effected a reconciliation, and they were permitted to reenter the community. The man who headed the household during its period of ostracism is still living; one of his sons recently held the office of buraku-chō. In 1951, the man who headed the other household involved in the dispute attended the wedding of another son of the former outcast family.

Although people admit that the force of such expulsion is somewhat less today than it was then, it is still regarded as a formidable punishment. Its effect is not physically to remove a household, but to exclude it from all personal and social contacts with the community. Only in the case of a funeral will a priest visit the outcasts. They are not spoken to by other villagers, and they can expect no help in case of trouble or a shortage of labor. There is little question among Kurusu residents that an uncooperative member would be expelled now as in the past. The practice was officially outlawed after the Meiji Restoration (1868); but it has continued. There is at least one mura-hachibu elsewhere in Yasuhara at the present time.

In addition to the more formalized aspects of cooperation dealt with above, Kurusu has demonstrated in other ways that it considers itself a distinctive social unit. One of these is the way in which the government requisition of agricultural products has been handled. Although in theory the requisition is submitted by individuals, it is the buraku which sends an estimate to the village office stating the maximum amounts of grain and vegetables it can offer. In the case of a widow or poor farmer or any other person unable to meet its requisition, other buraku members always have made up his share. The village records maintain the fiction that individuals always submit the amounts required of them. In this way, even in the difficult years of 1946 and 1947, the buraku was spared the disgrace of a forced sale, in which cases the government seizes the grain.

Finally, the buraku acts as a unit in local politics. Since the end of the war, it has become increasingly evident to Kurusu people that they need a councilman in the village assembly to represent their interests. They are, however, too few in number to elect a candidate alone, as demonstrated by repeated failure to elect a buraku man. In order to improve their position, they have formed an alliance with Takabatake, their neighbor to the east. The understanding is that the two communities will vote as a unit in the election of assemblymen. Candidates will be chosen alternately between the two buraku, and such candidates will act in the interests of both communities. A number of people who discussed this arrangement with me were apologetic about its "undemocratic" aspect, but they emphasized that a small community like Kurusu had no other choice.

The most interesting feature of the alliance to date is that Kurusu has upheld its end of the bargain to the letter, while Takabatake has not. In 1951 every household in Kurusu voted for a very unpopular Takabatake man, who was elected. In the election prior to this one, the Kurusu candidate was defeated because he failed to receive all the Takabatake vote.

As a result of such occurrences, people from Kurusu take some pride in pointing out that they have an especially strong community spirit (danketsu-shin) in contrast to many of their neighboring buraku. Already some of them are wondering, however, whether they will be able to maintain this close in-group feeling in the face of increasing mobility and the growth of a commercial cash economy.

ROBERT J. SMITH

Notes

1. See J. F. Embree, Suye Mura, A Japanese Village, Chicago, 1939, 112-157.

2. Embree, op. cit., 132-138.

3. Ibid., 138-153.

Chapter III

DAY-TO-DAY LIFE

What kind of life does the average citizen of Kurusu lead? What does his house look like? What sort of clothing does he wear? Does his wife use lipstick and have a permanent wave? Does he have a hobby or leisure activity? What does he eat? How much money does he make and what taxes does he pay? It is the purpose of this chapter to answer questions of this sort about the residents of Kurusu.

The average house in Kurusu is a one-story, wood and mud structure with a thatched roof. None of the wood on either the outside or the inside of the house is painted, but wood with attractive grain or unusual shape is often used, and even the most ordinary wood acquires beauty as it becomes weathered and polished with use. In the kitchen, years of cooking over open fires blackens the wooden ceiling to a dull ebony. The outside walls of the house take on an earthen color that matches the surrounding soil.

From spring until fall the houses of Kurusu are light and airy, but as the weather becomes colder the outside sliding doors are closed making the houses seem dark and close inside. This is less true of the newer houses, because they use glass doors around the outer walls. Sliding paper and wood doors (shoji) and sliding paper screens (fusuma) between rooms are universally used. But in all the houses of the buraku (except that of the sawmill owner) these fragile paper screens and doors are punctured and torn. Every spring an attempt is made to replace all the torn paper in the shoji, a job best done by professionals but one frequently attempted by members of the household. These homemade patching operations are often done with newspapers with the result that the shoji in the poorer houses are often nearly opaque. Members of the household also patch the fusuma, but when they can no longer do so successfully they hire a professional artisan to replace the paper covers.

TABLE 1

BUILDING UNITS BY TYPE: KURUSU, 1952

| Kind | Number | Roof Type | | | | Stories | | Floor Area* | | Age** |
		Thatch	Tile	Bark	Iron	One	Two	Total	Average	Years
Dwelling.........	21	14	6	1	-	17	2	449.5	21.4	47.50
Storage..........	19	10	9	-	-	17	2	186.5	9.8	45.68
Sawmill	4	-	2	-	2	4	-	132.0	33.0	31.22
Bath and Toilet ...	8	-	8	-	-	8	-	20.5	2.6	24.25
Stable	2	2	-	-	-	2	-	8.0	4.0	41.00
Fertilizer Storage	1	-	1	-	-	1	-	5.0	5.0	21.00
Chicken House ...	1	-	-	-	1	1	-	7.0	7.0	30.00
TOTALS.........	56	26	26	1	3	50	6	908.5	----	41.39

*In tsubo (1 tsubo = 3.95 square yards).
**Average age.

19

Priest from Shingon temple outside the buraku officiating at a Kurusu memorial service
for the dead. He is one of the many specialists called into the buraku.

A mendicant Buddhist pilgrim and
small boy who pass through Kurusu twice a year, asking for food
or money.

Another outsider is the "Ice Candy" vendor who comes through
Kurusu in warm weather three or
four times a week.

Stove of brick in one of the wealthier homes in the bura-ku. To the left is the kindling box.

On the other side of the kitchen is a stone mortar used for pounding glutinous rice. To the left is a work table.

Just outside the kitchen door hang a variety of utensils. The chimney and stove pipe are seen to the right.

When shōji open to the outside, it is usually onto a passage running along the outside wall and in comfortable weather left unclosed along its outer edge. In periods of extreme cold, however, or when there is a high wind or heavy rain, a kind of wooden shutter called amado is pulled across the outer edge to form a temporary but fairly firm wall. The amado are shut every evening, no matter how hot the night, as a means of gaining privacy and keeping out the night air.

Every house in Kurusu has electricity, and in most cases the light bulb is simply hung unshaded from the center of the ceiling. In some homes glass shades are used, but they are open at the bottom so that the full glare of the bulb is directed downwards. There are no floor lamps of any sort in the buraku, although in the cities many styles have been developed, from straight copies of Western lamps to adaptations of old Japanese forms to electricity. All houses have a supply of candles, and most keep one or two old kerosene lamps of the Western type for use in the inevitable electric power failures which have plagued all Japan since the surrender. In most houses, every room has an electric socket and bills are paid on the basis of the number of outlets.

Furniture is at a minimum and the use of a room is determined largely by the furniture which may temporarily be placed in it. All rooms of a house may be used for sleeping simply by laying bedding wherever it is needed, and similarly meals may be served anywhere a table or tray is laid. The floors of most rooms are covered with tatami, thick straw mats six by three feet in size, covered with closely-woven rush matting. The size of a room is determined by the number of mats it will hold; in Kurusu all rooms are either four and a half, six, eight, or (rarely) ten-mat rooms. The ordinary house in Kurusu has a kitchen (daidokoro), living room (i-ma), parlor (zashiki), and dining room (cha-no-ma). There are also an earthen-floored work area under the roof (dō-ma), the bath (furoba) and toilet (benjo). The i-ma and cha-noma are used for sleeping.

Most houses have three entrances, of which only two are commonly used in Kurusu: one through the kitchen and one through the work area. The door opening directly into the kitchen is only occasionally used by members of the household, for they generally come into the house through the work area at the front. From the work area one can go directly into the kitchen which is built on the same level. The living room, parlor and dining room are raised nearly a foot above the level of the kitchen and their floors are covered with tatami, on which one steps only after he has taken off his shoes. The entrance to the raised, mat-covered floor directly from the outside is rarely used. Guests use it on formal occasions, and at funerals the pallbearers use it when they carry the coffin from the parlor.

The houses of Kurusu are a reliable index of the economic status of the community. A great deal has been said about the post-war prosperity of the Japanese farmer, but it is well to use caution in estimating the lasting material gain from the period 1945-1949. It has been pointed out that the prosperity of this period was a money prosperity with the result that few farmers have enlarged their holdings, acquired new and better equipment, or built better homes or farm buildings. Of Kurusu's 908.50 tsubo (one tsubo = 3.95 square yards) of buildings of all types, only 84.50 have been built since 1945, a total of eight of the buraku's fifty-six units (see Table 2). Three new dwelling units have been constructed, but the one built in 1945 is a very modest addition to a small older house, and the shortage of materials is indicated by the fact that cryptomeria bark was used for the roof, the only such roof in Kurusu. The other two dwellings of post-war construction are slightly under the average floor area of 21.40 tsubo for buraku dwellings. One of them is an entirely new structure, built on a former paddy; the other replaced an older dwelling, occupying approximately the same area.

HOUSE PLAN

Scale ⊢━━━━━⊣
9'

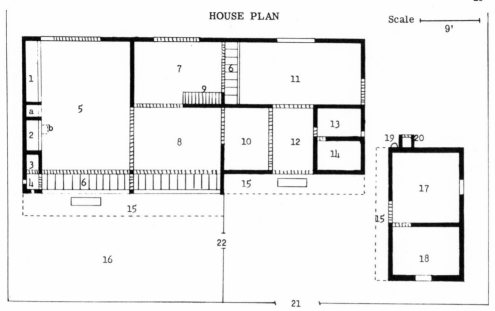

⊏━━━⊐ Solid mud and wattle or plaster wall   ⊏ⅠⅠⅠⅠⅠⅠⅠⅡ Sliding door of paper, glass or wood
⊏━━━⊐ Window

⊏\ⅠⅠⅠⅠⅡ Wooden flooring

Figure 1

KEY TO HOUSE PLAN

1.	Alcolve	tokonoma
2.	Closet	mono-oki
3.	Toilet	benjo
4.	"	"
5.	Parlor	zashiki
6.	Hallways	roka
7.	Dining room	cha-no-ma
8.	Living room	i-ma
9.	Stairs to second-floor attic	
10.	Entrance room	genkan
11.	Kitchen	daidokoro
12.	Earthen-floored area	doma
13.	Bath	o-furo
14.	Store room	oshi-ire
15.	Area under projecting eaves	
16.	Garden	niwa
17.	Store-house	kura
18.	" "	"
19.	Urinal	
20.	Toilet	benjo
21.	Entrance to compound	
22.	Entrance to garden	
a.	Buddhist altar	butsudan
b.	Shinto altar	kamidana

TABLE 2

BUILDING UNITS CONSTRUCTED IN KURUSU, 1945-1949

Type	Roof-type	Number of Stories	Floor Area (tsubo)*	Year
Dwelling	Cryptomeria Bark	1	6.00	1945
Storage	Tile	1	10.00	1947
Bath and Toilet...........	Tile	1	7.00	1947
Dwelling	Tile	2	17.50	1948
Dwelling	Tile	1	18.50	1948
Storage	Tile	2	13.75	1948
Storage	Tile	1	8.75	1948
Bath and Toilet...........	Tile	1	3.00	1949
TOTAL			84.50	

*1 tsubo = 3.95 square yards.

Construction skills have been rather consistently on the wane, if the recollections of buraku people are to be trusted. In former days more house construction was done by individuals, but today a man usually confines his labor to work on small outbuildings and minor repairs. Rough plastering such as is found in these outbuildings often is done by the farmer, and occasionally a young man from the village will find employment in the city or town as an assistant to a plasterer or carpenter. For most house building and repair professional carpenters will be hired, and for all oven and bath construction the farmer will call in professional plasterers and masons. In the past a family or an exchange-labor group might roof a house, but today roofing in thatch or tile is almost always done by professionals, although a man may himself put on a galvanized iron roof, of which there are only three in the buraku. Thatch roofs are made of barley and wheat straw, which is too stiff for the weaving of straw mats or the twisting of straw rope.

The average house of 21.40 tsubo would cost today about 325,000 yen with thatch roof, or 475,000 yen with tile roof. From 1934 to 1937 costs for dwelling construction were far lower, the thatch-roofed building of average size costing at most 1,070 yen, the tile roof an additional 400 yen. These figures give a measure of the vast inflation in prices, but it should also be noted that, with increased use of skilled labor, a higher percentage of building costs must be paid out in cash today than was formerly the case.

The amount of Western-style clothing (yōfuku) worn in Kurusu has increased considerably within the past fifteen years. Old men and women still wear Japanese kimono for the most part, but old men are likely to have a worn felt hat of Western type which completes their wardrobe. Kimono patterns and colors vary with the age of the woman, large gay prints for the young but more subdued browns, blues and grays for the old. Men wear duller hues at all ages, usually with a very small pattern. Summer kimono are of light cotton, but winter kimono are made of thick-padded material. Silk is expensive and not common except for formal black kimono which are worn at weddings, funerals and other formal occasions. One's "best" clothing is almost always Japanese.

Some small girls and boys wear kimono on festival days, but the rest of the time they are attired in Western clothing. In summer, very small boys may wear only a shirt, but most children are kept clothed the year round. School children wear Western dress exclusively—pull-over sweaters and slacks or a skirt and blouse combination for girls, and white shirts and inexpensive trousers for boys. A few children have black school uniforms, but the schools in Yasuhara do not require that they be worn.

Western garments are popular with young people to the extent that some youths even wear suits to formal occasions like funerals and weddings. Women say that dresses are far more comfortable and convenient than kimono, particularly in summer. However, women of thirty or more almost always wear kimono, except when working in trousers and shirts in the fields. Because they are so warm and because cold-weather Western clothing is so expensive, kimono are much more commonly worn in winter.

Kimono are made by hand by the women of the buraku, and all Western-style clothing is purchased ready-made. There are two or three sewing machines, but these are not much used even by their owners.

Shoes are worn primarily on dress occasions but only with Western-style clothing. Many old people do not own a pair, preferring to use the Japanese clog (geta) and sandal (zōri) exclusively. Young men and women wear shoes when going to town, except in the rainy season when everyone prefers high clogs. Rubber boots are worn by some farmers who can afford them, as are rubber Japanese "socks" (jika-tabi), with the characteristic split toe. Western stockings are worn with shoes; on formal occasions or in cold weather, socks (tabi) are worn with native footgear.

For rain wear, most farmers still use the native straw rain cape, open in the front so that the person's arms are free while he bends over to work in the field. Large conical rain hats of straw and bamboo are also used. A very few people now wear Western-style rain coats when not working, but they are expensive and uncommon. For work in the sun, a small sombrero-type hat is worn by both sexes, and almost everyone carries a towel around his neck or tied about his head.

Young women use cosmetics—powder, lipstick and rouge—and most of them have permanent waves. Youths are likely to wear their hair rather long and use heavy pomade to make it manageable after its frequent washings. Small boys have shaved heads or wear their hair very short. Girls' hair is bobbed short.

A few people, mostly the young, have inexpensive wrist watches. Almost no one has any jewelry, and my own ring and tie pin, when I wore them, were objects of admiration. A bride wears rented celluloid hair ornaments, imitations of the classic ornaments of tortoise shell, precious metals and semi-precious stones. Folding fans are carried on visits during the warm months. At work in the hot weather people use the ever-present towel to wipe their faces.

Everyone tries to bathe at least three times a week and would bathe oftener if fuel were more readily obtainable. Clothing may not always be spotless, but bodies are always clean. Teeth, however, are cleaned only occasionally. Clothes are washed in warm water and soap and scrubbed on a ribbed wooden board. Kimono are unstitched before washing and hung to dry in long strips on horizontal bamboo poles.

Few individuals in Kurusu have sufficient leisure time for artistic pursuits. The one conspicuous exception is the buraku Buddhist priest who does no work in the fields. He occupies his time with calligraphy, poetry and wood-carving when he is not performing his religious duties. Many of his poems have been published, and occasionally one is read on a Takamatsu radio daily program devoted to poetry. His ability as a calligrapher is widely recognized in Yasuhara. Primarily for his own amusement, he carves mottoes on wooden plaques, a form of decoration very popular in many Japanese homes. In addition, the man is a collector and connoisseur of sorts, with a keen interest in Japanese antiquities. His Buddhist altar is the finest and most expensive in the buraku, and all of its parts were purchased in Kyoto.

The only person in Kurusu who has had formal training in flower arranging, tea ceremony and the playing of musical instruments is a woman who formerly lived in Takamatsu. Apparently she seldom practices the former two, but is frequently called upon to perform on the samisen at parties in the buraku and in other parts of Yasuhara. Her enemies, perhaps jealous of the popularity she derives from this accomplishment, whisper that it is only a geisha who should play such an instrument professionally, not a farmer's wife. Partly because she is from the city anyway and partly because she is a widow, this talk does not deter her from seeking employment as a samisen player.

These brief remarks on the "artistic" accomplishments of Kurusu people do not do justice to the qualities of the objects with which all but the very poorest families attempt to surround themselves: a small tree strategically placed in the dwelling compound, two curious gate-posts of untreated natural wood considered to be of pleasing shape, a single flower and some grasses in a green bamboo vase and, in the wealthier homes, painted scrolls and a very few ceramic pieces. If they have the time, the people of the buraku take short trips to see the cherry blossoms and the autumn leaves. They are very conscious of natural beauty, and the natural woods and open airiness of their dwellings point up the efforts they make to bring such beauty as close as possible. Kurusu people obviously have an aesthetic sense but they have neither the time nor money to indulge it.

There is little evidence, however, of their aesthetic sensitivity at most of their meals. The food is prepared and eaten hastily and without relish or ceremony. In ordinary seasons the family eats three times a day, but in summer and in the busy season of rice harvest and wheat and barley planting, four meals are the rule. During these periods, breakfast (asage) is at 5:30 a.m., mid-morning meal (hiruge) is at 10:00 a.m., afternoon meal (o-cha) at 2:00 p.m., and evening meal (yūge) at 9:00 p.m.[1] Ordinary meals or those served on other special occasions tend to be lingered over and accompanied by much sake and camaraderie. Foods are usually served cold, or cool, largely because the housewife is unable to keep them warm while the rice steams or water for tea boils. Most people like hot foods, but the latter two are the only ones which seem consistently to arrive hot at the table. The head of the family is served first, and all the men eat together at a low table. Women and children usually eat later or, if they eat at the same time, sit at the side of the room and frequently place their dishes on the floor. They are expected to bring anything the men ask for, such as second portions or tea.

Before the surrender in 1945, farmers in this part of Shikoku ate barley almost exclusively, rice being bought only for very special occasions. However, since that time there has been an individual rice ration in Japan which, coupled with the decrease in rice rents due to the land reform, has made it possible for virtually everyone to eat at least a mixture of rice and barley. Many families eat rice alone. Adults who do a full day's work usually eat three bowls of rice at each meal.[2]

Polished rice is served in many forms, the most common being boiled and steamed rice without seasoning. Glutinous rice is steamed and pounded to make mochi, a sticky white cake which is toasted over the fire and eaten with sugar or with sugar and soy sauce (shoyu). Mochi, besides being an important festival food, is the principal offering for both

Buddhist and Shinto ceremonial occasions. Sake of varying grades, all of it containing approximately 17 percent alcohol, may be purchased across the river in Chutoku-buraku. No
one now manufactures his own, and Kurusu people tend to buy the lowest quality wine because it is so inexpensive, about 400 yen for one shō (3.18 pints). Sake, like mochi, is
an important festival food and is sometimes offered to the Shinto gods.

Wheat is used in making a kind of noodle (udon), which is often prepared for special
meals. Kurusu people say that when wealthier families in other buraku prepare rice with
red or black beans for ceremonial occasions, they usually serve udon because it is cheaper. The noodles are served hot with pieces of boiled fish loaf, leeks, shaved bonito and
chili pepper.

Another basic item in the diet is soy sauce, which can be purchased in Chutoku, but
about half the families in Kurusu still make their own. It is generally prepared during the
dog days (dōyō) in June. The principal ingredients are equal parts of roasted wheat and
boiled soybeans, which are mixed with yeast and fermented. A household of five persons
consumes about thirty-two gallons annually. Only the yeast, which costs about 30 yen,
must be purchased.

Miso, a fermented paste of rice and soybeans with about 40 percent of salt, is prepared in December and January by almost every house in Kurusu. The paste is used to
give flavor and body to soups, particularly for breakfast. A family of five uses approximately eighty gallons a year. For ama-miso (sweet miso), which is the base for a special
New Year's dish, only 15 percent of salt is used. Almost no one in the buraku makes tōfu
(soybean curd) because of the complicated process involved. Soybeans and brine are mixed
to form the curd, and the product is eaten in soups or as a side-dish on special occasions.
Konnyaku, made from the tuberous root of the devil's tongue, is a kind of paste which
solidifies when dropped into boiling water and may be stored until ready to be boiled again
and eaten. The paste is made in the home from late spring until autumn. It is usually
eaten as a side-dish. Broad beans (sora-mame), Irish beans (azuki) and other varieties
are less important in the diet than soybeans (daizu), perhaps, but they are often served,
particularly at festival meals. Pickles and relishes (tsukemono) appear at every meal;
most common varieties are made of white radish (daikon), Chinese cabbage (hakusai) and
eggplant (nasu). The vegetables are first dried in the sun, then placed under pressure in
a cask with a mixture of rice bran and salt. The tangy pickles are said to be best when
about three months old, but they may be eaten a week after the process begins. A family
of four requires about thirty gallons of tsukemono a year.

Kurusu farmers buy only a little meat and fish in a year. Meat is expensive and is
not sold in warm months by the shops in Chūtoku across the river. Fresh fish are sold
by peddlers who come through the village by bicycle from Takamatsu. There is only one
regular fish vendor who passes through Kurusu. Eggs are eaten occasionally, and chicken
is sometimes served. An ordinary meal, prepared in haste by the women of the house,
consists of a soup, vegetable, relish, and rice. The beverage is green tea. Fruits are
sometimes eaten in season, but infrequently. For festival meals much more elaborate
dishes are served, for which the farmer must buy dried seaweed (nori), dried small sardines (tatsukuri), herring roe (kazunoko), fish roll (kamaboko) and special relishes and
sweet cakes.

Water and tea are the most common beverages. Some children from the buraku get
milk at the primary school, for which their parents pay eight yen a day, but the principal
estimates that not more than half of the Kurusu children are normally included in the milk
program. Several varieties of carbonated drinks, chiefly ginger-ale and sweet soda, are
sold in the stores in Yasuhara, as are candies and candy bars. Chewing gum is popular
with children.

Young people who go to Takamatsu sometimes eat "foreign-style" food there, but restaurants which have such menus are usually too expensive for the farmer. If a trip is planned to last all day, the traveler takes a lunch with him. This is a small box packed with rice and pickles, or a more elaborate one may include some fish roll or small pieces of vegetable and chicken. When it is time to eat, a person looks for a spot where he can get a pot of tea, which may be had very cheaply. Changes in the diet have been marked in recent years due to increased prosperity in the village, but non-native items still are unknown to most buraku people.

Estimates by Kurusu families about the average income in the buraku vary widely. Ordinary people will not let it be known what they have earned in a given period, so that accurate accounts are not often seen. Some of the wealthier men give the following estimates: About 85 percent of a family's income is derived from the three cereals—rice, barley, and wheat. The remaining 15 percent comes from cash crops, day labor and home industry. An average family of five persons cultivating four tan of land obtains about 70,000 yen worth of rice in a good year. Since he cannot double-crop all his land, the cash value of his mugi is probably no more than 25,000 yen. Home industry and day labor bring in not more than 10,000 yen annually. A household selling a cow receives less than 10,000 yen in profit, according to most farmers.

A gross annual income of about 110,000 yen for five people seems a safe average estimate. Excepting, for the moment, the family of the sawmill owner, it appears that the highest income is about 180,000 yen, the lowest 40,000 yen. Chemical fertilizer, which costs the farmer about 15,000 yen annually, is his biggest cash expense. Clothing for a family of five costs about 8,000 yen, if there are no extraordinary expenses. Each child in school is reckoned to require from 2,500 to 3,000 yen annually. Other average expenses, like taxes, government crop insurance and cooperative dues, are not readily arrived at.

One informant claims that the average net profit from one tan of land in rice is no more than 6,500 yen, for mugi 4,000 yen. This would indicate that after purchasing fertilizer, paying for rental of a cow, etc., the average family would have a net profit of about 40,000 yen from its cereal crops.

Only a few households in Kurusu derive a substantial income from subsidiary industries (fukugyō), part of the reason being that the buraku is too far from Takamatsu's ready markets. Straw mats, straw rope, and bags of straw for salt and fertilizer are manufactured in the home for sale in the village. Some informants say that the motivation for undertaking a home industry is not so much desire for a big profit, but the pressing need for some cash income. Such a subsidiary occupation is carried on only during slack seasons of the agricultural year. Households engaged in a subsidiary business are said to get about 10,000 yen in cash annually from this source.

Two households in Kurusu weave straw mats (mushiro), one for its own use, the other to order for local people. Most of the customers are from nearby, but not all are from Kurusu. Both households own their own foot-powered vertical looms. If the customer supplies the materials, the cost is 60 yen per mat. If the weaver must supply the straw, the price is one hundred yen each. A skillful person can weave ten mats in one day, but both households have only recently undertaken the business and their production is much lower than this. The household which currently weaves only for its own use plans to market its products when members of the family have more experience and can make more efficient use of the equipment. The best machine for making mushiro costs about 12,000 yen new, but cheap ones may be had for as little as 5,000 yen at the Agricultural Cooperative Union. Both looms in Kurusu are very old and were bought second-hand. The same household which makes its own mushiro also uses the same loom for the manufacture of straw bags (kamasu) for fertilizer and salt. These are of far coarser weave than mushiro and can be woven at the rate of twenty per day. They are sold to the village Agricultural Cooperative Union under contract.

By far the most common home industry is the manufacture of straw rope (nawa). Eight families engage in its production, all but one of them owning the machine on which the rope is twisted. These machines cost about 7,000 yen. Four of the households which make rope sell it, two by contract with the buraku sawmill for use in tying bundles of box parts, one to the mountains to the south where the rope is used for bundling fuel; the fourth sells it indirectly as binding for the kamasu he provides the Agricultural Cooperative Union. As far as I could determine, the other four families make the rope in small quantities for their own use. A skilled worker can make a net profit of about 100 yen per day at rope twisting. Both weaving and making rope are usually done by women while the men of the household gather fuel and green manure during slack seasons.

During 1951 and 1952 people from the buraku found day labor chiefly at the sawmill, the dam and on the roads. The sawmill hired four buraku people full-time and two part-time. Six men from Kurusu were employed at the large dam construction project in Shionoe-mura to the south during my stay. They worked from fifteen to twenty days a month for about 200 yen a day, a good wage in the opinion of buraku people. Three of the men are family heads; the other three are young unmarried men. Since they are employed virtually full-time, they are not always able to get leave for the busy seasons and the women of their families say that this means much extra work for them. The jobs do bring in the all-important cash, however.

The construction work is on an eight-hour day and employs about seventy permanent laborers and as many as three hundred temporary workers on some occasions. Employees are given free transportation by truck or they may ride to and from work by bicycle if they prefer. Informants say that when farmers are not busy in the fields they can almost always get employment at the dam simply by going to the hiring office and asking for work. One or two improvement projects on the prefectural road to the south from Yasuhara to Shionoe provide occasional work for Kurusu men, and there is a forestry road being built in the mountains of the mura on which at least one Kurusu man has been employed as a dynamiter.

The son of one buraku family and the head of another work outside the village as turpentine collectors from April to October, during which period a man may earn 150,000 yen in a good year. The work is considered difficult and buraku people feel that it is altogether a risky business. Some young men hire themselves out for about 200 yen per day to work fields of families who have a shortage of agricultural personnel, but such work is only for short periods during the busy seasons. People employed in repairing irrigation ponds, of which there are only a few in Yasuhara, are paid about 180 yen a day.[3]

The sawmill, which is the largest employer of day labor within the buraku, stands at the entrance to the buraku near the Kangetsu Bridge. It was established in 1938 as a private enterprise by a long-time farming family of the community. Besides members of the family, the mill employs ten persons on a full-time, year-round basis, although they do take time out briefly during the busy agricultural seasons. Four of these steady employees are young men from Kurusu, and two Kurusu women do occasional part-time work there. Wages for men are about 190 yen per day, for women about 140 yen. All machinery at the mill is electric, requiring additional power to supplement the weak current supplied dwellings.

Rolling out the dough for noodles (<u>udon</u>). The dough is wrapped around the thin rod before rolling, never laid out flat on the board to be rolled thin.

Preparing to drop noodles into boiling water on stove.

Pounding glutinous rice for New Year's. The mallet is of wood, the mortar of stone.

Threshing early barley by hand on an old-style machine. The heads are pulled off by the long iron teeth and fall into the bamboo basket below.

Weaving straw mats on a foot-powered upright loom.

Twisting rice straw rope on a foot-powered machine. Straw is fed into the two extensions on the left.

Since the surrender the problem of getting timber has become increasingly difficult. Occasionally the owner of the mill buys a piece of forest land which he hires cut by his own men, but the hills around Yasuhara were so badly cut off during World War II that he more frequently is forced to buy timber in Tokushima Prefecture and have it hauled in rented trucks across the mountains to his mill site. Under such circumstances, the seller of the wood pays the transportation costs.

Products of the mill are quite varied. Most of the lumber is sold to the Farm Implement Manufacturing Company in Ichinomiya near Takamatsu, which places orders for boards in standard lengths. Although this company sends its own trucks to carry away the finished product, the sawmill must pay the transportation fee. The mill owner says that the existence of his enterprise depends largely upon orders placed by this firm.

For several years the mill has been making lacquered trays for sale in the Kyoto-Osaka-Kobe area. One of the sons of the family is traveling agent for the mill, obtaining orders from wholesalers and merchants in the urban areas. The work of turning the trays on a lathe, sanding them and applying the clear lacquer is done primarily by one individual from one of the buraku across the river from Kurusu. The demand for trays is seasonal, being especially heavy in March and September, according to the agent. Staves for wooden boxes, chiefly egg crates, are another important product, most of which go to Takamatsu or the prefectural agricultural cooperative. These are bundled and tied at the mill for later assembly elsewhere.

On one occasion since the surrender, the mill acquired a contract to supply building materials for construction of a large school elsewhere in Kagawa. People in the buraku say that this was the first time the family ever made a really handsome profit from the business. Although the owners have a fine home, built during the war,[4] and spent a great deal of money on a wedding while I was in Kurusu, many people feel that their financial position is insecure, for "a businessman can lose money as well as make it."

Taxes are a subject of universal complaint in Kurusu. My informants estimated that from 10 to 15 percent of their income went for taxes. Perhaps the most burdensome of these is income tax, which they have never had to pay until recently. Before the surrender peasants paid a land tax, house tax and various local taxes, but as one authority puts it:

> Now they pay income tax; inhabitant tax—500 yen plus a certain percentage of income; land tax—twelve percent of rental value plus surtaxes for villages; house tax; business tax—five percent of net income in the preceding year; special tax on income; admission tax; tax on sake; tax on electricity; tax on trucks; tax on receipts from real estate; tax on timber; taxes on cows, horses, apples, felling of the trees; tax on prime movers; sewing machine tax; bicycle tax; cart tax; tax on slaughter of cattle; (village) tax on houses; taxes on radios, dogs, weights, water wheels, land use, sleighs, medicines, special crops, orchards and fruit gardens; taxes on various agricultural machinery. This list of taxes, existing in 1949, is far from complete.[5]

Personal exemption for income taxes is 25,000 yen with a further exemption of 12,000 yen for each dependent. The tax is paid to the central government, but I have no figures for the amounts paid by Kurusu residents. Figures for 1950 indicate that thirty-one individuals paid a total of 52,115 yen in head tax (son-min-zei). The same thirty-one paid a property tax (kotei-shisan-zei) of 31,270 yen. Seventeen persons paid a total bicycle tax of 3,400 yen (200 yen for each vehicle). One individual paid the 600 yen cart tax. Three persons paid a total special income tax (shotoku-zei) of 4,900 yen. Of the thirty-one persons paying the inhabitant tax in 1950, thirteen paid more than the minimum of 400 yen collected from all taxable residents. The largest such additional payment was 32,706 yen, the smallest 18 yen. The average additional payment by twelve individuals, excepting the owner of the sawmill who paid the 32,706 yen, was 584.08 yen. The highest property-tax payment was 3,090 yen, the lowest 110 yen. All taxes are paid in three bi-monthly installments at the village office, or to the buraku official in charge of tax collection (zeikingakari).

The data do not seem to warrant the construction of a detailed income-outgo balance sheet either for the community or for individual families. Perhaps the major point to be made concerning the foregoing data is the increasing stress on the problems of obtaining enough cash for expenditures of all sorts. Occupations which do not yield a cash wage tend to be slighted in favor of those which will supplement cash income derived from other sources. In any event, few families have a really large surplus, and there is a narrow margin between going into debt and breaking even.

It is this precarious balance which makes the individual reluctant to take any risks in agriculture; procedures which are known from experience to give reliable yields are preferred to untried ones which are alleged to be more productive. If the Kurusu farmer is conservative, it is because he cannot afford to experiment.

The failure of a family to make ends meet is a potent factor in the re-acquisition by landlords of lands which they lost in the reform program. Only they can offer adequate loans to individuals with a small security, and it is often much safer to revert to a tenancy status than to try to make one's own way. This is particularly true now that under the law a man may lose his land to the government, whose privilege it is to resell it. Striking an illegal bargain with a landlord makes for greater economic security in the long run, in the view of many farmers.

Although the majority of Kurusu farmers plainly live at a level higher than mere subsistence, there are few who have achieved any sense of lasting security. With the emphasis on wage-paying work and the accompanying dependence on outside sources of employment there develops increasing interest in matters of national finance, particularly as this meets the ordinary citizen through taxation. People recognize that their savings are inadequate for an extended emergency; many feel that the best they can hope for is to continue to break about even, saving a little one year or going slightly into debt another year.

Why is it that these farmers who only a few years ago turned over fully 50 percent—and in some instances as much as 90 percent—of their crop as rent, today complain when their tax bill eats up a mere 15 percent of their income? The answer lies at the heart of the change that is overtaking day-to-day life in Kurusu. The buraku, like most of agricultural Japan, is depending more and more on cash and less on barter and credit. Cash is used to purchase the services of professional carpenters and craftsmen to build and repair one's house, cash is used to buy clothing, permanent waves and certain foods that the farmer used to make. And, most painful of all to the farmers of Kurusu, cash is used to pay taxes.

Notes

1. Meals sometimes are called asahan, hiruhan, o-cha and yuhan, but the names given in the text are more common in Kurusu.

2. The estimated caloric intake per person per day is from 2,160 to 2,300. The Occupation has taken 2,250 as a reasonable average estimate. See M. B. Williamson,

Agricultural Programs in Japan: 1945-1951, Supreme Commander for the Allied Powers, Natural Resources Section, Report 148, Tokyo, 1951, 18.

3. Forty years ago the daily wage for this type of work was one sho (3.18 pints) of rice, then worth about 18 yen.

4. A very unusual case, since materials were very short and austerity was being urged upon the nation. Their insistence on going ahead with the construction aroused much ill-feeling at the time.

5. See A. J. Grad, Land and Peasant in Japan, New York, 1952, 71.

Chapter IV

LAND REFORM

In October, 1946, the National Diet passed a law limiting the amount of agricultural land a person can hold and outlawing large holdings of agricultural lands. Under the law only so-called "agricultural persons" can own land. Moreover, their holdings are limited to land within the mura in which they reside, a provision intended to get rid of absentee landlords. In Kagawa, the maximum holdings permitted are 2.6 chō (6.37 acres), of which only 6 tan (1.47 acres) may be rented. The enforcement of the provisions of this law is a complex administrative undertaking with innumerable economic, social and political ramifications.[1]

The law in Yasuhara was put into effect by a land commission set up on December 12, 1946. It was composed of three landlords, two owner-cultivators and five tenants, each of whom was elected by the group he represented. The composition of this commission was changed after the major portion of the land had been transferred; in Yasuhara this was on August 12, 1949. The second group was composed of two landlords, six owner-cultivators, and two tenants. Four of the owner-cultivators were former tenant members.[2] The provisions of the land reform law and the composition of the commissions empowered to enforce the law both gave promise of rather sweeping changes. As we shall see, that promise has been fulfilled to a great extent but not entirely.

Before discussion of the effects of the land reform law, it should be made clear that it was put together against a background of many decades of strife between tenant and landlord. Tenants were not uncommonly allowed to exist just at the level of subsistence and no higher. Some landlords would relent, however, when there was a crop failure. It was a common practice for the tenant to confer with his landlord in an attempt to reduce the rent after a bad year. According to many informants, including both former landlords and tenants, most landlords were willing to reduce rents in years of crop failure; those who did not were subject to general disapproval. But it was not at all uncommon among those who did reduce rents under these conditions to insist that the tenant make up the difference in the following year.

From about 1921 until 1928 there were tenancy disputes (kosaku sōgi) all over the prefecture of Kagawa. If Yasuhara was not directly affected, as seems to have been the case, the spirit of the times was one which apparently penetrated into every city, town and village in the prefecture. Tenant protests were confined chiefly to requests for the lowering of high rents. The widespread nature of the disturbances seems to have contributed to their partial effectiveness.

Rents had been as high as two koku of rice per tan, often the entire yield of the crop, leaving the farmer only his wheat, barley and vegetables for subsistence. Nearly all rents were collected in rice, regardless of the crop grown on the land. The effect of the tenants' protests was to bring about reduction of rice rents by 20 percent over a seven-year period, during which time a total of 383 disturbances were recorded by the prefectural government. The following list presents a revealing classification of the reasons behind the 383 disturbances as they were officially viewed:[3]

High rents................................. 130
Influence of new thoughts[4] 112
Natural damage unrepaired by owner 62
Increase in cost of living and rise of
    production costs........................ 16
Decrease in price of grains............... 7
Government inspection of rice crop......... 5
Land rationalization 2
Increase in rents......................... 1
Other.................................... 48
                                                           383

Both tenant unions and landlord unions were formed during this period, and at their
peak the former claimed 135 branches with 15,000 active members in Kagawa alone. The
first trouble came in June 1921 when 256 tenants formed a union to oppose sixty-five landlords in Tsuda-shi and were successful in negotiating for the abolition of rents on land
planted in barley and wheat. In 1922 the Japanese Farmers' Union (Nippon Nōmin Kumiai)
was formed, and Maekawa Shoichi of the Socialist Party, a resident of Takamatsu, was influential in making Kagawa a stronghold of the union. In the years which followed there
were 58 court cases in which 349 persons were arrested.

It was the central government's break-up of the Japanese Communist Party in the
spring of 1928 which ended the activities of the Farmers' Union. Its eleven offices were
ordered closed in the crackdown on all left-wing and liberal organizations, and the 2,000
members who had not already seen the warning signals and resigned were instructed to
cease their activities at once. The union never attempted a comeback, yet its objective of
lowering rice rents may have been achieved though the results were wiped out soon after
in the price collapse accompanying the depression (see Table 5). Now, under the new law,
rice rents are outlawed. Only cash rents are legal. Thus it can be seen that the land
reform law was enacted against a background of many years of friction and agitation.

What was the nature and extent of the land in Kurusu that was subject to the land
reform law? Within the geographical limits of ko-aza-Kurusu, which coincide with the
social limits of Kurusu-buraku, there are 170 plots (ippitsu) of land, other than houseland
and forest lands, which are registered in the Land Record Book (tochi daichō) in the Yasuhara village office. (See Map IV.) This record is maintained for tax purposes, and all
land transfers must be noted in the book. The tochi daichō was set up in 1890 as a kind
of informal register and in 1899 became the official record book. The name of the owner
of each piece of land is entered and a number assigned each plot; the kind of land is also
indicated, i.e., whether it is paddy, dry-field, cemetery, wasteland, or grassland.

There are 118 paddy fields in Kurusu totaling 5.196 chō, an average of about .044 chō
(524 square yards) each. The largest is .213 chō (slightly less than one-half acre), and
the smallest is 1 bu (3.95 square yards). There are thirty-three dry fields (hatake), having a total area of .706 chō, an average size of .021 chō (250 square yards). The total
area of all 151 fields is 5.902 chō, an average of about .037 chō (.09 acres). Other registered plots include cemeteries, wasteland, grassland, etc., and total nineteen in all. Their
area is .085 chō, an average size of .005 chō (55.9 square yards).

Of the 151 agricultural plots, 56 percent changed hands during the land reform. The
following figures are for all the lands within the boundaries of Kurusu, whether cultivated
by buraku residents or by outsiders: Prior to the reform, 120 plots were cultivated by
tenants, a total of 4.325 chō (about 10-1/2 acres). The remaining fifty plots, totaling
1.662 chō (about 4 acres) were owner-cultivated. Thus, 72 percent of the land in Kurusu
was tenanted.

At the completion of the land transfers, in which 3.339 chō (slightly less than 8-1/2 acres) actually changed hands, only twenty plots remained tenanted land. Their total area is .926 chō (2-1/2 acres) 15 percent of the buraku's lands. In all but one case, the pre-land reform tenant purchased the land which he formerly had rented. The single exception is a small field whose owner formerly rented it to a tenant but who now cultivates it himself.

Equally striking changes were brought about in the status and amount of land held by Kurusu farming households. The following figures concern these families, not necessarily the lands in the buraku: Prior to the reform, seventeen farming households cultivated a total of 6.308 chō (15.45 acres), or an average of .37 chō (about .91 acres) each. Of this amount, 28 percent was owned by the cultivators, and the remaining 72 percent tenanted. It was said of Kurusu that it was a buraku of tenants. (See Map IV and Table 3.)

TABLE 3

AREA CULTIVATED BY KURUSU RESIDENTS
PRIOR TO THE LAND REFORM: 1947[*]

| House- hold | Owner-Cultivated[**] | | | Tenanted[***] | | | Percent Tenanted |
	Paddy	Dry Field	Total	Paddy	Dry Field	Total	
1	-----	04 04	04 04	46 01	01 00	47 01	92
2	-----	-----	-----	09 12	01 04	10 16	100
3	10 00	01 07	11 07	30 19	00 10	30 29	72
4	-----	-----	-----	63 04	19 04	82 08	100
5	-----	-----	-----	47 26	08 00	55 26	100
6	10 10	02 00	12 10	-----	-----	-----	-
7	-----	-----	-----	56 03	00 28	57 01	100
8	17 25	09 26	27 21	21 28	00 07	22 05	45
9	-----	-----	-----	43 15	03 00	46 15	100
10	-----	01 15	01 15	31 28	00 20	32 18	94
11	26 09	-----	26 09	26 19	01 13	28 02	52
12	04 29	10 00	14 29	32 20	21 00	53 20	78
13	22 25	07 21	30 16	06 15	-----	06 15	17
14	01 04	09 24	10 28	-----	-----	-----	-
15	-----	-----	-----	05 27	06 23	12 20	100
16	-----	-----	-----	-----	02 28	02 28	100
17	-----	-----	-----	-----	02 12	02 12	100
TOTALS	92 12	47 07	139 19	422 07	68 29	491 06	78

[*]Figures taken from Land Register in Yasuhara Village Office.
[**]Jisaku
[***]Kosaku

Note: The figures in columns should be read: tan, se, bu, meaning that Household #3 was owner-cultivator of 1 tan 1 se 07 bu of land.

30 bu = 1 se
10 se = 1 tan
10 tan = 1 chō

38

MAP IV LANDS CULTIVATED BY RESIDENTS PRIOR TO THE LAND REFORM

Field boundaries
Irrigation ditches
Owner-cultivators
Tenants

N

Scale in feet
0   1800

The situation following the land reform reveals how far-reaching were its effects in Kurusu. For the same number of farming households, the post-reform cultivated area is 6.27 chō (15.36 acres), a very slight decrease. The average holding for these households is now .3697 chō (.9 acres). This represents an insignificant decline in the average amount of land cultivated, but tenancy figures have dropped to 20 percent. The remaining 80 percent of land which is farmed by Kurusu households is owned by them. (See Map V and Table 4.)

Actually, fifteen households in the buraku purchased land, a total of 4.182 chō (10.24 acres), or an average of about .28 chō (.68 acres) each. Small amounts of household, pond, and grassland which the land transfer committees judged to be essential to the cultivation of certain fields were sold with those fields in a few cases. As pointed out above, virtually all the land which Kurusu people bought was land on which they formerly had been tenants.

TABLE 4

AREA CULTIVATED BY KURUSU RESIDENTS
FOLLOWING THE LAND REFORM: 1952[*]

House-hold	Owner-Cultivated[**]			Tenanted[***]			Percent Tenanted
	Paddy	Dry Field	Total	Paddy	Dry Field	Total	
1	46 05	04 04	50 09	-----	01 00	01 00	2
2	09 12	01 04	10 16	-----	-----	-----	-
3	40 19	01 17	42 09	-----	-----	-----	-
4	59 02	05 06	64 08	04 02	13 28	18 00	22
5	47 26	08 00	55 26	-----	-----	-----	-
6	10 10	02 00	12 10	-----	-----	-----	-
7	20 90	-----	20 09	26 24	00 28	29 22	58
8	17 25	10 03	27 28	21 28	-----	21 28	43
9	28 17	-----	28 17	14 28	03 00	17 28	37
10	31 28	01 15	33 13	-----	00 20	00 20	05
11	39 16	01 13	40 29	13 12	-----	13 12	24
12	37 19	31 00	68 19	-----	-----	-----	-
13	29 10	07 21	37 01	-----	-----	-----	-
14	01 14	09 24	11 18	-----	-----	-----	-
15	05 27	06 23	12 20	-----	-----	-----	-
16	-----	02 28	02 28	-----	-----	-----	-
17	-----	02 12	02 12	-----	-----	-----	-
TOTALS	428 20	95 20	524 10	81 04	19 16	102 20	16

[*]Figures taken from Land Register in Yasuhara Village Office.
[**]Jisaku
[***]Kosaku
(See preceding table for explanation of land measures.)

As of May 1952 the following were the amounts of land owned by residents of Kurusu, according to the Land Record Book. They probably are not entirely accurate, but the inconsistencies are minor and the figures as a whole present rather a good picture of the situation as it exists in the buraku today: Eighteen families are registered as owning a total of 5.726 chō (14.03 acres) of paddy land; 1.298 chō (3.18 acres) of dry fields; 2,403.37 tsubo (1.96 acres) of houseland; 15.785 chō (38.67 acres) of wood lots. This last

MAP V LANDS CULTIVATED BY RESIDENTS FOLLOWING THE LAND REFORM

Field boundaries

Irrigation ditches

Owner-cultivators

Tenants

Scale in feet

0   1800

N

figure was unchanged in the land reform, as forest lands were subjected to provisions of the reform only in unusual cases. Although the area is relatively large, one should bear in mind that ordinarily little income is derived from wood lots, which serve chiefly as sources of fuel and green manures.

The scattered distribution of the holdings of Kurusu farmers presents a major problem from the standpoint of the wasted time and energy required to travel from field to field. About half the land they cultivate is located within the buraku limits and half in other communities. All but two families own some land outside Kurusu. Fifteen non-residents cultivate land in the buraku; their fields account for a total of 2.121 chō (5.2 acres) or about 36 percent of the fields in Kurusu. Eleven of these families come from the commercial buraku, which are strung out along the highway in such a way as to limit severely the amount of arable land within their borders.

TABLE 5

RENTS PER TAN* IN RICE AND CASH: YASUHARA
(SELECTED YEARS FROM 1925 to 1952)

| Year | Paddy | | Dry Field | |
	Highest	Lowest	Highest	Lowest
1925	2 koku**	1.4 koku	1 koku	.7 koku
1937	1.6 koku	.8 koku	.8 koku	.5 koku
1945	1.6 koku	.8 koku	.8 koku	.5 koku
1948	120 yen***	60 yen	60 yen	37.50 yen
1950	600 yen**** (maximum)	420 yen	420 yen	262.50 yen

*One tan = .245 acres
**One koku = 4.96 bushels
***The official price for rice was set at 75 yen per koku. The cash rents were obtained by multiplying the number of koku formerly collected by the official price.
****The same procedure was used, with an official price of 525 yen per koku, but a maximum of 600 yen per tan cash rents was imposed.

Before the land reform, eight of Kurusu's seventeen farming households were pure tenants, owning none of the land on which they worked. Five families rented out land to other farmers, but with one exception these rentals were on a minute scale. The one fairly large landowner in the buraku, who is now dead, rented out about five acres of land. He was known as a difficult man with whom to deal and is said to have been very strict with his tenants.

How have the "little" farmers reacted to land reform? A matter of increasing concern to farmers in the village, and particularly to those in former "tenant buraku" like Kurusu, is the accumulating evidence of a trend toward recentralization of land holdings. The three or four years of good income and inflationary prices for farm produce just after the surrender in 1945 made it possible for almost all farmers in the village to retire their debts and to purchase a great many things which they had never been able to buy before. The boom has been leveling off in the past two or three years with many families once more in financial distress. This decline in post-war prosperity, a period called the farmers' paradise (hyakushō-tenkoku), has placed the farmers in an economic position somewhere

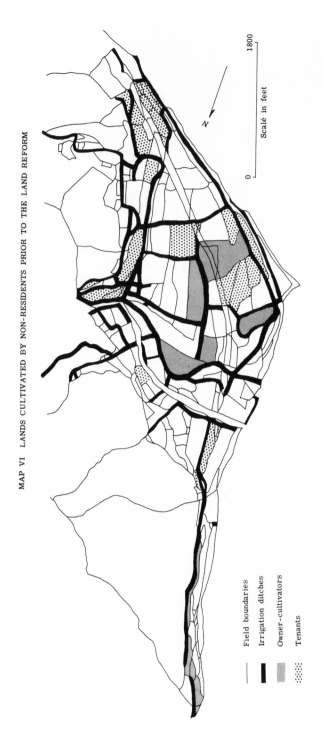

MAP VI   LANDS CULTIVATED BY NON-RESIDENTS PRIOR TO THE LAND REFORM

Field boundaries

Irrigation ditches

Owner-cultivators

Tenants

Scalé in feet

0   1800

N

between their pre-war level and the post-war peak. Almost all Kurusu people agree that they are now better off financially than at any period before 1937, but most of them fear a quick return to the old, familiar days of high rents and general poverty.

The urgent need for cash for taxes and other expenditures appears to have led some families to make sub-rosa agreements with former landowners. The latter, as pointed out above, have retained most of their forest and grasslands, and are occasionally engaged in enterprises of one sort or another. They can lend money and will make loans to families who could secure funds nowhere else. The desire and necessity to retain the right to live on the land at any cost are so great that farmers often will agree to very severe rental terms in return for the landlord's promise that the farmer will be permitted to stay on the land as long as he submits the required rents. Since he can never hope to raise enough cash to repay the debts he incurs, his tenancy becomes a permanent arrangement, with all the pre-war features. These illicit rents are never in cash, as are legal rents, but in kind, a fact obviously to the advantage of the landlord. They are, of course, also advantageous to the farmer who could not pay cash if he wished to, but seriously detrimental to him in that their actual value is far higher than official cash rents.

In 1952 there were several cases of illegal tenancy under investigation involving a total of about three acres. Informants at the official level and among the legal tenants are unanimous in the belief that the landlords are attempting to make a strong comeback. Some illegal tenancy is allegedly on an annual basis, as in the case of a widow who hires a man to cultivate part of her land from year to year. She pleads insufficient labor; if there were to be an investigation, the tenant would insist that he is actually only working on a temporary basis. Even more flagrant are the few cases in which landlords have rented out the entire two chō which they were allowed to keep for cultivation by their own households.

Since the enactment of the land reform law prices for land have increased enormously, but chiefly because of the depreciation of the yen. In 1937 good paddy land in Kurusu sold for about 1,000 yen per tan. The same land is now reckoned to be worth about 50,000 yen, although the official price is much lower. In more mountainous areas of Yasuhara, good paddy land sells for about 100,000 yen per tan. There is a great discrepancy between official land prices and those paid in actual transactions. All sales must now be made through the government, represented in the village by the Agricultural Committee (nōgyō iinkai). Parties to the sale, while fulfilling all the legal obligations, also reach a private understanding regarding the actual amount of cash which will change hands over and above the official price.

In the continuing struggle between tenants and landlords, the Agricultural Committee plays an important role. Created by law in 1951, all its members are elected by the village. In Yasuhara this body is strongly conservative, consisting primarily of former landlords. Nor is the strength of this group of former landlords limited to this committee. The mayor, deputy mayor and several important village officials are also of this class. Part of their power lies in the fact that they lost almost none of their non-agricultural lands in the reform. This permits them to retain considerable control over farmers who must rent the right to cut grass and gather fuel on these lands.

All farmers in Kurusu have verbal agreements with persons who own grass and forest lands under which they may gather fuel and cut green manure, both so essential to the farmers' existence. The general impression is that their rents, already too high, are increasing, perhaps as a part of the former landlords' gradual efforts to regain some of their lost holdings. Significantly, although there has been some tendency towards payment of cash rents for these rights, they are still primarily paid in rice.

44

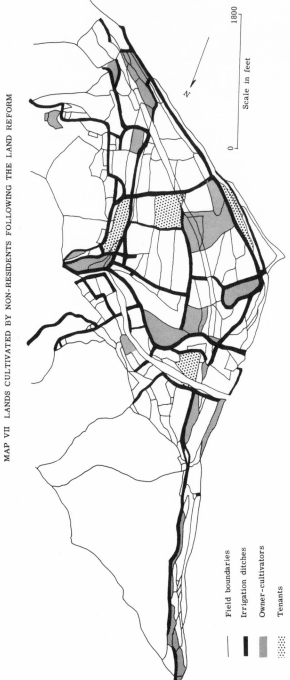

MAP VII LANDS CULTIVATED BY NON-RESIDENTS FOLLOWING THE LAND REFORM

Scale in feet

0   1800

N

Field boundaries

Irrigation ditches

Owner-cultivators

Tenants

Throughout Yasuhara, there is a practice relating to non-agricultural lands adjacent to the paddy fields which operates to the benefit of the cultivator. These areas are called hotori-bai, and although the custom has no legal basis it is almost universally observed. If the border of a field is in a sunny place, a width of about 13 feet (2 ken, 1 shaku) of the adjacent land is the hotori-bai. If the border of the paddy is in a shaded spot, the hotori-bai is a strip about 19 feet (3 ken, 1 shaku) in width. Within these strips of land the owner of the forest has virtually no rights. He may plant no trees there, and the cultivator of the field is permitted to gather grass and fuel without paying rent. Often a few trees are left on the hotori-bai, trimmed very high for use as poles around which to pile rice straw. Some farmers in Kurusu claim that they get as much as 50 percent of their annual fuel requirements from the hotori-bai. There are frequent disputes between the cultivator of the field and the owner of the adjacent land, and public opinion is often brought to bear if the two men are unable to reach an agreement.

A similar kind of customary usage obtains in the areas of terraced field (dan-batake). The growth on the walls of these fields is divided in the following manner: If the wall is very high, all the grass within an extended arm's reach from the lower field belongs to the cultivator of that field. The remainder goes to the cultivator of the upper field. In cases where the wall is low, and the top can be reached from the lower field, all the grass belongs to the man cultivating that field. This system tends to give most of the grass from the terraces to the lower fields, because it is felt that the lower field is almost always partly shaded by the upper, necessitating additional manuring for a good yield. When repairs must be made, the owner of the upper field usually is held responsible for maintaining the walls, which in some cases he has built. In a few cases, agreements for cooperative repairs have been made.

Closely related to the problem of land reform is the problem of land rationalization. In those areas of Yasuhara where the land is chopped up into numerous narrow strips, it is not uncommon to find one tan of land divided into fifty different fields. Most of these strips are so narrow that an ox-drawn plow cannot be used to cultivate them. Long, narrow paddies only two rows wide are also not uncommon; dry fields may be even smaller. Not only are individual land areas small, but one's total land holdings are likely to be comprised of several of these small fields widely separated in the village. Half of the land cultivated by Kurusu residents is located somewhere outside the buraku, some as far as two miles away. The time and effort consumed in traveling from one field to another, especially in a hilly area, is not inconsiderable.

But in spite of the inconvenience and seeming irrationality of the present arrangement, and in spite of the complaints against it, rationalization will probably make little headway in Kurusu or in Yasuhara. One of the chief reasons is the variation in the quality of the land from field to field. A man with a good paddy, no matter what its location, is loath to trade it for poorer land more conveniently located. He probably would trade if the cost of chemical fertilizers necessary to raise the productivity of poor land were not so expensive. As one farmer put it to me, "I can't afford to risk insufficient production simply to save on production costs, however high they may be."

Another reason that land rationalization will make little headway is an emotional one. Because of the farmer's complete dependence on his small land holdings, they assume a position of supreme importance in his existence. Often his family has depended for its survival on the same piece of land over many generations. Many fields in Kurusu have names of their own. Some typical ones are sema-chi (narrow land), umagatani (said to be "just a place name"), uchi-gaki (used for a large field with a small shed on it), and san-se (a three-se field, usually prefixed by "lower," "middle" and "upper"). Most of these names are said to be very old, having been used in a family over several generations in some cases. Because he has cultivated the same field so many years, a farmer comes to "know" the field and how to use it most efficiently. There is a feeling, too, that the rice grown in Kurusu possesses a special excellence that makes it superior to rice grown elsewhere in Yasuhara.

For all these reasons it is unlikely that the land in the buraku or the mura will be redistributed on a more rational basis in the near future. Perhaps the example of land reform is instructive here. Like land rationalization, land reform involves a basic change. Before the latter could be enacted into law by the Diet in 1946 there were hundreds of disturbances ranging over more than a quarter of a century, a cataclysmic war and occupation by a foreign power.

Notes

1. A detailed account of the history and development of the land reform program, from the point of view of the Occupation, will be found in L. I. Hewes, Jr., Japanese Land Reform Program, Supreme Commander for the Allied Powers, Natural Resources Section, Report 127, Tokyo, 1950.

2. Both these commissions were too small to do all the work connected with administering the reform, so one man was selected from each buraku in Yasuhara to act as adviser on his community's affairs. One of Kurusu's most progressive farmers was chosen for the job.

3. See S. Matsuura, A series of thirty-four articles in the Osaka Mainichi, November 12 through December 27, 1929, Number 21.

4. Jidai shisho moko, which meant "liberal" or "left wing" in this period.

47

MAP VIII. KURUSU: LANDS HELD BY THE VILLAGE IN 1952*

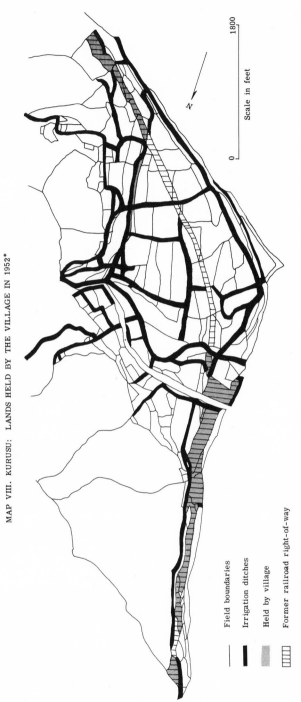

Field boundaries

Irrigation ditches

Held by village

Former railroad right-of-way

*Ownership in doubt or undisposed of in land reform

N

0   1800

Scale in feet

48

MAP IX. KURUSU: FOREST AND GRASSLANDS IN 1952

——— Field boundaries

▬▬▬ Irrigation ditches

▦ Forest and grasslands

N

Scale in feet

0   1800

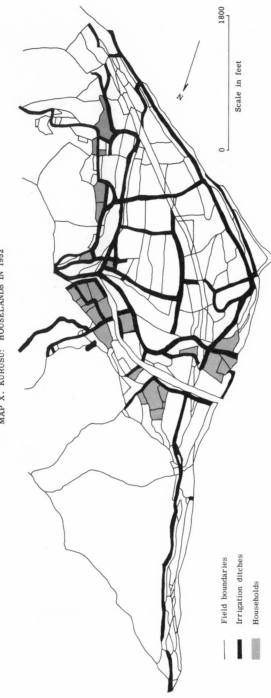

MAP X. KURUSU: HOUSELANDS IN 1952

Scale in feet

0   1800

N

—— Field boundaries

━━ Irrigation ditches

▓ Households

49

Daikon (large white radish) drying along the main road through Kurusu. Note the small two-wheeled cart.

Seeder for wheat and barley resting on a tray of woven bamboo used for carrying seed. Behind it is a limp straw carrying basket used for compost.

Chapter V

AGRICULTURAL METHODS AND PRACTICES

A farmer in Kurusu needs only six tools: a wooden plough, a hoe, a rotating harrow, a straight-toothed harrow, a weeding machine and a sickle. Actually any farmer owns more than these six tools, but they constitute his basic equipment. In addition he is likely to have such tools as a hand-operated seeder, spray equipment and, perhaps, a power-driven threshing machine. But, generally speaking, the Kurusu farmer's equipment is quite primitive, simple and inexpensive compared to the apparatus with which the average U.S. farmer attacks the soil.

Most of the farming equipment in the buraku is purchased from the retail store of the Agricultural Cooperative Union (Nōgyō Kyōdō Kumiai) in the village. The cooperative also sells the larger, more expensive machines used to process grains after harvest. Of these, the threshing machine (dakkokki) is used for rice, wheat and barley; it also serves to thresh the wheat and barley. For hulling rice a special machine called momi-suri-ki is required. There are five dakkokki in Kurusu, bought at a cost of about 30,000 yen each. All have been purchased since 1950. In Kurusu there is only one momi-suri-ki, a far more costly and complicated machine costing about 70,000 yen new. This one was bought secondhand for less than 35,000 yen.

All the threshers and the huller in Kurusu are powered by small one-cylinder gasoline engines, said to cost about 20,000 yen each. Other older machines are foot-powered and are still used by many families, although some farmers prefer to rent the newer varieties. In 1951, rental was 500 to 600 yen per tan, which included the services of an operator to run the machine. Several households still use a very old threshing method for the barley which is intended for use as chicken feed. After the harvest, the plants are drawn through a row of long iron teeth and the heads fall into a basket below. They are then pounded with a short wooden mallet to break the husks. This is a slow, tedious process not otherwise used today. No one in Kurusu uses the flail.

Three or four families use small manually operated seeding machines for wheat and barley. These are a simple perforated rotating drum attached to a fairly long handle; the drum is filled with seed and the machine is rolled down the rows of the field. Sowing by hand is far more common, however.

One of the most modern agricultural innovations is the insect lamp (keikōtō); the cooperative which owns it is discussed in detail in Chapter II. A great deal of controversy surrounds this lamp, and the debate as to its effectiveness still continues. The following statements sum up the pros and cons of the argument: The effective range of such a lamp is said to be the 4.5 chō around it, if the light is in a flat area. Opponents of the use of the lamp say that if there is only one such light in a larger area, as is the case in Kurusu, it attracts many insects, not all of which are killed in the pan of oil and water beneath the fluorescent bulb. Those which fly towards the lamp but are not trapped are said to do great damage to fields nearest the light. It is estimated that in 1951 the rice harvest in the paddies nearest the lamp was about .5 koku per tan lower than in comparable distant fields; this is about one-fifth of the total yield from a tan of good land. Another disadvantage to using the lamp is that in autumn the birds congregate on the wires which lead from the lamp to the power line and eat much of the grain in the fields below.

It is, of course, very difficult to obtain accurate information on the amount of time which a farmer spends at his various tasks, but on the basis of several estimates and much

51

observation, the figures given in Table 6 are offered as approximate requirements. In theory a farmer can cultivate one tan (.245 acres) of land per day, but the average is probably not more than eight se (about .2 acres). It is estimated that a Kurusu farmer spends about twenty-six twelve-hour days annually per tan of land cultivated, exclusive of the time required to take equipment from field to field. Since the average family culti-vates about four tan of land, some member of the household will be working in the fields about one hundred days a year.

Three kinds of fertilizer are used in Kurusu, in varying proportions as the farmer requires them or can secure them. They are chemical fertilizers, night soil and green manures. All chemical fertilizers must be bought for cash. They usually can be obtained at the Agricultural Cooperative Union in Yasuhara, which formerly handled rationed ferti-lizers. Night soil is applied both to field and to garden crops. Kurusu farmers empty the tank under the family toilet periodically and place the contents in a sunken tank along the edge of the field. These are usually left uncovered and are a danger to everyone, es-pecially to small children. If allowed to stand for several days, the night soil loses much of its odor, but if it is spread too soon its odor is almost overpowering on a hot summer day. There is a shortage of night soil in the villages as far removed from cities or towns as Yasuhara, but farmers near cities like Takamatsu can buy night soil from sewage cart-ers on a contract basis. Only two Kurusu households obtain night soil from public build-ings in Yasuhara; the two schools sell it to them. The mixture of 40 percent night soil to 60 percent water is poured on the fields from wooden buckets by means of a long-handled dipper. Chemical fertilizer and green manure are spread by hand, the former from pails, the latter from baskets slung on shoulder poles.

Green manuring is the third important method for getting high yields from worn-out land in Japan. Some farmers say that adequate green manure for a field requires the grasses from an equal area of uncultivated land, but this seems too high an estimate for Kurusu. Rights to cut such grass are obtained from owners of grassland. Because the only good spots in Kurusu are the old orchards on the hills behind the settled area, buraku farmers must also secure cutting rights on other land distant from the community. Ideal-ly a grassy area should be allowed to stand for one to two years after cutting.

Composting is done by everyone, and all houses have a place for the compost heap somewhere about the buildings. Fresh rice straw is used for green manure, as is straw which has served as bedding for cattle. Some people say that because rice straw is so important for fertilizer the farmer often does not undertake home industry involving its use. On a very few single-cropped paddies, a kind of winter vetch is grown for plowing under.

The major crops raised in Kurusu, as in the rest of Yasuhara, are wet rice, naked barley and winter wheat. A large number of vegetables are grown in small quantities the year round, but the only purely cash crop raised in the buraku is a kind of reed (i) which is used in making mats for the floors of dwellings. Only very small quantities of this reed are grown, however. Tobacco is not raised today by Kurusu farmers, although one or two did cultivate the crop in the past. Fruit trees are to be found in almost every yard, but the chestnut and persimmon orchards in the buraku have been abandoned.

About 55 percent of the land cultivated by Kurusu households is double-cropped in cer-eals; even garden areas seldom lie fallow. Unlike the situation described in Suye-mura,[1] double-cropping has been practiced in Yasuhara for as long as anyone can remember.

Rice is, of course, the principal crop. In mid-January the fields which will be used for rice seed-beds are broken with a single plowing. Sometimes green manure is spread on the field before plowing, but most farmers wait until after the ground is broken. The area of a seed-bed is about one-twentieth of the area to be planted.   Good farmers are said to plow the beds three times before sowing the seed, but most do so only twice. About the twenty-fifth of April, water is let into the prepared bed and raised mud banks (aze) are built.   The bed is harrowed, plowed, harrowed again, and carefully hoed to break up the small clods still remaining; then the seeds are broadcast.   From the completion of the mud banks, it takes about six hours to complete a one-se (119 square yards) seed-bed.   By about the first of May all beds are sown.

Ordinarily a farmer plants more seed than will actually be needed in the final transplanting to offset possible loss or damage to part of the bed.   A man plants about four shō (12.72 pints) of seed for every tan (.245 acres) to be planted, although the actual amount needed is not more than 3.5 shō (11.13 pints).

Shortly before time for transplanting, the beds are weeded to remove the hie grass, which so closely resembles the rice seedlings.   The wheat and barley are harvested, and the paddies completely plowed and irrigated within a period of ten days.   Transplanting, with all its gaiety and laughter in the fields, begins about June 10 and is almost completed by June 15.   A rope is used to lay out a straight line down a field, and portable measuring devices are used by the transplanters to lay out the ranks.   In an ordinary paddy, two or three rice seedlings are transplanted in a bunch.   A few farmers plant seven or eight together for a higher yield of straw for feed, fertilizer and home industry.   Great care must be taken to keep the rows absolutely straight, for later a plow and weeding machine will be used between them.   From the middle of June until the rice harvest begins very late in October, people are almost constantly in the fields, applying fertilizer, weeding, hoeing, plowing, clearing the irrigation channels and in a few cases spraying insecticides. Shortly before the harvest, the farmers working bent down among the tall rice plants cannot be seen from the roads.   Although this work is very hot, both sexes leave as little skin area as possible exposed to the burning sun.

One farmer gives the following schedule for fertilizing his fields: About June 20, apply superphosphate of lime, and about ten days later add potassium or caustic potash. Twenty-five days before the rice is due to ear out, apply two kan (16.54 pounds) of ammonium sulphate to each .245 acres of paddy.   When the grain heads appear, apply about five and one-half kan (45.48 pounds) of ammonium sulphate to each .245 acres of paddy. Thirty days after the head appears, spread eighty kan (about 660 pounds) of night soil. The above figures are an ideal, for in most cases the farmer spreads the fertilizers in various combinations and in amounts which he can afford to buy.

Crop damage by insects is sometimes serious, and aki-ochi, a condition in which the grains of rice fall from the ear shortly before harvest, is not uncommon.   Two or three Kurusu farmers became particularly concerned about this disease in 1951 and asked the Agricultural Cooperative Union to conduct research on methods for combating the difficulty. In other parts of Yasuhara, some have tried ferromanganese in an effort to prevent the rice from dropping, but its effectiveness is unknown as yet.   Currently the only proven prevention of aki-ochi is kyakudo, a laborious process involving the replacing of the soil of an entire paddy by removing the earth to a depth of one to two feet and filling it in with fresh topsoil got from forest land.   It is believed that rice grown in old, worn-out fields is particularly susceptible to aki-ochi.

Kurusu has the highest yield of any buraku in the village, averaging about 2.4 koku per tan (49.07 bushels per acre).   Very good paddy will yield up to 2.6 koku per tan; poor land may yield as little as 1.2 koku per tan.   The average yield in Yasuhara is 1.75 to 1.8 koku per tan.

54

TABLE 6

ANNUAL MAN-DAY REQUIREMENT FOR VARIOUS AGRICULTURAL PRACTICES: KURUSU 1951

This schedule kept by a young man interested in agricultural problems is for his own household. No comparable data from other families are available.

Type of Work	Jan.	Feb.	Mar.	Apr.	May	June	July	Aug.	Sept.	Oct.	Nov.	Dec.	Total	Own Family	Helped by others
Paddy rice.......	1	1	1	2	5	25	10	10	5	10	15	5	90	75	15
Barley and wheat.	10	10	10	5	5	15	5	-	-	1	15	10	86	80	6
Other cereals....	2	2	2	2	2	3	3	2	3	3	3	3	30	30	-
Vegetables.......	5	5	5	5	5	5	5	5	5	5	5	5	60	60	-
Composting	5	3	3	3	5	2	2	2	3	3	2	3	36	36	-
Bamboo forest*..	15	5	10	5	5	10	15	20	15	10	5	10	125	100	25
Forest care** ...	2	2	3	5	3	1	1	1	1	2	1	2	22	20	2
Gardening	2	2	3	3	2	2	2	2	2	3	2	2	27	27	-
Fruit trees	2	2	2	2	2	2	2	2	2	2	2	2	24	24	-
Grass and fuel***	1	1	1	1	1	1	1	1	1	1	1	1	12	12	-
Poultry..........	5	5	5	5	5	5	5	5	5	5	5	5	60	60	-
Miscellaneous****	13	11	10	10	20	10	5	15	10	5	5	2	116	63	53
TOTALS.........	63	49	55	48	60	81	56	65	52	50	61	50	688	587	101

*Includes cutting bamboo for drying racks, irrigation pipes, etc.
**Cutting dead wood, clearing small brush, etc.
***Gathering green manure and fuel in forest.
****Including supplementary industry (fukugyō), construction, etc.

According to the official figures for 1950, sixteen farming households in Kurusu had a total area of 52.75 tan (a little over 12-1/2 acres) planted in rice. Not all of this area is in the buraku itself. From these fields, the sixteen families obtained a total yield of 105.55 koku (almost 41 bushels per acre). Of this total, the householders estimated that they would require about 70 percent for their own use, or 73.11 koku. This figure indicates that each of the sixty individuals in these sixteen households was expected to consume about 1.2 koku of rice annually.

Although a little glutinous rice is grown by every household in Kurusu, the many varieties of wet rice are the most important in village rice culture. Known in Kurusu as ma-ine (true rice), the variety of wet rice which will be grown in a given field changes from year to year. The village office asks for volunteers to make experimental beds with new seeds, for which the farmer receives a subsidy payment from the government. Changes in soil character dictate trials for new seed, which may be bought from the government's agricultural experiment station in Busshozan, a town to the south, or from farmers in other buraku.

The rice harvest begins about October 28 and ends approximately one week later. The grain is hung up to dry on bamboo racks in the fields. Threshing may be done in the fields with a portable foot-powered or motor-driven machine, or in the house compound with the larger threshers and hullers. Straw is stacked along the edges of fields or piled around the trunks of trees and bamboo if forest lands border the field. Threshed grain is dried on straw mats spread out in any available flat place—house compounds, along the roads and paths and along the outer hallways of houses. Vehicular traffic through the village is seriously hampered by the encroachment of mats on either side of the road. After drying and hulling, the grain is placed in the storehouse in large galvanized iron containers which protect it against rats and mice as well as against damp and mildew.

As soon as the rice is cut, the fields are plowed in preparation for sowing naked barley (hadaka mugi) and wheat (ko-mugi). This plowing begins about November 2 or 3, and by about November 21 the plants in the early fields are about one inch high. It is not uncommon to see men plowing and harrowing one field in the buraku while men and women in other fields are still harvesting the standing rice.

The entire process of preparing a field for sowing is an elaborate one. First, the rice stubble is chopped out with a hoe and the field plowed from eight to twelve times. It is then hoed twice again to break up the clods, and the rotating harrow is used twice. Next the rows are made. In Kurusu the winter cereals are planted in two rows on one broad ridge with deep furrows between the ridges. When the plants are about a foot high the ridge is divided by plowing. Four or five families use the small, manually operated seeding machine, but most still sow by hand. In planting, about 3.5 sho (11.13 pints) of seed are needed for each tan of land to be planted. None of the gaiety and spirit of rice transplanting is to be observed in the mugi planting. It is cold and the people are tired.

Wheat and barley, like rice, require much fertilizing; one tan needs eight kan (66.16 pounds) of a mixture of one part calcium phosphate and three parts ammonium nitrate. Throughout the growing season, a total from 300 to 350 kan (2481 to 2890 pounds) of compost is applied to a tan of land. On warm days in December the mugi is plowed and weeded, and dirt is raked over the small plants to protect them against wind damage. The plants grow only one or two inches before April, at which time much more rapid growth begins.

Harvesting of barley begins about June 4; farmers start cutting wheat about June 8. The latest fields in Kurusu were cleared by June 15, and most were done by June 10. Wheat and barley frequently are harvested before they are fully ripened, for the farmers

Wearing rice-straw rain garb, this man is breaking clods in newly plowed paddy.

Woman channeling water in flooding paddy.

Women bundling rice seedlings in seed-bed prior to transplanting.

In the work of transplanting, these women raise the scales by which they lay out the ranks and rows, preparatory to moving back to set out the next rows.

Threshing rice in late October.
The machine is foot-powered.

Spreading rice grains on straw
mats along the main road
through Kurusu.

Rice straw stacked around bamboo on the hotori-bai.

are afraid to be caught by the onset of rainy season if they delay too long. These winter cereals are not dried before threshing, but are sunned two full days after hulling to prevent their sprouting.

Vegetables are grown the year round in Kurusu. A fairly complete list includes eggplant, white radish, cucumber, onion, leek, cabbage, Chinese cabbage, pea, spinach, sweet potato, rape seed, Irish potato, chili pepper, turnip, burdock, broad bean, soybean, Irish bean and squash. The beans, which are a major source of protein in the diet of Kurusu, are usually not raised in plots, but along the banks (aze) of the rice paddies. In spite of the variety of vegetables grown in Kurusu, they are raised solely for the farmers' own consumption. I-rush is the only cash crop grown in Kurusu.

In the fall of 1951 two Kurusu farmers planted two small experimental fields of i, a rush which is used in the manufacture of covers for the mats for floors of dwellings. The seed used in these fields came from Okayama Prefecture across the Inland Sea, where i is grown in large quantities. Both farmers hoped to try the crop in 1952 on the mountain paddies which are at present single-cropped because they are too wet for the dry winter cereal crops.

A seed bed for i is one-thirtieth the area of the proposed field. The field itself, which which is flooded at the time of planting, is surrounded by a mud bank about six inches high. On this bank are placed the plants which will serve as seed the following year. The reed in the field grows rapidly and straight, due to the lavish application of fertilizer, but the plants on the bank attain only about half the height of those in the field. The amount of chemical fertilizer used is about twice that needed for winter grain; ammonium sulphate is spread four times during the growing season.

Other farmers have a major objection to raising the crop at all, complaining that it requires too much manual labor just after the initial plowing following the rice harvest. The i is transplanted in late December, using the same methods used in the transplanting of rice. Following the harvest in early July, the reed must be dried and treated with lime. Both men plan to sell their entire output to a small factory in Yasuhara which weaves the tops for floor mats. As yet, neither is planning to undertake the weaving himself, although this has become one of the major home industries in Okayama.

Although i-rush is considered the buraku's only cash crop, government crop requisitions also are a source of cash. Since 1940 the central government has maintained a system of requisitioning certain crops at fixed official prices. This system, called kyōshutsu, has been modified from time to time.[2] In 1951, the procedure was as follows: The Ministry of Agriculture of the central government established a national quota and allocated a certain delivery quota to each prefecture, based on a pre-planting estimate of yields. The Ministry then assigned the quotas to the prefectures, and the local governments divided up their quota among the regions (chihō), a kind of loose administrative unit within the prefecture.[3] The regional offices send quotas to the village offices, but it is actually the mura Agricultural Committee (nōgyō iinkai) which makes the final allocations for each individual household on the basis of past production and estimated needs. Although it is not officially sanctioned, the buraku is in the final analysis the unit which submits the requisition.

The buraku-chō is called to the village office where he consults with the Agricultural Committee about the quota for his buraku. He returns with this figure, and on about October 15 the farmers take samples of the rice crop from scattered spots in their fields. From these spot checks (kemmi) each farmer arrives at an estimate of what his total yield will be and submits this figure to the buraku-chō. The heads of all households in the buraku then meet to review these estimates; if there is a dispute, a group is sent to the fields in question to make its own check. When all household quotas have been agreed upon by the buraku men, the figures are taken to the Agricultural Committee at the village office. Should this body question the estimates, another check of a buraku's or a household's ability to supply a certain amount will be made. Usually these buraku estimates are accepted, although deliveries under the system are officially credited to individuals. In one or two instances in Kurusu when an individual was unable to meet his quota, others in the buraku made up the deficit, thus filling the buraku's quota. Official records maintained the fiction that each farmer submitted the amount required of him.

Kurusu in 1950 sold a total of about 140 bushels of rice to the government of a total yield of about 525 bushels. This was an average delivery of 7.7 bushels for each of the seventeen households reporting. In the same year, about 135 bushels of mugi were requisitioned, of a total harvest of about 345 bushels for the same seventeen households. In the following year, 1951, the amount actually collected had dropped to about 75 bushels, or an average delivery of 4.36 bushels.

An advantage to the requisition of rice and mugi in recent years has been the payment of bonuses for early delivery and delivery in excess of quota. The bonus for the former in 1952 was 1,000 yen per koku, for the latter about 2,000 yen per koku. Official prices per koku for rice delivered in filling the regular quota were about 7,500 yen for first-class rice, 7,000 yen for second-class rice. For mugi, prices were about two-thirds those for rice. The grade of the grain is determined by a government expert at the delivery station of the Agricultural Cooperative Union. The farmer may sell any grade of grain he chooses, and he often prefers selling the high-quality product because of the higher prices paid for it, keeping the lower quality for his own consumption. Perhaps the major disadvantage to the system, at least from the farmer's point of view, is that it makes possible a fairly close village-office check on an important share of a family's income, thus making it difficult to conceal true earnings for purposes of evading the income tax.

Although he can obtain his tools and seed from the Agricultural Cooperative Union, the Kurusu farmer buys his work cattle from itinerant dealers or rents them from a neighbor. The eight farmers in the buraku who own cows, all of which are used for work and none for milk, are inconvenienced by the absence of grazing lands in Yasuhara. The rice straw, wild grass, rice bran, wheat bran and barley mash that the cattle eat must be carried to the animals' stalls. Only their salt needs to be purchased, however.

In the spring and autumn the cattle dealers come through the villages, bringing calves with them. These men are from Kagawa, and are said to belong to outcast (eta, in this case) groups for the most part. The average price for a good female calf is from 35,000 yen to 45,000 yen; the farmer receives from 45,000 yen to 60,000 yen for the two or three year old ox he sells the dealer. Even a very old ox, which will be taken to the slaughter house by the dealer, brings a slightly higher price than does a calf. It is estimated by some farmers that the highest gross profit a man can make on a cow is about 10,000 yen.

For breeding, farmers take their cows to a place in a village to the north where there is a stud bull whose owner charges 1,000 yen for the services of the animal. A very few take their cows to the government agricultural experiment station at Busshozan, about eight miles away, where artificial insemination is practiced. There is a veterinarian in Yasuhara who is usually called when an animal is sick, for few farmers are willing to risk losing the animal through improper care.

The number of work oxen owned by Yasuhara farmers has so increased since 1945 that Kurusu people find it possible to rent animals from neighbors rather than from itinerant cattle dealers. The charge currently is 1,000 yen per tan of any kind of land, plus food

Plowing a field prior to planting wheat or barley in early November.

Using the rotating harrow in the same field.

Spreading compost on a field just before seeding with wheat or barley.

for the owner of the cow, for a man does not let another farmer use his animal, but hires himself out with her. Before the use of cash became so widespread about twenty years ago, the rent for an ox was one to (3.97 gallons) of rice for one tan of paddy; one to three sho (5.27 gallons) for dry-field cultivation.

Now that Kurusu people can rent local cattle, no one in the buraku rents the oxen brought over from Tokushima Prefecture at the planting seasons by the cattle dealers. These oxen, called kariko-ushi, are still seen on the roads in strings of three to a dozen, being led across the mountains from grassy, sparsely settled Tokushima to the densely crowded plains of Kagawa. Their owners find fewer customers in the mountain village like Yasuhara today, but these oxen are much in demand farther north on the plain. It former-ly was the custom for the dealers to contract with Kagawa farmers to supply an animal for a fixed period of time and at an agreed-upon price, and then to make the trip to the Tokushima border, high in the mountains, to negotiate for the animals.

There are no horses, pigs, goats, or rabbits in the buraku, and very few in other parts of Yasuhara. The only domestic farm animals kept in Kurusu besides oxen, are chickens, which are raised by five or six families primarily for their own use. Some eggs are sold to neighbors and in other parts of the village, but the buraku is too far from Takamatsu for successful marketing of poultry products in the city. About fifteen years ago the present sawmill buildings were part of a large poultry enterprise conducted by the family that now owns the sawmill. That enterprise was subsequently abandoned in favor of the more stable lumber industry.

Besides offering the farmer a good selection of agricultural implements, the Agricul-tural Union will sell him seed, fertilizer, feed and clothing. It will also purchase his produce, process his grains and lend him money. The history of agricultural cooperatives in Yasuhara is a long one. In 1910, two cooperatives were established, both based on legal regulations passed at the national level. One of these was the Production Union (sangyō kumiai), the intent of which was to foster trade and business in rural areas by of-fering marketing, purchasing, processing and credit services to farmers. At the same time the Agricultural Society (nō-kai) was set up, the purpose of which was to propagate new and improved agricultural techniques. Financial support for these two "cooperatives" was obtained from the government, and membership was compulsory.

In 1943 the central government combined the two into the Agricultural Society (nōgyō-kai). Williamson presents a concise summary of the functions of these organizations:

> One such organization existed in each village, town and city, and member-ship was compulsory for all farmers. The village agricultural associations in each prefecture were federated into forty-six prefectural agricultural associa-tions which, in turn, were federated into a single national agricultural associ-ation. This integrated system of agricultural associations served as the means through which agricultural prices and production were controlled, food collec-tions and rationing were accomplished, and rural capital was collected for the war effort.[4]

Following the surrender in 1945 the present Agricultural Cooperative Union was estab-lished throughout Japan. In theory this is a membership-controlled organization, but ac-tually it seems to serve as little more than an arm of its prefectural counterpart. Mem-bership is voluntary, however, and regular membership is open only to farmers, while non-farmers may become associate members. In the Yasuhara organization, which was established in 1948, there are about 700 members holding 829 shares.

All officials of the Union are elected by a vote of all regular members. One of the first heads of the organization was a village "boss" who was, according to many Kurusu

people, a communist. He lent money to many bad risks and is alleged to have misman-
aged the funds of the cooperative to such an extent that people lost confidence in the organization during his administration. The present head is very popular, however, and
savings have actually doubled since he took office in 1950.

Since its establishment in 1948, the Cooperative has not paid a single dividend, and
some people claim that it must still have a huge debt. Nevertheless, most people prefer
to put what savings they do have in the Cooperative. One reason for this is that if they
wish to borrow money for good reason, it may be obtained more readily from the Cooperative than from any local bank. The feeling is very strong that since the Cooperative
lends only within the mura, a man can be more sure of the uses to which his money will
be put than he can with a bank which in theory may lend to any comer, no matter what
his place of residence.

There are, of course, complaints about the Cooperative, also. It is frequently said
that the farmer gets no real benefits from its services, and that its accountant "always
has red fingers." Some of the reasons given for the financial difficulties of the Cooperative are: (1) that employees' salaries are constantly having to be raised to keep pace with
rising prices; (2) that farmers are able to buy less and less through the Cooperative due
to falling income; and (3) that the Cooperative has made some bad purchases, e.g., large
quantities of cotton cloth purchased at inflated prices and now being disposed of at a loss.

The rate of interest on savings is six percent annually; on loans it is 12.8 percent.
These are fixed by law and are identical with bank rates. The maximum loan which may
be made is decided upon by a vote of all regular members. In 1951 the total savings de-
posited in the Cooperative was about ten million yen; outstanding loans amounted to about
three million yen.

Just prior to the 1945 surrender, the old Agricultural Society (nōgyō-kai) bought electrical machinery for processing grains. Immediately after the introduction of this machinery, individual processing of grains declined sharply. During the past two years, however,
Kurusu farmers have acquired a number of privately owned, motor-driven hullers and
threshers, a situation which apparently is once more decentralizing the processing of
grains. However, the Cooperative plant still offers several processing services. It will
polish rice, press barley, polish both wheat and barley, make wheat flour and noodles,
and make rice or mugi dumplings. The most expensive of these processes is making
wheat flour. Although a few households make their own noodles, it is not uncommon for
farmers to take the grain to the Cooperative for quick processing.

The twenty-two households of Kurusu all belong to the Cooperative, but in any given
year not all of them will have savings deposits with the organization. At the end of 1948,
sixteen buraku households had a total savings of 125,911 yen. In 1949, fourteen households had a balance of 114,574 yen. By the end of 1950 this balance, for fourteen households, was 112,847 yen. At the close of the 1951 fiscal year, all twenty-two households
had a total balance of 239,913 yen, more than double that of the previous year.

Notes

1. J. F. Embree, Suye-Mura, A Japanese Village, Chicago, 1939, 38.

2. A. J. Grad, Land and Peasant in Japan, New York, 1952, 65.

3. Ibid., 66.

4. M. B. Williamson, Agricultural Programs in Japan: 1945-1951, Supreme Commander
   for the Allied Powers, Natural Resources Section, Report 148, Tokyo, 1951, 111.

Chapter VI

FAMILY AND HOUSEHOLD

Without doubt the most important record maintained by the village office is the village register (koseki) in which vital statistics are entered as required by law. Each buraku in Yashuhara has a special section in the register, the only copy of which is kept in the village office itself. Officially the sections are for ko-aza, but buraku names are used in almost all cases where the two units are not identical. Births, deaths, marriages, adoptions, changes of residence and succession to household headship are recorded in the koseki.

When a man marries, both his family and that of his bride must affix their seals to the koseki, and the date entered is not that of the actual marriage, but the date of registration only. Often, in the past, a marriage was not registered until the birth of the first child, and under pre-war legal provisions, if a woman bore no children she could be sent back home. Consequently, her register frequently was not transferred until she had established the permanency of her marriage by the birth of the first child. At present, the government requests that registration be made not later than six months after the ceremony is held. Other time limits for the registration of certain vital statistics are: birth—two weeks; death—one week; divorce—six months. Currently a strong incentive to register the marriage within six months to a year of the ceremony itself is that the husband then can claim income tax exemption for his wife as a legal dependent.

If application for registration of a birth is submitted before the marriage application, the child becomes legally the wife's illegitimate offspring. It may be legitimatized by filing a marriage application, at which time the couple applies to the civil court to change the child's family name for entry in their register. Should a woman be more than four months pregnant, miscarriages, abortions and still-births must be reported, but they are not recorded in the koseki. If the child is born alive, no matter how short the period of life, both birth and death applications are filed in the village office. All children born alive are registered in sequence in the koseki, e.g., "first son," "fourth daughter."

Under the new post-war Civil Code, there is no householder (koshu) insofar as legal privilege is concerned. There is, however, a ranking family member (hittōsha), who is the nominal head of the family. The registration in the Kurusu koseki conforms closely to the actual situation of household headship in each family. Thus, in the case of an adoptive marriage, the wife is registered as the ranking member, for it is the family name taken by a newly-married couple which determines the holder of this position.

There are some things which the koseki, useful as it is, does not contain:

1. Any marriages or adoptions which are dissolved before being recorded.

2. Later marriages, divorces, and deaths of a son or daughter adopted or married out are not recorded because such sons and daughters are blotted out of the koseki and entered into their adopted family's koseki.

3. Deaths or divorce in the family before the koseki is established in the village office to which the koseki is transferred.

4. Population of the mura. Many people live elsewhere without removing their koseki, and many have moved into the mura without transferring their koseki.[1]

The first entries in the Kurusu family register are for the year 1872, when the koseki were established throughout Japan. Some interesting points emerge from perusal of this eighty-year record of vital statistics for the community. A great many marriages are listed, but for only thirty-six of them are the ages of both spouses given. The average age at registration of marriage for men is 27.3 years, for women 22.1 years. Actual age at date of marriage is impossible to determine, but it probably is from one to two years younger for both sexes than the above averages. Fifty-five percent of the men registered married between the ages of nineteen and twenty-four, while 69 percent of women were in this age group at registration of marriage. For the Kurusu marriages reported, men are 5.2 years older than their wives, a differential slightly higher than the 4.12 years reported for all Japan in 1930.

The following information on the present status of the households of Kurusu is drawn from an actual census taken early in 1952, and from the koseki itself. A certain number of inconsistencies were found, usually resulting from failure of a household to record a de facto change. The koseki lists twenty-five households in Kurusu, whereas there are twenty-two actually functioning. In all three cases in which the koseki fails to reflect the true state of things, it is that of an older widower living with one of his children in semi-retirement, but still maintaining a separate register.

As of June 1952, the twenty-two households lived in eighteen dwellings in the buraku, there being one case of three households sharing one dwelling and another in which two households live together. Under current registration practices, each family which has registered a householder is listed as a single household, even though two "ranking family members" may thus be placed under the same roof. This situation is worked out in various ways in Yasuhara, the solution apparently depending largely on conditions within a given dwelling unit.

The case which has been defined as three households sharing one dwelling is quite complex. The father and mother, now very old, have maintained a separate register with their eldest son and his wife and children. This son, who is unable to function normally in social situations, is kept in the house. Two younger sons of the old couple have married and live with their families in the same dwelling, but both are listed as householders. How the group operates I was unable to learn, nor is it clear whether responsibility for decisions is held by one householder or shared by all three.

The complexities of adoption are found in Kurusu as in every community in Japan. The importance of preserving the family name and of having descendants to pay proper respect to the household's ancestral tablets cannot be overestimated. There are a number of ways of solving the problem of maintaining the name:

1. If a man has a son, he will marry in the course of time, and will provide heirs in the family line.

2. If a man has no sons, but an adult daughter, he will arrange for her to make an adoptive marriage, so that her children will carry on the family name.

3. A man with adult daughters but no sons of his own, may still adopt a son and arrange a marriage for him, letting his own daughters make regular marriages and leave the household.

4. Should a man have no children at all, he may do one of two things: (a) Adopt a son and arrange a marriage for him, or (b) adopt a daughter and arrange an adoptive marriage for her.

In Kurusu, all of these possibilities are found, but succession from father to own son is the most common. In one case, however, a man has adopted a son even though he had adult daughters and thus has caused the succession to pass through an adopted male. There are two cases of the childless head of a house adopting a son and arranging a marriage for him, and two cases of adoption of a girl, for whom an adoptive marriage has been arranged. A situation such as that described above in 4(b) occurs when the most readily available child for adoption is a niece, granddaughter, or perhaps an unrelated female child. Younger sons often will be adopted out while still youths, or as husbands for daughters of houses without sons.

By far the most common type of adoption is that which occurs in the extended family, e.g., adopted children are often nieces and nephews of the adopting couple, usually from the family of a brother of the household head. One Kurusu man adopted his daughter's daughter, and arranged an adoptive marriage for her, because his only son had been killed in World War II. Kurusu people prefer having property stay under the control of the extended family. They give this feeling as the reason for the occasional adoption of a female relative and the subsequent arranging of an adoptive marriage for her, as in the two cases above.

Like marriages, adoptions may be dissolved, and therefore are not ordinarily immediately recorded in the koseki. Even with this caution, Kurusu's register shows a number of broken adoptions. Such dissolutions are not always a matter of failure after a year's trial, but may take place as long as five to ten years after the adoption was recorded. There are no ceremonies surrounding adoption, except that in some cases the two fathers concerned exchange cups of sake to seal the bargain. Just as a bride maintains occasional contact with her family, an adopted child may pay rare visits to his own house. Embree makes the point that, "The family system is patrilineal in pattern but, through the custom of adoption, often matrilineal in practice."[2]

Attitudes towards becoming an adopted husband (yōshi) are by no means favorable. There is an old proverb, often mistranslated, Konuka san-go attara, iri mukō-ni yuku-na, meaning, "If you have as much as three go of rice bran, don't become an adopted husband." Men give a number of reasons for this feeling, but by far the most frequently heard is that it is very difficult to adjust to a new family. The adopted husband takes not only the name of his bride, but assumes the Buddhist sect of her household and is bound to obey her family in all things, as well as his own family in certain things. It is generally felt that only a mild and good-natured young man is capable of making this extensive adjustment, and the arrangement of such a marriage is considered to require somewhat more subtlety than is needed for the ordinary situation. The family of the girl is particularly careful, for they want to be certain that the young husband will stay. Stories of the adopted husband who spends his wife's money freely for a time and then leaves the family are common. When such a marriage is terminated, the reasons most commonly given are the difficulties between the girl's father and the adopted husband, and financial squabbles.

Though adopted husbands, like brides, come from outside the buraku, they are accepted on equal footing with men born there. Two of the three elected officials of the buraku in 1952 were adopted as husbands. The sole foreign resident, a Korean, is also an adopted husband. He has taken his wife's Japanese name, of course, and speaks the language with a slight accent. Not until I had been working in the community for a number of weeks did I learn of his background, and then only in passing. He is apparently universally liked. In 1952 he was given his turn as nominal head of his household to sponsor the buraku festival to Jichinsan.

Men who were born in Kurusu very occasionally express disapproval of an adopted husband's activities, especially when these concern community matters, and lay his failure to

Elderly couple in best clothing for New Year's.
This picture was taken to commemorate their
fiftieth wedding anniversary.

Small boy in new clothes, worn
on special occasions.

Elderly man, his adopted daughter
and her two children.

"behave well" to his outside origin. Such opprobrium is rarely heard, and seems to be used only as one more complaint against a man who is disliked anyway.

As indicated above, brides and adopted husbands come from outside the buraku. (See Table 7.) Of the fifteen brides for whom we have data, twelve come from within the area of the county (gun) in which Kurusu is located. Even the three who come from outside Kagawa are from a nearby section of the neighboring prefecture of Tokushima. Three of the five adopted husbands come from the same county, one from nearby Tokushima, and one from Korea. Two of the other immigrants into Kurusu are from Takamatsu; three are from the big urban center of Osaka. These last five are felt to be temporary residents. During my stay in Kurusu the three from Osaka left the community and returned to that city.

TABLE 7

PLACE OF BIRTH OF IMMIGRANTS TO KURUSU

Kind of Immigrant	Yasuhara	County	Shikoku	Other	TOTAL
Brides..................	4	8	3	-	15
Adopted husbands........	2	1	1	1	5
Other...................	-	2	-	3	5
TOTAL	6	11	4	4	25

Under pre-surrender law, a household consisted of the head, his wife and unmarried children, his eldest son and his family, and often retired grandparents and a servant or two. Within the household the head's power was unchallenged and in theory his will was deferred to on all occasions. In actuality, the head of a household was, and is, expected to serve the interests of the family as best he can and it is his primary duty to consider those interests rather than his own. What he perceives to be the proper course of action for any one member of the family is determined in large part by the relationship between such action and the welfare of the family.

No one in Kurusu now has servants, but in pre-surrender days the wealthy families occasionally took in a boy or girl servant whom they never officially adopted, but for whom they arranged marriages when they came of age. At a memorial service for the dead that I attended, one of the guests was a man who had been taken in and cared for by the man for whom the service was being held.

Households and families in a community like Kurusu stand in rather vaguely defined status relationships to each other. A prominent family is one with money or one with a good, or old, name in the community. Wealthy families may be unpopular, but they wield undeniable power and live on a grander scale than do their neighbors. It has not happened in Kurusu, but in other communities in the area, wealthy families may dissociate themselves from the cooperative relationships ordinarily obtaining in their buraku. Occasionally, a wealthy man may even be ostracized from the community, but this has not happened in Kurusu, either. When a formerly wealthy family comes upon hard times, their prestige and political power may continue due to the long-standing relations of obligation which they have established with less prosperous neighbors.

Families which have long been associated with power and influence in the village are usually rich, but members of families which were important in feudal times, before the

Restoration of 1868, are deferred to and exercise considerable influence over lesser families. In Yasuhara, one of the most influential priests of the village is a descendant of the former ruling family of the province which is now Kagawa Prefecture. Such eminent families (meika), some of which were formerly large landowners, often control village politics.

Within Kurusu itself there are a number of interesting interfamily relationships. Former tenants of a buraku family frequently help their erstwhile landlords to prepare festival meals or do other small services for them. These subordinates are called de-iri-mono, indicating that they have a well-established relationship to their superiors. There is only one really clear-cut case of this sort in Kurusu. An old man now living was in the distant past aided by the father of a contemporary householder. The nature of the help was such that the recipient has placed himself and his children in a de-iri-mono relationship to the son of his benefactor. The latter told me about the arrangement himself, and added, "It is unusual for these things to go on so long. When the old man dies, the children (who are adopted) probably won't feel obligated to keep it up."

Other families are friendly or antagonistic as personal preference dictates. Occasionally, when there is some degree of blood relationship there may be a carry-over of family feuds into inter-family relationships in Kurusu. The two families related by the closest of the blood ties in the buraku today have almost no social intercourse, and there is said to be bad feeling between them.

Notes

1. J. F. Embree, Suye-Mura, A Japanese Village, Chicago, 1939, 62-63.

2. Ibid., 85.

Chapter VII

THE LIFE CYCLE

Although sex activities figure in many popular songs and form the basis for innumerable stories and jokes, the sex act itself is very private. Young men may upon occasion among themselves boast of sexual adventures, but a person's own private sex life is discussed far less frequently than is that of others. Indulgence in extramarital relations on the part of a male should be carried on discreetly if at all; such activities are generally tolerated if they are not carried to extremes. On the other hand, a woman who is found out in an adulterous relationship will be divorced and sent back to her family; the community is severe in its judgment of her.

Widows seldom remarry, although they are in theory free to do so. Since it frequently happens that a widow occupies a house alone with her children, she is relatively free of access to local men if she is so inclined. Again, condemnation of her activities may become general if she is too open in them. There was much gossip in Kurusu and in the mura when two men who were involved in affairs with the same local widow met at the poll on election day and had a fight over her. Since all the parties concerned are fairly prominent people in village affairs, it was felt to be an unusually embarrassing situation. If a young widow chooses to stay in the home of her husband's family under their supervision or if she returns to her own family, her opportunities for such exploits are limited by the strong disapproval of her elders.

Although privacy is highly desirable in sexual matters, it is not always attainable in Japanese dwellings. Sexual intercourse is performed as quietly and as quickly as possible at night after the children are asleep, and neither partner disrobes fully. There are many jokes which deal with the variety of sounds made by wooden floors rattling in the night. It is not thought essential that intercourse be pleasurable for the wife, and there is almost no foreplay. Sex is a business to be got over with quickly. It is somewhat embarrassing, no matter how pleasant.

Modern methods of contraception are not practiced in Kurusu, according to available information, but I have no data about native techniques. The local drug store carries one or two varieties of contraceptives, but the owner states that very few are sold through his store. It is unlikely, as a matter of fact, that anyone purchasing contraceptives would do so at the village outlet, for such matters become common knowledge quickly. There are many opportunities to get them personally or through friends in the anonymity of Takamatsu. A few people whom I asked gave three major reasons why contraception is not practiced in rural areas like Yasuhara: (1) children are wanted; (2) contraceptives are troublesome and inconvenient; and (3) the expense of contraceptives is prohibitive. In "A Survey of Public Opinion in Japan on the Readjustment of Over-population,"[1] the first two of these reasons were given by almost two-thirds of those surveyed as reasons for not practicing contraception.

A few houses in Kurusu possess pornographic photographs, wood block prints, paintings on silk and ceramic pieces. However, it should be emphasized that there is no general circulation of such objects about the house among family members. Several people who were asked about such practices were genuinely shocked at the idea. But, on the other hand, no particular shame is attached to possessing pornographic items; they are interesting and amusing. A major limiting factor in the number of such things a man may own is their not inconsiderable expense. They are found today chiefly in Kurusu's wealthier homes, or homes of former means.

69

Birth and Infancy

There are some folk beliefs concerning pregnancy to which older people still cling, citing an array of cases to prove their truth. If one's first guest on New Year's Day is a woman, and if there is a pregnant woman in the household, the child will be a girl; if the first guest is male, the birth of a boy is assured. The desire for male children is so strong that on the first day of the New Year, women are supposed to sleep late while the men of the house prepare the morning meal. Before the women arise, men exchange visits from house to house, thus insuring both good fortune and male offspring if the family visited includes a pregnant woman. In recent years, this custom and others associated with it have declined; it is estimated that no more than half the households in the buraku observe them at all.

In her fifth month of pregnancy, the family of the woman holds a household observance called the ceremony of the sash (obi-no iwai). The obi is the wide, elaborately tied belt worn with kimono. A small party for close relatives is given, to which the midwife is invited, and the pregnant woman is presented with an obi ten shaku (about ten feet long), made of red and white silk. the conventional congratulatory colors. She puts on the belt to insure an uneventful pregnancy and successful delivery. Mochi is made at this time and given to relatives and near neighbors.

There is no midwife in Kurusu, but there are four licensed ones in the mura. It is not unusual to call a woman from outside the village; one midwife who is currently very popular is not a resident of Yasuhara. According to Kurusu women, they seldom relied on midwives before 1945, usually calling in an experienced old woman from the neighborhood. Only landowners and other wealthier families called in midwives, while in most other families neighbors helped with the whole affair. Partly because sanitation has been emphasized by public education, and partly because of the strict laws enforced by the Ministry of Welfare, employment of midwives has increased; most families have felt able to afford them for the first time in the post-surrender period of prosperity.

Professional midwives are now licensed, but the fee they charge is dependent upon the financial circumstances of the family. It is estimated that the average fee is about 1,500 yen, which includes some pre-natal service, delivery and caring for the child until its naming ceremony seven days after birth. Women credit the reported decline in the number of miscarriages and stillbirths to the licensing of midwives.

Delivery takes place in the home, in the room in which there are no household god shrines; one informant said the delivery room (sanshitsu) should be the "darkest, dirtiest and least-used" room in the dwelling, and many stressed the unclean nature of the event. Water used in bathing the mother and child must not be poured in a sunny place, for that would defile the gods (the Shinto kami) and bring punishment to the offender. The water usually is poured under the elevated floor of the sanshitsu. There is no agreement about the proper way to dispose of the afterbirth and umbilicus. In a very few households there is some concern about the direction in which a woman lies during childbirth, but there seems to be consensus only that she should not face north, the direction from which evil comes.

After the birth of the first child, the husband and wife will sleep apart. The baby, whose bed is near the mother's, does not sleep with her for almost his first year in most households. On the eighth day after birth (the seventh by our reckoning, since in. Japan the day of birth is counted the first) the family holds a small party, inviting close relatives and friends and the midwife as guests. It is customary for the women of the community to present a gift to the child. The Women's Club of Yasuhara has sub-branches, in one of which Kurusu is a subordinate unit. The woman in Kurusu who is elected (or occasionally appointed) representative of the buraku in this organization, makes the rounds of the houses to collect 30 yen in cash from each towards the purchase of a gift for the child. In theory she also spreads word of the birth, but usually this has been done by the buraku-chō before her. Sometimes relatives give clothing to the child when it is born, in return for which they receive a gift of three white and two red manjū, a kind of cake filled with bean paste. On the cakes is placed a piece of paper bearing the child's name. At the naming ceremony itself, a tray of food is simply offered the child and his given name is pronounced over him.

For thirty-three days, the new mother is subject to a number of restrictions and taboos, for she is considered ceremonially unclean to a greater degree than a menstruating woman. Practices relating to this period differ considerably from house to house in Kurusu, and there seems to be a steady drift away from any special observances at all. If there is an old person, especially a woman, in the house, the young people will go through with some of the practices, but lacking such pressure they largely neglect them.

It is felt that if the mother has much milk, the child will grow strong and healthy. Although the child usually is not weaned until the arrival of the next baby, he will be given solids long before that time. Actually, solids are formally introduced into the baby's diet on the hundredth day. If no children follow, a child may ask for the breast until he is ready to go to school when he is six, and although there are accounts of how, until about twenty years ago, children sometimes nursed until they were eleven or twelve, such permissiveness in breast-feeding is rarely found now. An important weaning technique is to tell the child that other children and adults will laugh at him, and the force of the fear of ridicule is a strong deterrent in most cases. If the mother still has trouble in weaning, she smears her nipples with chili pepper juice.

By the time a child is a year old, and somewhat earlier if possible, he has been taught not to soil his clothing, having been instructed to warn with words or sounds that he must eliminate. It is common to see very small children being held out over the doorstep or the side of a path or road, clothing pulled up, with the mother urging elimination by the appropriate sounds. Eventually the child learns to respond to these, and then to anticipate them. Children are expected to have full control over elimination processes by the age of two, but because toilets in rural Japan are so dangerous, most parents do not permit the child actually to use the toilet alone until he is three or four years old.

Mistakes and lapses in elimination control are not severely scolded, nor is any physical punishment meted out. Not one woman in Kurusu to whom I talked about the subject remembered instances of such punishment, nor did they see the necessity of concern over the issue.[2] The heavy cotton wrappings of the young baby are not changed when he cries, nor even when the parent knows that they have been soiled, but the baby is washed frequently. Rural women give as one reason the fact that they are far too busy with household and agricultural work to attend to the child every time he cries. This is especially true during planting and harvesting seasons, when feeding also will depend largely upon how much free time the mother has.

During slack seasons, however, nursing babies are given the breast whenever they demand it. There was initially some hesitancy about letting children nurse when I was about, but the uneasiness lessened considerably with the passage of time. All children, especially boys, go frequently to their mothers and open their kimono to get at the breast and unless the mother is unusually busy the child will not be sent away until the woman feels that he is satisfied. A favorite posture is lying prone across the mother's lap, nursing at one breast and grasping the other with the hand.

When the baby is old enough to be carried on the back, usually at the end of the thirty-two day period of its mother's restrictions, the heavy cotton is today frequently replaced by a kind of rubberized cloth which is calculated to protect the garments of the person carrying him. The baby is held on the back by means of a double length of cloth under his buttocks and under his arms; in cold weather he is covered by a loose padded garment worn by his bearer. From this vantage point the infant, when he is old enough and sufficiently strong, pulls himself up to a comfortable riding position and surveys much of what is going on about him. When he cries, he is bounced lightly while the person carrying him croons to him. If he persists in crying, efforts may be made to talk to him and stroke his head. If all this is to no avail he will be laboriously unstrapped and given the breast.

One hundred days after the birth of a child, he formerly was taken to the local Shinto shrine, but this custom (called momoka-mairi) is dying out among the young parents of the buraku. Today it is customary to go to the shrine with the child on the first Fall Festival following his birth, although some people take him on the first New Year's after birth. The child is dressed in new, very gay clothing, for this first pilgrimage (hatsu-mairi) is an auspicious occasion. The priest at the shrine gives the child a wooden nameplate, recites a prayer over him, and enters his name in the shrine register of parishioners (ujiko).

From this time on the child will attend the shrine, primarily on festival days, when he goes with his family. When he grows older, he may go there to play, for except for the two school yards the shrine compound is the only place flat enough and big enough for group games like softball, tag and races. The child is also taken to the family's temple early in life, but most people in Kurusu feel that there is even less urgency about this first pilgrimage. The child may go to Buddhist festivals, although there are few of them at the temple, but the local establishment does not have as large a play area as the shrine.

As has been pointed out in the chapter on religious life, the child learns what he knows of both Shinto and Buddhism at home, not from priests. He is acquainted with the ritual and purposes of both systems through attending home ceremonies and from observing those activities connected with the home's sacred places.

Childhood

As has been stated in virtually every book on Japan which treats the subject at all, children are indulged. Correction takes on severity only in serious breaches of manners or discipline; I never saw an adult strike a child during my stay in Kurusu. They are not encouraged to creep, but once they learn to walk, usually between a year and a year and a half (the latter is quite late), there are very few things that they do not explore. Although the young are cautioned not to poke fingers through the thin paper of the sliding doors, a house with small children can always be recognized by the tattered lower portions of the doors. The open hearths for cooking and heating are actually most dangerous for small children, and fear of fire is so great that scolding and physical removal are very apt to take on more serious tones in the matter of keeping away from fire receptacles. Play with matches is similarly discouraged.

In my opinion, the number and importance of the prohibitions directed at children in a Japanese house have been overstated in various Western works touching on the subject. There are virtually no bric-a-brac with which the child must endlessly be cautioned not to play. Stairs are rarely encountered, and although he may hurt himself if he tumbles from one of the elevated rooms to the ground level, the drop is less than two feet. If he does push holes in the paper sliding doors, the damage will not be repaired until autumn, or may even be left until there is no further danger to it from small fingers. The doors to the zashiki are kept in reasonably good repair, but others are only occasionally re-covered. The damage a child in our Western house can do to papered or painted walls with a few strategically placed crayon or ink marks far outstrips, in terms of financial loss, the damage a Japanese house suffers from its young occupants. Should he burn himself in the fire, the Japanese child's parents assume that he will soon learn not to touch such dangerous things again. At least that is the assumption in Kurusu.

As mentioned above, the toilet is a dangerous place, and one into which the child is not permitted to go until it is felt that he can take reasonable care not to fall through the opening into the tank below. There is, on the other hand, no danger of his breaking the plumbing or letting the water run until he floods a portion of the house. All in all, in matters of household conduct, the child is given much latitude, for the damage which he can do is quite limited.

If a child demonstrates an unseemly temper, or if he is stubborn to the point of being unmanageable, his mother or grandmother will give him the moxa (mogusa) treatment. A small cone of powder is placed on the skin, and while the child is firmly held, the powder is lighted. This method of cauterization is believed to relieve a variety of muscular aches and is regarded as a certain cure for misbehavior. The scar it leaves is for life, and the efficacy of the treatment is indicated by the fact that it is a rare child who must be given it a second time.

Instruction in adult techniques is carried on through ceaseless, patient demonstration, the child being encouraged to do the thing himself, imitating the movements of the adult as best he can. I noted striking examples of this process on several occasions. A four-year old boy, who because he was the youngest child was constantly with his widowed mother, was present once when his mother was making tea and serving it with cakes to two guests. There was a charcoal brazier in the room, a box of charcoal and iron chopsticks with which to handle it. She had a tea set, a kettle and tea and water. As she talked, she was building a fire over which to heat the water. Her small son watched her lift the charcoal from the box into the brazier a number of times and then wrested the chopsticks from her faintly resisting fingers and continued the process himself.

When he dropped a piece she would, without interrupting the flow of conversation, adjust the chopsticks to his fingers and help him pick it up, after which he would continue unaided for a time. This same procedure took place with pouring the water, putting the kettle on the fire, cleaning the tea cups, putting tea into the pot, pouring on the boiling water, pouring the tea and serving it. When she got up to get the cakes from the kitchen, he pulled at her, demanding to know where and why she was going, and hung on to a kimono sleeve until she told him. Thereupon he demanded to be told where the cakes were and learning, insisted on getting them himself.

His mother finally gave in and sat down again while he went off to the kitchen. After much clatter and delay he appeared with a tray bearing two plates of cakes, some obviously just rescued from the dirt floor of the cooking area. The guests smiled indulgently; the widow praised him for his efforts; the boy beamed and proceeded to devour most of the cakes, including those offered him by the guests as a reward.

This sort of permissiveness extends into the area of sexual activity, too. Infant sexuality is accepted unless it occurs in what is regarded as inappropriate surroundings. Small children indulge in sexual play without censure, several common games having clear sexual overtones. Masturbation is regarded as harmless in very small children, but as the child grows older he is likely to hear warnings from elders and stories about the adverse physical and mental effects the practice has on growing youth. This advice stresses the increased nervousness and fatigue that allegedly result from masturbation.

Parents are likely to be comparatively rigid in matters of etiquette. All parents are deeply concerned that their children learn to show respect properly. This training begins before the infant can talk. Strapped to his mother's back, his head and shoulders will be inclined when she bows in greeting. He learns to welcome guests and relatives as soon as he can walk, if not before, and at the elders' signal of the proper verbal greeting, he will bow. All this is some time before he can remember or even articulate many of the conventional phrases of greeting, of course. Great latitude is permitted young children in matters of etiquette, but they are constantly reminded of what they should do, even if they are not actually expected to conform to the patterns.

Shortly before a child starts to school, when he is six years old, he begins to associate more and more with children of his own sex, but mixed gangs still play together for the first two years of school. Buraku children often play together, so that there may be a spread of two to four years among members of a play group. There begins to be differentiation in the kinds of games played also, for girls learn early to be restrained, while boys continue their pleasant freedom somewhat longer. Boys' games are noisy and strenuous, while girls learn less rough-and-tumble activities.

There are three schools in Yasuhara, the primary school and its branch and the middle school. All three are housed in separate plants, constructed largely with the combined use of national, prefectural and village tax funds. The primary schools comprise the first six grades; the middle school makes up the last three of the nine grades of compulsory public-school education. All are co-educational.

In 1951, the main primary school had fifteen rooms and a total enrollment of four hundred, while its branch had an enrollment of thirty-five. Only one of the sixteen primary school teachers is employed at the branch school, and both are under the same principal. Because of the great size of Yasuhara, which is fourth largest of Kagawa's 147 mura, it was necessary to establish the small school to serve those communities located at a considerable distance from the main school. In Yasuhara, as in most villages, the central primary school is near the village office and other public buildings. The structure now in use is old, having been constructed some years before the 1937 China Incident.

The middle school was completed in April 1949, and has nine teachers supervised by a principal. Teachers at this school carry a very heavy work load; all must combine teaching and secretarial duties as there are no funds for secretarial help. There are no branches of the middle school, and some of its two hundred and sixty pupils walk for two hours to reach the school from their homes.

The year is divided into three terms: the first term, from April 5 to July 25; the second term, from September 1 to December 25; and the third term, from January 3 to March 20. Besides the regular legal holidays, rural pupils receive about fifteen days a year for "harvest vacation" usually divided equally between the spring wheat and the autumn rice harvests.

The educational system of Japan has undergone far-reaching changes during the Occupation, some of which have raised adverse criticism in Yasuhara, as in other areas of the country. Revision of texts has not excited much interest in the village, although an occasional middle-aged person expresses regret that the children are no longer taught Japanese history as it was given in pre-surrender education. It seems to them unnatural that a child does not know of Amaterasu-o-mikami, the Sun Goddess, and it is surprising even to the foreigner to realize that a whole generation of children are almost wholly ignorant of their country's mythology.

that children learn nothing much at all in school
ed on several factors, most important of which is
ns for passage into middle and higher schools.
iildren do nothing but play, quite unlike the days
ed hard so that they could go on to middle school
ipline is laid to the inexperience of new teachers.
sory education (formerly six, now nine years),
is practically automatic. As both Benedict[3] and
back a grade, especially in primary school.

in 1880, offered a four-year course, which is
er people of the village. About forty years ago,
years, and most of the residents of Kurusu have
oximately twenty years ago an additional two-
as introduced under the name of youth schools
hing to vocational instruction ever available to
ent to the evening classes in military drill,
ouths of the village were expected to attend.
wing and other homemaking skills were offered.

is there a uniform, for they would be too ex-
pils in city and town schools and most of these
iiforms. The fact that Yasuhara children do not
s of the village.

has been the introduction of co-education, which
is not popular in Yasuhara. In the annual fall athletic meet in 1951 the final number was
a mixed square dance exercise about which the students themselves complained afterwards.
But it is the older people who are especially critical of the new system as it applies to
the middle school, claiming that it lowers the morals of the youth and leads to trouble
later when it comes time to arrange a marriage for a girl or boy. There was a stir of
indignation throughout the prefecture with the revelation in the spring of 1952 by the Board
of Education of Kagawa that several middle-school girls had been discovered to be pregnant. No such occurrences have been reported from Yasuhara.

It is certainly true that co-educational schools present an anomalous picture. In no
other activity do boys and girls participate so closely. What folk dancing is still performed is done in separate groups. Work in the fields may involve both men and women,
but they are almost always siblings, relatives or married couples. Social events always
separate male and female. Dating is, of course, entirely absent and marriages are largely arranged, frequently over the protests of the principals. It is no wonder that the young
people are "embarrassed" by co-education, fitting as it does so poorly into life outside the
school.

Another important post-surrender reform has been the establishment of parent-teacher
associations under the name PTA (pronounced in Japanese pi-chi-ei). Dues in the association are 15 yen a month per student, not per family. Before the surrender, Yasuhara had
an organization somewhat comparable to the PTA, but its chief function was the raising of
funds for the schools. The present PTA concerns itself with educational problems as well
as fund-raising, but in Yasuhara as in most communities in the area, the latter is by far
its most important activity.[5] The group meets on the twenty-third of every month, and it
is estimated that about fifty percent of eligible parents come. It is at PTA meetings that
much discussion of the possibility of offering more vocational courses takes place; such
meetings are also good sources of information for parents about their children's chances
for further education.

About 35 percent of the graduates of the middle school attend higher schools, according to the principal of that school, but this probably is much too high a figure. Those who do go attend the Ichinomiya Kōtō-gakkō, about eight miles to the north of Yasuhara.

Annual events of the middle school include two excursions, one in spring and another in autumn, on which all pupils are supposed to go. They usually take place during the first ten days of May and the first ten days of October and are commonly visits to places of interest in the prefecture. During this season public transportation facilities are jammed with traveling students who are hurried from one spot to another in what seems to be a continuous state of exhaustion.

During the summer vacation those students who can afford it are taken on a trip to more distant spots—generally to Kyoto or Osaka—to visit factories, business establishments, famous shrines and temples, and other places of interest. Few students from Yasuhara can pay the expenses of such a journey, but it is made by some each year under the supervision of a male teacher. No Kurusu students went on this trip in 1951 or 1952. During the first ten days of February there is an annual school play which is always performed to a full house of parents and relatives of the children.

A total of twenty-seven Kurusu children now attend secondary school in Yasuhara, twenty-two in the primary school, five in the middle school. There are no Kurusu children currently attending higher schools, but one boy was sent to Osaka in 1951 to live with relatives while attending a middle school there, an extremely unusual case.

A man's closest friends throughout his life are those he makes at school in his own age-group, and those with whom he has played in the buraku. Although the bonds are strong for girls, they lose contact after marriage to a far greater extent than do men, since they leave their buraku. This factor alone makes the position of a young wife coming into the buraku difficult, for her husband is surrounded by childhood friends, while she is an outsider and intruder. The school yard becomes a place for recreation after school hours where softball games are organized and other games can be played on its broad flat surface. Since promotion from grade to grade is automatic, and admission to the village middle school virtually guaranteed, these age groups remain fairly constant in membership.

Adolescence

Adolescence is a trying period for both sexes, but evidence seems to indicate that the girl has less difficulty with this period than does the boy. She has been taught to obey the members of her family; only her younger sisters are subordinate to her in the immediate family. Adolescence is a period of preparation for marriage, for during adolescence she is expected to obey her family as she will obey her husband. The boy, however, is expected to develop adult qualities of behavior and attitude; ideally he remains under the control of the head of the household, a control which frequently thwarts his wishes and constantly reminds him of his primary obligations to the family. It is, after all, the family which is the important unit; the problem is for the youth to be made aware of the extent of his involvement in it.[6] Boys just out of school pass through a period of very difficult adjustment, but usually accept their responsibility to the family in the matter of arranged marriage.

That the above is a somewhat over-idealized picture in Yasuhara is indicated by the number of unsuccessful adoptions and arranged marriages. Unfortunately the family register does not record the majority of these broken contracts, because a period of waiting, during which time the arrangement is tested, has become the rule. Should the union prove unsuitable, it can then be dissolved without taking legal steps.

Marriage

In Japan today there are two kinds of marriage, the arranged marriage (miai-kekkon) and the love-match (renai-kekkon). The latter is far less common than the arranged marriage and is generally disapproved. Arranged marriages are made in accordance with the wishes of the family, while the latter is characterized by family strife and absence of customary negotiation and ritual. All marriages in Kurusu for the past fifty or sixty years except one have been of the miai variety, the only true love-match having been made some forty years ago under unusual circumstances. Informants are emphatic in their statements that it is easier for a young person to make his own wishes known in the matter of choosing a mate now than it was before the surrender. Many heads of households claim that they would never force a young man to marry a girl for whom he expressed violent dislike. Girls apparently are given far less choice unless they happen to be daughters for whom the family is seeking an adoptive husband. In such instances the boy is likely to have less say in the matter than the girl.

Miai marriage in this area is often merely the form used to validate a choice which the young people themselves have already made. Although there are few activities in which both men and women participate, it is obvious that they do meet and occasionally are able to speak to one another. A young man who takes an interest in a girl may approach his family and ask that they try to arrange a marriage for them. If there are strenuous objections, he may drop the matter. Should the suggestion meet with favor, arrangements may proceed. Negotiating for a marriage contract involves the use of the go-between (nakōdo), for business of such delicate nature is rarely undertaken by the principals, whether it be a political, financial or criminal undertaking. The go-between in marriage is often an older married couple, a widow, or a relative of either sex. Professional nakōdo such as are found in the cities are not known in the village, although some old people have been go-betweens many times. There is financial reward for performing the job, usually 10 to 20 percent of the dowry, as well as a vague belief that a successful go-between will profit in the afterlife.

In urban centers it is sometimes the custom to have a kind of "honorary" go-between attend the wedding ceremony itself in the place of the person who actually negotiated the match. In such cases it is a superior in one's office, an important political, academic or business contact, or an older relative with prestige or position in the family. Such substitutes are not customary in Kurusu, although it occasionally happens that if two married couples participate as go-betweens in marriage negotiations, the husband of one and the wife of the other will attend the ceremony as representatives of the four actual negotiators.

It is customary for the go-between to approach the family in which there is a male of marriageable age. Even in cases where the boy has expressed a preference, the first visit of the nakōdo will be made to appear to be the first step. He brings a photograph of the girl, if she is unknown to the family, a history of disease in her family, and information which he has obtained from her family concerning her lineage and financial status. He also estimates their reputation and generally pictures it as a very advantageous match. I have heard it said, half as a joke, that a marriage exists when the lies of the go-between end and those of the couple begin. If the family of the boy expresses interest, the nakōdo goes to the girl's family and they will set a date for the miai (marriage interview).

This formal meeting of the boy and girl, which is theoretically their first, but not necessarily so, usually takes place in her home. In Kurusu, the boy goes with the go-between, with or without his parents. In the ordinary miai, the guests talk for a time with the parents of the girl, who then enters to serve tea and cakes, after which she is supposed to enter into the conversation. The girl is notoriously shy at such meetings, but if her parents think that she will talk to the boy they occasionally leave them alone for a half an hour or so. Conversation tends to be stiff and formal, and, according to reports of both young men and women, very painful. The parents and go-between meanwhile exchange polite conversation, and eventually reenter the room where the young people have been conversing.

When the guests have left, there follows a round of earnest discussion within both families, and the go-between is commissioned by each to investigate the other more thoroughly. Should he discover some distasteful or disqualifying information about either family, negotiations will be halted and the burden of gracefully breaking them off falls to him. If one of the young people objects with spirit to the cessation of negotiations, a second miai may be arranged, but informants agree that a third is very rare. However, if both are favorably inclined, negotiations will be concluded swiftly, and when both families have indicated a willingness to go through with the marriage, the betrothal presents (yuinō) are discussed. In Yasuhara, contracts for this exchange of betrothal gifts are rarely drawn up. In the urban areas contractual agreements are the rule.

The gifts are delivered on an auspicious day (kichi-jitsu) to the house of the bride by the go-between alone. They consist of three sums of money, and an ornamentally wrapped piece of dried pressed abalone, an indispensable part of the larger gift. The three sums of money are: (1) an amount for the bridal costume, called obi-ryō; (2) a sum for sake; (3) a sum for various items of food, called sake-no sakana. These are wrapped in decorative envelopes ornamented with pine, bamboo and plum (shō-chiku-bai), an auspicious symbol.

Included with the gifts is an inventory (moku-roku) written by the bride's father. When they have been placed in the tokonoma of the zashiki, the father of the bride writes out a receipt, puts it in a special envelope tied with red and white strings (mizuhiki), and requests the go-between to deliver this to the groom's family. On this day the concern of all is to meet only with good omens (engi); any untoward event is a matter of serious concern to the older family members. On one occasion, the receipt was sent back to the groom's family with the paper folded from right to left, as the garments of the dead are folded. This struck the mother as such an ill omen that she had it returned to the sender with a request that he rectify the error. This was done with profuse apologies.

There is no fixed lapse of time between the presentation of the yuinō and the date of the wedding. Arrangements are made to suit the convenience of both families. September and October are regarded as ideal marriage months throughout Japan, although spring has some popularity, also. On the day of the wedding, the bride's family sends to the groom the o-kaeshi ("the return"), which is their reciprocal betrothal gift. This consists also of three sums of money: (1) money for the groom's clothing (hakama-ryō) which is an agreed percentage of the groom's gift for the bride's clothing (obi-ryō); (2) a sum for sake; and (3) a sum for certain foods (sake-no sakana). The latter two are roughly equivalent to the sums given by the bride's family for the same purposes. The hakama-ryō is usually less than 50 percent of the obi-ryō, but if the latter is very small there may be no reciprocal at all.

An inventory of the bride's dowry is furnished with the o-kaeshi; the dowry itself is sent ahead of the bride to the groom's house, in which the ceremony is held. Today the furniture and clothing which she brings are carried by hired truck and unloaded by the bride's relatives. This is done before her arrival. Night weddings used to be the custom, but today's bride arrives by automobile with members of her immediate family and the go-between about mid-morning. She is met at the road by a young (ordinarily teen-age) girl from the family of the groom or from among his relatives, whose duty it is to greet the bride and to show her the way into the house. This office may be performed by a hired geisha in more affluent families, but professionals are never used in Kurusu.

Such a wide range of practices in the marriage ceremony are found from buraku to buraku, and even within the same community, that it seems preferable to sketch its features in broad outline, rather than to attempt a detailed description. Over the past twenty-five years there has been a gradual simplification of the ceremony, aimed at reducing the financial burden imposed upon both families. For example, there is no longer a formal display of the bride's dowry, although visitors are always anxious to know what she has brought.

The bride is taken into the house through the kitchen, from which she enters the room in which the family altar is located. There she burns incense in token of the fact that she now belongs to the sect of her husband's family. When she retires, the women of the buraku assemble to be served the wedding meal, and the bride is taken to a separate room. In smaller homes, she simply goes behind a screen at the far end of the zashiki. There or in the separate room the go-betweens and the groom join her for the first part of the ceremony called fūfu-gatama-no sakazuki, the exchange of sake cups between the couple. The woman who performs most of the ceremony (o-shaku-onna) administers this exchange. It is interesting to note that the bride is served before the groom at the beginning, but in the last portion of the ceremony she is served after him, indicating her shift from the status of guest to that of wife in the house. She has previously entered the room first; now she leaves it when all the others have gone.

The second step in the ceremony is the introduction of the bride to the assembled buraku women, one from each household. Formerly this meeting was at a party held on the day following the wedding, but the custom has changed, perhaps as part of the effort to simplify the procedure. The introduction is short; neither the bride nor the women speak. An exchange of sake cups takes place between the bride and the representative of the women present, who in Kurusu is the oldest married woman present. The bride then leaves the room, after which the women go home, taking with them the gifts of food brought out with the banquet.

Following this reception is the combined oyako-shinseki-gatame-no sakazuki, the exchange of sake cups among parents and relatives. This represents a fusion of two very similar portions of the wedding ceremony, one in which the bride and groom were acknowledged as child of the other's family, the second in which both groups of relatives acknowledged their new relationship. The o-shaku-onna performs this ceremony, as she did the exchange of cups between the women of the buraku and the bride. After a series of exchanges between the go-betweens, the new couple and their parents, each person present drinks, and then is introduced individually to the assembled group by the o-shaku-onna by name and relationship to the bride and groom. Occasionally she does not know all the names, in which case the person comes to her rescue and introduces himself. With this, the families are united and the formal ceremony ends.

Later, when the more distant relatives have gone home and when all have rested, there is a wedding party. People say that the number of guests is so limited not because of any lack of conviviality, but for financial reasons. A large number of special foods are served, and the bride changes costumes during the course of the party, displaying her trousseau. Apparently this latter practice is by no means universally observed, the reason given being that few brides have enough kimono of sufficient quality to carry off the display. There is music at these parties, provided by a local musician, often the o-shaku-onna, or by geisha. No one in Kurusu is wealthy enough to have a real geisha even if there were one in the vicinity, so frequently a widow substitutes as entertainer. The party lasts for several hours, but even if it ends very late, the bride's family returns to their home rather than pass the night in their daughter's new house.

Bride drinks ceremonial sake during the first part of the wedding
ceremony while a woman attendant
looks on.

In the second part of the ceremony,
shaku-onna exhibits yuinō to the
guests.

Shaku-onna offers a cup of ceremonial sake to representatives of the dōgyō during the conclusion of the
reception of the bride.

Weddings in Yasuhara are strictly household affairs, in contrast to the present urban custom of holding the ceremony in a Shinto shrine and following it with a party at a tea house or restaurant.   The bride's costume is extremely elaborate and usually is rented, for few families can afford to buy the necessary brocades and fine silks.   Formal Japanese dress is customary for all persons attending the ceremony, with the exception of boys who may wear their school uniforms and an occasional young man in a Western-style suit. The groom wears hakama, a very formal Japanese garment, in Yasuhara.   In the cities and towns most men are married in rented, ill-fitting Western morning attire.   Buraku women wear good clothing, but not formal kimono, when they appear for the reception.

The cost of a wedding to the groom's family is formidable, sometimes' amounting to one-third of a family's annual income.   A large wedding which took place in Kurusu in 1952 cost about 65,000 yen, the largest expense being 15,000 yen for the yuino and 30,000 yen for food for relatives and guests.   These are higher than average expenses, for the family in question is the owner of the sawmill.   A farmer's less elaborate ceremony would cost about 40,000 yen.   The bride's family is spared the cost of food, but must provide her with a suitable dowry and a rented kimono, in addition to the reciprocal betrothal gift. Estimates of the cost of a wedding to the bride's family vary greatly, but it seems to be normally less than half the cost to the groom's.

Three days after the marriage, the bride's mother visits her daughter at the house of the groom, a custom called heya-mi-mai, known in other areas as hiza-naoshi.   When she leaves, she takes her daughter with her for a visit to her former home.   This is called sato-gaeri (returning to the native place), and the girl stays only one night, returning alone to her husband the next day.   A month or two after this the groom goes with his bride to her home to pay his respects to her parents.   Muko-iri, as this visit is called, used to take place on the fifth day after marriage, but is regarded as so unimportant at present that a whole year may elapse before it is made.   With a growing feeling that the girl's parents should not interfere, the custom of heya-mi-mai also is disappearing, and is observed only in scattered instances.

Unless they live close by, the girl has almost no contact with her own family following her marriage.   The bride of the eldest son takes up her duties as the newest and lowliest member of her husband's family, and devotes much of her time to coping with her mother-in-law.   The plight of the new bride is celebrated in Japanese story and proverb, for the difficulties placed in her way by her husband's mother are considerable, although Kurusu women say that the power of the latter is now much diminished.   With the birth of her first child, even if it is female, she takes on added stature and has more authority in her dealings with other women of the family.   But it is the arrival of the first male child which firmly establishes her as second only to her husband's mother. in the affairs of women in the household.

Adulthood and Old Age

A young man does not become the head of the household merely by achieving a certain age or by acquiring a wife.   If he is to succeed his father as head of the household he almost invariably lives with his parents in the same house until he attains that position. There are two ways in which this may come about; one is through the death of the head of the household, the other through his retirement.   Inkyo (retirement from active life) is both a legal and social status, entered into by heads of households who feel that their advanced age indicates the necessity of surrender of active headship to a younger person. Such an elderly person registers his withdrawal from family affairs in the koseki at the village office and turns over to his successor all responsibility for the family.   He is consulted in some matters, for experience is felt to have given him wisdom, and he continues to work in the fields as long as his strength permits.   In Kurusu there are four men who

Elderly woman harvesting wheat
in early June. In the background
is a poor Kurusu house.

Young man carrying barley from
the field to the thresher.

Woman and son threshing wheat.
The grain is placed in straw
bags like that shown. The machine is powered by a kerosene
engine.

have effectively retired from active life in their households. If such a man is still married, his wife goes into retirement with him, giving over to the wife of the son who succeeds her husband.

Old age is regarded as a pleasant time in which there is opportunity for relaxation and many leisure hours. But the onset of old age is regarded in Kurusu as a dangerous period full of psychological strains. Women are believed to reach the beginning of old age in their thrity-second year, men in their forty-second. This is such a dangerous year (yaku-doshi) that when women achieve thirty-two and men forty-two they go to the Shinto shrine to ask the aid of the gods in making a safe passage through the dangers ahead. After having safely negotiated the year, the grateful survivor again goes to the shrine to give thanks. Certain other years in a person's life are also regarded as dangerous ones. A man's twenty-fifth and sixty-first years and a woman's nineteenth and thirty-seventh years are so regarded.

But once old age has finally been reached, it is an enjoyable period. The burden of responsibility, so heavy during active adulthood, can be shed. Old people use their new-found freedom to devote more attention to religious matters. Visits to the temple, rarely made by men in their prime and only slightly more frequently by women, become more common, and a kind of preoccupation with death leads to more strict observance of Buddhist prayers and ceremonies. An aged person is not expected to maintain the rigid etiquette patterns demanded of younger people, but neither old women nor old men in Kurusu exhibit the extreme freedom of behavior to which Benedict[7] and Embree[8] refer. Conversation may become broader with reference to sexual matters, and older persons are clearly less bound by the sense of shyness which so frequently immobilizes the young, but the kinds of behavior observed in old people do not differ markedly from that of younger adults.

Illness and Disease

Sickness, unless it is felt to be very serious, is treated at home by the family or by the individual himself. The most common remedies are patent medicines, many of which can be purchased at the drug store near the village office. In Japan, such establishments still deal largely in drugs and medicines. A striking exception to the general reluctance to call for the services of a doctor is the widow who was born and raised in Takamatsu. It is said of her that she learned to rely on doctors and will not or cannot treat all her family's ailments.

The relative ease with which new medicines like penicillin have come to be accepted is traceable in part to the influence of the urbanites who fled the cities during the closing phase of the war. These people brought with them attitudes towards such matters which were quite foreign to their rural relatives and friends. Although the stay of most of the refugees was brief, their influence on the countryside seems to have been profound. Unfortunately, we have no systematic investigations of the full nature and extent of this forced rural-urban contact and must depend now upon reliable reconstruction of the period.

Before World War II, medicines were commonly bought from itinerant peddlers. These men, medicine vendors from Toyama Prefecture, traveled about the nation on foot. It was their practice to leave a kit containing a variety of medical supplies with a household. When they came again the following year they checked what had been used, charged for that amount and replaced the exhausted items. These men no longer come to Yasuhara, forcing reliance on the modern drug store and home remedies.

When a person feels ill, the most common treatment is to go to bed, and to begin a diet of rice gruel (kayu) and plums pickled in brine (ume-boshi). If he has a stomach ache, he keeps his abdomen warm and stays in bed. He will not enter the very hot

Japanese bath until the pain is gone. A rather common complaint, called kembiki locally, is an ailment characterized by a slight fever, headache, sore muscles and a general feeling of exhaustion, occasionally accompanied by a toothache. Such a condition is laid to overwork for a long period; if it is possible a person will rest for a day or two. Recommended treatment includes the taking of aspirin and the massaging of the neck and shoulders. Almost any time a person is tired, he will have a family member rub his neck and shoulders, especially ·to relax him at the end of a hard day's work. Children perform this service for each other and the women of the family, while the latter treat the men.

There are three "hospitals" in the area to which Kurusu people can go, but they are actually little more than isolation wards for contagious diseases. One such establishment, which operates only during the summer months when such diseases are particularly common, is located a few hundred yards from the bridge leading into the buraku. Another smaller one is about two miles from Kurusu and has almost no equipment. No Kurusu person has gone there in recent years. The best of the three is in the next village to the south, Shionoe. It has beds, a doctor and one or two nurses in fairly constant attendance; it has a reputation for good service. However, Kurusu people prefer to remain at home if it is at all possible, for if a man is sick it is believed to be better for him to be with his family where he is assured of constant and tender care.

This attitude is clearly evidenced in Kurusu in the case of a man described as mad (shinke). I never saw this man, but it was reported to me that though he recognizes people his actions are irresponsible. He has been kept in his family's house, for the most part in bed in an isolated room, for the past fourteen years. His wife and children live in the same household and although most of the responsibility for his care falls to her, his parents and siblings do help her. The wife in another household behaves in such an odd fashion that she is not permitted to attend public functions, but around her own home she performs domestic tasks competently. No one in Kurusu, including the city-born widow, would consider sending such a person to an institution as long as he could possibly be cared for at home. People say that it would bring much shame on a family who did send a member away.

Sanitation practices have changed considerably since the surrender in 1945. Government agencies such as the Ministry of Welfare and the Ministry of Agriculture and Forestry have conducted fairly extensive programs explaining the use of DDT and other insecticides, the necessity for care to prevent water pollution, the technique of washing, cooking and eating utensils, and other public health matters. As one woman put it, the government became very yakamashii (noisy, clamorous) about sanitation under pressure from the Occupation authorities, but she felt that such emphasis has been largely to the good.

These programs have by no means universally revolutionized the villager's life, however. Apparently more care is taken about some sanitary measures now than formerly was the case, but cold water and careless washing generally rule in the kitchen; food is often not covered even in the summer, and wells are frequently startlingly near the outdoor privies. Diarrhea, which is especially common in summer, often incapacitates a person for a day or two, and when one member of a family gets a communicable disease it almost invariably is passed on to the others. Given the small size of the houses, however, and the close contact in which people live, this would not be surprising even were sanitation a compulsive concern in the buraku. Similarly, in the winter months, nearly everyone has a cold, particularly the children, whose noses are permitted to run freely. Ringworm is seen occasionally, but it is by no means common, and informants say that its incidence has very much decreased in recent years.

Unfortunately, I was unable to obtain conclusive data about the causes of death. Tuberculosis, pneumonia and infant dysentery were cited frequently. The last is especially feared, but reports indicate that infant mortality from this cause has much decreased since 1945. There are a number of very old people in the community, and it is said that the complications of old age are largely responsible for the death of the elderly. (See Table 8.)

TABLE 8

AGE AT DEATH OF KURUSU RESIDENTS 1872-1952*

Ages	Male	World War II	Female
Less than 1 year	18	-	8
1 year-5 years	13	-	11
6 years-10 years	4	-	2
11 years-20 years	4	1	5
21 years-30 years	9	6	2
31 years-40 years	3	-	5
41 years-50 years	-	1	2
51 years-60 years	5	-	-
61 years-70 years	5	-	4
71 years-80 years	2	-	3
More than 80 years	-	-	3
TOTALS	63	8	45

*These figures are taken from the Kurusu family register (koseki) kept in the Yasuhara village office.

Death

Attitudes towards the death of an individual appear to vary somewhat with the age of the deceased. A very young child is mourned, but he is not felt to have developed a firm hold on life. His funeral is simple. The death of adolescents and youths is felt to be very sad, but when a man or woman in the prime of life dies, it is said to be hardest to bear. The aged are also mourned, but the feeling seems to be that they were prepared for death, having lived a full life.

The buraku and the extended family come together in the event of a death, at least for the funeral ceremony itself. This is a period of extremely difficult transition for the family, particularly if the deceased was the active head, and the support received from relatives and friends is felt to be absolutely essential. It is significant that the intra-buraku ties are revealed most clearly in funeral preparations. (See Chapter II.)

The following is a description of a funeral service I attended in February 1952. The funeral was that of a woman who had died two days previously of an overdose of worm medicine. Because she was only thirty-nine, her unexpected death was a shock to her family and the community, and preparations for it were fairly elaborate. The household belonged to the Shingon sect of Buddhism, whose funeral service differs from the Shinshū to which several houses in the buraku belong.

At noon of the day of the funeral, people began arriving from neighboring buraku and villages to pay their respects to the deceased and the family. It was a cold, gray winter day, and buraku men sat warming themselves about a fire in the yard of the house. Since the dwelling was small, the overflow of guests was being accommodated in a nearby home,

loaned by a neighbor for the occasion. Relatives and very close friends arrived in formal
Japanese garb. They went to the zashiki and remained seated by the corpse while they
waited for the ceremony to begin. Other visitors, wearing ordinary work clothes or slightly better everyday garments, spoke briefly with members of the family, expressed their
sorrow and retired to the neighbor's house to wait, or stood about in the yard and on the
road, waiting for the procession to begin. Meanwhile, the funeral feast was being served
in both houses by women of the buraku.

There was desultory conversation, but neither laughter nor tears, and people stood hud-
dled in small groups close to the walls of buildings for protection from the cold wind. All
about the house yard were items of funeral paraphernalia, the special standards carried in
a Shingon procession, the stand upon which the coffin is borne, the chairs and umbrellas
of the priests and the decorative artificial flowers seen commonly at almost all public ceremonies in Japan. The priests themselves began to arrive about 1:30 p.m. by bicycle,
each man's equipment having been carried up previously by someone from his own buraku.
There were twelve priests in attendance—nine adult males, two adult females and a boy
apprentice.

The ceremony was begun about 2:20 p.m., after the priests had eaten and changed
from traveling clothes to their ceremonial robes. Only relatives were in the zashiki when
the services started, all but one or two men in formal Japanese dress, and all the women
in black kimono and black obi. The women wore a small triangle of folded white paper
pinned to their hair at the back. The room was packed, with the mourners seated in all
the available space not occupied by the semi-circle of priests in front of the offering-laden
butsudan (Buddhist altar). To the right of the Buddhist altar, in the tokonoma (alcove), the
seat of highest honor in the home, was the white pine coffin. In Yasuhara, a barrel-
shaped coffin is used, in which the corpse is placed sitting in a foetal position. It is made
of new wood, bound with fresh withes of bamboo and the top tied with clean straw rope.[9]

The zashiki ceremony, which requires about thirty minutes, was conducted by the chief
Shingon priest. None of the mourners participated in his prayers and ritual activities, although the other priests joined in on a number of occasions. There was no weeping. When
it was over, the mourners and priests filed out, and two men in work clothes came in to
carry the coffin out of the zashiki to the outdoors. They used the entrance to the house
reserved for formal or special occasions. These men placed the coffin on the palanquin
(koshi) with its ornamental cover, and carried it out to the road where the procession was
forming for the next portion of the ceremony.

The priests led off, wheeling their bicycles and accompanied by the helpers who carried their chairs and parasols. Next came the coffin on the palanquin suspended from the
shoulders of two male relatives, followed by the bearer of the memorial table, the stand-
ard-bearers and a group of women walking together. At the end of the procession were a
large group of children and adults, straggling out along the road to the rear.

The second part of the funeral, called the farewell ceremony (kokubetsu-shiki), is held
in a flat place where a large number of people can stand, and where there is room to
array the priests and their paraphernalia. For Kurusu, it is in the river-bed, and it was
to this place that the procession went. The coffin in its palanquin was set at one end of
an imaginary rectangle, surrounded by flowers, lanterns and standards. The family sat on
benches to the right of the coffin. The priests, with the head priest in the center, were
arranged in a large arc from the group of relatives around to the left side of the coffin.
They were seated in large folding chairs and shielded with great red parasols held over
them by their helpers. During this portion of the funeral observances, which began about
fifteen minutes after the procession left the house, relatives burned incense before the deceased and the chief priest offered a number of prayers. When this was finished all the

House in buraku near Kurusu
with funeral paraphernalia in
yard.

Priest recites a sutra before
the coffin in the tokonoma. To
the left is the butsudan.

The koshi in which the coffin
has been placed. The woman
to the rear carries the ihai.

The priest reads a prayer before the koshi at the "farewell ceremony." Relatives of the deceased sit to the right.

Tipping the coffin over into the crematory pit. Note the rough clothing of the dōgyō workers.

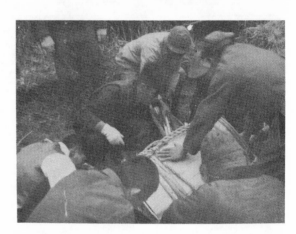

The coffin has been covered with wood, straw and two mushiro soaked with kerosene.

priests left, and the mourners crowded around the palanquin from which the ornamental cover had been removed. The lid of the coffin was taken off for a very brief period, during which people tried to get near enough for a last glimpse of the deceased. There were loud sobs and several women and young girls went away weeping, the first open demonstration of grief I saw during the entire funeral.

The coffin lid was replaced almost immediately, and a helper brought a bamboo pole from which the coffin was suspended. While this was being done all the funeral equipment was bring gathered up. The buraku people started back, accompanied by the group of relatives, who were instructed to change their clothes and come to the crematory as quickly as possible. Six or seven buraku men started with the coffin and, on the way up the very steep narrow path to the top of the hill where the crematory is located, changed over several times, making jokes about the weight of the corpse, the length of the trip and the coldness of the day.

After a fifteen-minute climb they reached the spot. To one side of the path is a stone-lined circular hole about six feet in diameter and from two to two and a half feet deep. Piled up beside this hole were bundles of straw and firewood cut in short lengths. The men filled the bottom of the hole with bundles of straw over which they laid pieces of wood in two or three layers. Next the ropes holding the lid of the coffin were re-tied so that one-half of the lid had no ropes across it at all. This half, which may be called the front, was then tipped forward and down, so that the corpse within the coffin was placed head down and face down, at about a thirty degree angle in the hole. The coffin was then completely packed about with bundles of wood and straw.

The first of the relatives to arrive had changed to work clothes, similar to those worn by the cremators. He brought with him two large straw mats soaked with kerosene which were placed over the entire pile in the pit so as to completely cover the coffin. After a short wait, during which the group sat down to wait, the apprentice priest arrived accompanied by the remainder of the family, most of whom were in everyday clothes. When they were arranged at one side of the pit, two helpers lit the pyre. The family took out their rosaries and as the priest prayed the smoke from the kerosene-soaked mats billowed up black in the high wind.

Ordinarily it takes about twelve hours to cremate a body, and family members stay as long as they can, not leaving until late in the evening in some cases. It is considered necessary to leave someone at the crematory all night to see that the fire does not die out and to keep it from spreading. At present these watchmen are most often relatives, for it is a job relished by no one.

The following morning, when the corpse has been consumed, the family arrives at the crematory, accompanied by a priest. There is a brief prayer, and the gathering of the bones (haisō) begins. Formerly the collection began with the bones of the feet and moved up, but nowadays only a token collection is made, often only the three top bones of the spinal column. The remains are placed in a small jar (kotsu-tsubo) and carried to the home, where they are placed in a section of the butsudan called the chū-in dan for a period of forty-nine days. At the end of this period, known as chū-in, the jar is taken to the cemetery and placed in the base of the family's gravestone. Formerly it was customary for members of the Shingon sect to bury their dead in the foetal position in large pottery urns. The chief reason for their shift to cremation seems to be scarcity of land. Every household in Kurusu now cremates its dead, except for very small infants who occasionally are buried.

The death of an individual is registered at the temple, and it is the priest of this temple who gives the deceased his posthumous Buddhist name (kaimyō). This is the name which is inscribed on the memorial tablet which was carried in the funeral procession and which later is placed in the household Buddhist altar. Most gravestones have the name of the family on the face, with the individual's given name, Buddhist name and date of death on the side. Some families in the buraku have their own cemeteries, often a small plot of land with a common gravestone, but there are four small cemeteries which contain the stones of a number of families, including one for two who actually live outside the buraku. As is true for statues of the Buddha, it is felt that the gravestones should not face north.

The Ancestors

The funeral ceremony itself is the first in a long series of household observances for the deceased. These memorial services, called hōji, are in theory observed on the following anniversaries of a person's death: 7th, 14th, 21st, 28th, 35th, 42nd, 49th and 100th days, and thereafter on the 1st, 2nd, 7th, 13th, 17th, 25th, 33rd, 50th, 61st and 100th year-anniversaries. For the hōji the services of a priest or number of priests are required, but if there is any observance at all of the ordinary monthly observances of the date of death (meinichi or otoki) and the annual observances (shō-tsuki), it will be very minor and done by household members only.

In actual fact, it is an unusual family which marks the hōji after the thirty-third year, for with the passage of such a span of time, another important family member usually has died and his rites take precedence. Memorial services for women are held for an even shorter period. It is the heads of the household who receive the most expensive, protracted series of observances. Both the meinichi and shō-tsuki are dropped after several years, usually long before the hōji are discontinued.

The dates upon which memorial services are actually held may not correspond to the true date of death, frequently being adjusted to suit the convenience of the family or guests and relatives who are to be invited. Thus, a woman who was to attend a buraku wedding on the actual anniversary of her husband's death, postponed the hōji to the following weekend. This arrangement not only permitted her to go to the wedding, but her relatives from Takamatsu could come to the memorial service for her husband.

TABLE 9

MEMORIAL SERVICES FOR THE DEAD (HŌJI): KURUSU 1952

		Number of	Cost	
Shingon Sect	Shinshu Sect	Priests	Rice*	Yen**
Dosha-kaji	Sem-bu	8-10	1 koku	4,000 yen
Han-dosha-kaji	Go-hyaku-bu	5	5 to	2,500 yen
Kōmyō-shingon dosha-kaji	Go-nen-iri	3-4	2 to	1,500 yen
Risshu-san-mai	Sam-bi-kyō	2-3	1 to	1,000 yen

*1 koku = 4.96 bushels
 1 to   = 3.97 gallons
**Minimum yen costs.

In Table 9 are given the names, number of participating priests and the cost in rice (with yen equivalent) for the hōji of both sects of Buddhism found in Kurusu. The most expensive hōji employs over eight priests and costs a minimum of 4,000 yen (one koku of rice). The least expensive costs 1,000 yen (1 to of rice) and employs from two to three priests. These figures are minimal, and sometimes the price is about one and a half times the amounts quoted. In Kurusu and the surrounding communities the least expensive observances are most commonly held, not only because of their inexpensiveness but because they are considerably shorter. The priests' fee usually is paid directly to them following the services, and all such payments are today made in cash. To illustrate the extent of the time differential, the longest Shinshū ceremony is said to require two nights and three days to perform, involving eight to ten priests who recite the prayer called the Amida-kyō one thousand times. The least expensive Shinshū ceremony requires the recitation by two or three priests of three prayers of some length, the services lasting one night and part of one day.

On the eve of a hōji, family and other relatives gather in the house to listen to the priests recite sutras before the butsudan in which the memorial tablet is kept. The following day, usually in the late morning, the same group, sometimes augmented by individuals who were unable to come the night before, gathers in the zashiki for a more elaborate ritual, in which all participate to a degree, and during which more sutras are read. There is often much conversation among those attending the ceremony, and a great deal of coming and going, notwithstanding the fact that this part of the service lasts less than an hour. Everyone present, including neighbor women and friends, who may have come to help in the kitchen, offers three pinches of incense to the deceased at the close of the ceremony.

Shingon hōji are characterized by a visit to the grave of the deceased following the zashiki ceremony; those of Shinshū are not. The group finishes the observance by dining together, and much sake is consumed. During these parties, which are held in the zashiki, priests, guests and kitchen workers all are entertained, and the trading of sake cups among the guests is a common sign of conviviality. At the typical memorial service there are from ten to fifteen guests, and four or five people will help in the preparation of the food. There is no fixed fee for such work, and the only person who ordinarily receives a wage is the man who makes the noodles (udon). Others receive extra food and a very small fee. Often the women who help on such occasions are buraku women, but outsiders may be called in if they are good friends or have the time to devote to the job. It is customary for those invited to the observance on the seventh day after death to bring a quantity of steamed rice with Irish beans (seki-han) and a small sum of money, usually about one hundred yen, in an envelope tied with black and white strings—in contrast to the red and white strings which bind a wedding gift or money given on a similarly happy occasion. At other hōji, each guest and caller will bring a sum of money.

For those services held for former household heads, the range of those who are invited to the hōji is quite wide, including those members of his immediate family who can possibly come, members of the extended family to whom he was close, and friends and business acquaintances with whom he had especially close contact. During the closing moments of the ceremony, a few of the older people may weep, but when the party is begun, there is no occasion for melancholy. Often very old women will not attend these parties, but will eat in silence in another side room. The aged tend to take the Buddhist services far more seriously than do others.

A man's memorial tablet is kept in the butsudan as long as the household exists, but ceremonies for him are discontinued when a number of others have died after him and his memory becomes dim within his own family. When that occurs, he passes into the category of very distant ancestors, honored in the large but forgotten as an individual.

Notes

1. Mainichi Shimbun, Population Problems Research Council, A Survey of Public Opinion in Japan on the Readjustment of Over-Population, Report No. 3, Tokyo, 1951, 24.

2. Conversation with a number of Japanese social scientists and psychiatrists brought out the interesting viewpoint that their own toilet training and weaning techniques seem to them far less severe than our own. They found the suggestions of some Western psycho-analytically oriented writers both ill-founded and amusing.

3. See R. F. Benedict, The Chrysanthemum and the Sword, Boston, 1946, 155.

4. J. F. Embree, Suye-Mura, A Japanese Village, Chicago, 1939, 188.

5. See F. N. Kerlinger, "Local Associations of Shikoku," Occasional Papers: Center for Japanese Studies, No. 2, Ann Arbor, 1952, 68.

6. This point is made very forcefully in R. K. Beardsley, "The Household in the Status System of Japanese Villages," Occasional Papers: Center for Japanese Studies, No. 1, Ann Arbor, 1951, 68.

7. Benedict, op. cit., 254.

8. Embree, op. cit., 214.

9. In the cities, the so-called "sleeping coffin" (ne-kan), like our own, is used.

Chapter VIII

RELIGIOUS AND CEREMONIAL LIFE

Virtually all the rest days and holidays in Yasuhara-mura are reckoned by the lunar calendar. The following explanation of that calendar is taken from Doolittle as quoted by Embree:

> The Chinese year contains thirteen or twelve months, according as it has or has not an intercalary month. Consequently the great annual periods, as the winter solstice or vernal equinox, do not fall in successive years on the same day of the month. Generally, in five successive years there are two intercalary days. The months are spoken of as the first month, the second month, etc., no distinct name for each month being in common use. The month which is intercalary is known as such in common conversation and in legal documents. For example: if the sixth month is intercalaried, there are two six months in that year, viz., the sixth month, and the intercalary sixth month.
>
> A month has never twenty-eight or thirty-one days, but always either twenty-nine or thirty days. A month is one moon, the character for month and moon being identical. The number of days in a month is intended to correspond to the number of days which it takes the moon to make one complete revolution around the earth; and as one such revolution requires between twenty-nine and thirty days, some of the months are reckoned to have twenty-nine and others thirty days. It follows that the number which indicates the age of the moon at any particular time also denotes the day of the month, and that the moon on the same day of successive months from one year to another always presents the same appearance. For example: on the fifteenth of every month the moon is full, on the first there is no moon; the first quarter ends about the evening of the seventh, the third quarter ends about the twenty-second of every month.[1]

National holidays, all of which are reckoned by the new calendar, are not observed by most villagers, for they frequently fall in the busy seasons for farmers. Some, like New Year's, are celebrated at another time by the lunar calendar; others, like Adults' Day, simply have no meaning in the rural areas, having been created since the surrender in 1945. Government offices and schools in the village do close, and the national flag is displayed, but in Kurusu as in most neighboring buraku, the national holidays pass otherwise unnoticed. National holidays are:

January 1	New Year's Day (O-shōgatsu)
January 15	Adults' Day (Seijin-no Hi)
March 21	Vernal Equinox (Shumbun-no Hi)
April 29	Emperor's Birthday (Tennō Tanjō-bi)
May 3	Constitution Day (Kempo Kinen-bi)
May 5	Children's Day (Kodomo-no Hi)
September 23	Autumnal Equinox (Shūbun-no Hi)
November 3	Culture Day (Bunka-no Hi)
November 23	Labor Thanksgiving Day (Kinrō Kansha-bi)

The following listing is of those festivals and rest days still observed by Kurusu residents. There are no festivals in an intercalary month, at either the buraku or mura levels.

93

First Month

A few people from Kurusu go to the Hachiman Shrine at midnight of the day before New Year's, or early in the morning of New Year's Day in order to be there to watch the sun rise (o-hi-machi). Virtually everyone in Kurusu goes to the shrine some time during the first day of the new year to drink before the gods the sacred sake that has been prepared and served by the priest, and then to return home to visit friends and neighbors, rest and eat a festival meal. Festival foods for the New Year's celebrations are varied. On the eve of the first day, a meal of buckwheat noodles (soba) is eaten. The dishes served on the first day itself are quite elaborate, and include soba served with boiled fish loaf and boiled chicken topped with onions, a salad of shredded radish and carrots in vinegar, black beans, herring roe, small dried sardines, and bean paste soup with boiled mochi, mushrooms, radishes and carrots. Sometimes a clear soup with shellfish and eggs is served, and sake is a feature of the meal in every household which can afford it. The second, third, fourth and fifth are also rest days, but the latter two are often not observed by buraku people.

One of the most interesting customs surviving in New Year's observances is that called saku-otoko by Kurusu people. For the first three days of the new year, women in the buraku do not work, spending their time visiting neighbors and going to the local shrines and temples. People sleep late on New Year's Day, except for the few who go to the shrine to see the sun rise. It is the custom for the men of the household to rise about 9:00 a.m. and fix the morning meal while the wife lies in bed for another hour or so. This practice is dying out with the passage of time, and today only about half the households still observe it. In those which do not, the women make wry jokes about their hard lot. Where the custom prevails, the men do what housework there is to be done, and all the cooking. At one house where I had a New Year's meal, both the father and eldest son apologized for the poor quality of the food they had prepared, but I suspect that they had not managed the elaborate menu without assistance from their wife and mother. However, they did serve the food, while she sat in the next room chatting with some neighbors who had dropped by, in sharp contrast to her usual industry in serving the males of the family and their guests.

Characteristic games at New Year's are top spinning for boys and battledore for girls. Some smaller girls dress in special holiday kimono for the day, but not all do, nor do all the adults. It is customary to wear "best" clothing when visiting, however: Kimono for women, but either a Western-style suit or formal kimono for men. There seems to be about equal division between the latter two styles, with a slight preponderance of Japanese dress on this holiday.

The seventh day of the first month is supposed to be the first upon which one can go into the forest to collect grass and fuel, but few wait this long to begin work in the new year. On the tenth falls the traditional visit to the great Shinto shrine at Kotohira in western Kagawa. This first call at the big shrine in the new year is called hatsu-Kompira or Kotohira-mairi, but is seldom made by anyone in Kurusu, although some informants recall a time when a few people went almost every year.

The fifteenth day, which is the end of the period known as matsu-no uchi, the first to the fifteenth of the first month, is marked by a small party held in the home at which special foods are prepared. This day is the end of New Year's celebrations and the importance of the occasion is revealed by the expensive dishes served. In Kurusu the kinds of food and their elaborateness depend largely on the financial state of the house, but they include those served at New Year's, supplemented in some houses by toso, a spiced sweet sake, and red Irish beans mixed with rice (seki-han).

February 17 is the new calendar date of the Memorial Ceremony (kinen-sai) at the Hachiman Shrine, which is attended by many Kurusu people. According to the priest of the shrine, the observance has three purposes: people give thanks for passing safely from the old year into the new; they pray for a good harvest of all crops for the coming year; and they pray for the safety of the nation (kokka antai). No one else mentioned the last of these when asked about the ceremony, and few had any clear notion of the reasons for the service beyond asking for successful harvests.

Second Month

The first day is a rest day, and is called taro-tsuitachi. Some houses serve special dishes on this day, but its importance has declined and young people do not know the reasons for its observance. Some say that this really is the last day of the New Year's observances, but others dispute this, saying it is only a day for rest.

On the third day, the last day of winter (setsubun) is observed in some houses in Kurusu, principally those of the Shingon sect of Buddhism. On the night of setsubun, roasted beans are thrown outside the house through the door of the zashiki and into the corners of the room by the head of the household, who says, "Demons outside; good luck inside!" The children gather up the beans scattered in the house, and each member of the family eats a number of beans equal to his own age. The fourth day, called risshun, is the first day of spring, but like setsubun is not a rest day. A very few old people go to the temple on the fifteenth day of the second month, which is the anniversary of the death of the Buddha, but other observances of the day are not made.

Towards the end of the second month comes the period of the vernal equinox (higan). It is on the middle day of this three-day period that Kurusu holds the first of its buraku religious functions. Every house participates in the festival, which is held first at the house of the sponsor and later at the buraku's own Shinto shrine to Jichin-san, "patron" of farmers in this area. No one works on this day and although the observances have lost much of their former importance, older people and most of the children of Kurusu attend the ceremony, which is performed by the priest from the Hachiman Shrine. When asked why so few adults were present at the 1952 spring festival, people laughed and said that as long as each household sent someone, even its children, it was sufficiently well represented.

Third Month

The third day of the third month, called momo-zekku or hina-matsuri, is the day of the Girls' Festival, March 3 by the new calendar. On this day a family in which there are girls ordinarily displays dolls in the tokonoma, and this custom is observed by some wealthy families in Yasuhara. No households in Kurusu displayed the dolls in 1952, and the one or two families who owned them at one time said that they had long since been eaten by mice.

The eighteenth day is a rest day for most Kurusu people, being the festival day in honor of Kōbō Daishi, founder of Shingon Buddhism. There is a special service at the Saimyō-ji, the Shingon temple in nearby Ongawa-buraku, which is attended by a few older people and some children from Kurusu. On April 20, by the new calendar, the Spring Festival of the Hachiman Shrine is observed, and although few Kurusu people actually visit the shrine itself they do not work but spend the day visiting in the buraku and nearby communities. The purposes of the observances at the shrine are to ask for a good wheat and barley harvest, and for successful completion of the rice transplanting.

The first of the three annual ceremonies held at the house of Kurusu's Buddhist priest is called the eitaikyō ho-onko, and is held at the end of April (end of the third month or early in the fourth). The services attract people from both sects of Buddhism in the buraku, although the priest himself is Shinshū. Most of those who attend are women, but some old men come.

Fourth Month

The eighth day, the birthday of the Buddha, is not widely observed in Kurusu, but a very few old people do go to the temple. Otherwise the day passes unnoticed. From about the tenth to the twentieth of the fourth month rice seed beds are made. The work usually is completed by the eighty-eighth day after the beginning of spring, and in 1952 all seed beds in Kurusu were finished by May 1 or 2. Following their completion, farmers put offerings to Jichin-san on the edges of the new rice seed beds. The offering is a bamboo holder about three feet tall with a written prayer and three kinds of flowers in the top. On the ground beside the holder is placed a piece of white paper containing several grains of rice and some small pieces of dry mochi. These offerings are to insure a good rice harvest.

On May 3, by the new calendar, a memorial service for the war dead of Yasuhara is held at the Saimyō-ji. This all-mura service has been held annually for many years, although no one seems quite sure when it began. Formerly the ceremony was performed in front of the monument to the war dead which stands in the yard of the temple, but following World War II there were too many people, so the services were moved into the temple itself for greater comfort and larger accommodations. There are a total of one-hundred and eighty-six war dead in the mura, including the very few killed in wars before 1937.

From 1946 through 1951, the memorial service was sponsored by an association of bereaved families (I-kazoku Kōsei Kai) because the government was forbidden by the Occupation authorities to engage in such activities as it had done previously. In 1952, following the signing of the Peace Treaty, the services were sponsored by the village office for the first time since the surrender in 1945, and the conspicuous decorations in the temple were two large wreaths of artificial flowers from the prefectural government in Takamatsu. The major part of the ceremony was attended by about three hundred persons, and almost every Kurusu family was represented. Most of those who came were old men and women, but numbers of young people from all over the village were present. Following prayers for the dead led by six priests, the mayor and other political figures, one representative from each buraku was called forward to burn incense for the dead of his community. After the ceremony the village youth association presented a play on an improvised stage in the court of the temple.

Fifth Month

The fifth day, Boys' Day (tango-no sekku), was observed by only one family in Kurusu in 1952. Traditionally a boy displays a warrior doll and other paraphernalia associated with the day, and the house flies one or a number of paper and cloth carp from tall bamboo poles. There are no dolls for this day in Kurusu, but one house did fly two carp, one for each male child, for a two-week period.

Near the end of May by the new calendar, the village office sponsors a day of sports contests and recreational activities at the middle school in which mura children participate. This meet is attended by nearly every person in Kurusu who has a child in school, and even if they cannot stay for the entire day, one or both of the parents appear for part of the activities. Grandparents and younger siblings often spend the entire day watching the foot races, relays and other field events. Recently, in an effort to promote acceptance of co-education by the pupils of the middle school, the teachers in charge of the day's events have closed the performance with a square dance in which carefully drilled boys and girls participate. Immediately following the dance they line up separately to receive prizes and gifts.

June 10 to 15, by the new calendar, is the end of rice transplanting, and all farmers in the buraku rest from noon of that day. Formerly the completion of this arduous task was marked by elaborate parties and a three-day holiday, but although special food may be prepared in most homes, casual visits for half a day have replaced the former practices. This day is called han-geshi, and is the eleventh day after the summer solstice.

Sixth Month

On the fourteenth day the Hachiman Shrine holds its only strictly lunar festival, the natsu-matsuri (Summer Festival). This is very little observed by Kurusu people and almost no one visits the shrine on this day. Whether or not it was ever of very great importance in Yasuhara is a matter of dispute; even the Shinto priests regard it as a minor celebration.

There is a rest day on the forty-ninth day after the seed beds are planted. It is regarded as a very unlucky day because it is on the forty-ninth day, after a funeral that the family takes the bones of the deceased to the cemetery. On this day, which is called nae-bi, no farmer enters the fields.

Formerly, on the twenty-third day there was a festival in honor of Jizō, The Buddhist protector of children. This featured much activity by the children and young men of the mura, but today only a few people go to one of the Jizō statues in the mura (there are two in Kurusu) and tie white papers bearing prayers to a bush nearby. Another custom which has died out was a special festival on this day for the six Jizō in Ichiman-buraku in which Kurusu people formerly participated.

On the twenty-eighth day, Shinshū Buddhists mark the day of birth of Shinran, founder of the sect. Members of the sect from Kurusu formerly went to the temple in Chūtoku-buraku across the river to hear a sermon by a priest, taking with them wheat or barley to contribute to the making of noodles for a festival meal following the service. Everyone in the buraku rested on this day, but recently people have tended to take only a half holiday or to work throughout the day.

July 20, by the new calendar, is dōyō-iri, the beginning of the dog days, and farmers do not enter the fields in the afternoon. The period of the great heat (o-atsu) lasts about one month, during which time there are two or three days of the ox (ushi-no hi) on which buraku people rest all day. Most houses cannot afford to observe the custom of eating eel on these days, but some special foods are usually prepared by a few families in Kurusu.

Seventh Month

The seventh day is Tanabata, marking the closest approach of the stars Altair and Vega, which represent parted lovers according to an old Sino-Japanese legend. Kurusu people do not rest on this day, nor do they follow the urban custom of erecting a bamboo tree on which children tie strips of colored paper with poems, names and drawings.

The tenth day is supposed to be the day on which people go to the cemeteries to clean them for the approaching Bon Festival. This visit is called sennichi-mairi, and is the only time of the year that graves are cleaned. Actually many people do the work after this day, especially if pressure of other work interferes on this particular day.

Bon, variously called the Festival of Lanterns or the Festival of the Dead or the Feast of Lights, begins on the night of the thirteenth and ends on the night of the six-teenth. It is believed that the souls of the dead return to their homes during this period, and members of the Shingon sect of Buddhism light welcoming fires (mukae-bi) in front of their houses. The Buddhist altars in every home are decorated with lanterns and special offerings of fruits and cakes. Everyone rests for the three days of bon, which ends when the souls begin their return journey on the night of the sixteenth day. Many older people visit the temples on the three days.

On the nights of the fourteenth, fifteenth and sixteenth, the Bon Dance (bon-odori) is held in Yasuhara on the athletic ground of the primary school. In 1951 the dance was sponsored by the Agricultural Cooperative of the village, which offered prizes to the bura-ku group which performed best. First prize was 2,000 yen. The buraku performed as units in the circle dance around the central platform. In spite of the prize, young people, if they dance at all, are always embarrassed and perform reluctantly.

The biggest dance is usually on the night of the fifteenth. No special costumes are worn, and no old songs or particular local dances survive in Yasuhara. The dancing is standardized and usually is accompanied by popular songs such as "Tanko-bushi" ("The Coal Miners' Song"). Records are played over a public address system for part of the evening, but there is a large drum which is brought out later, and older men sing songs, which are old but not local, to its accompaniment after the dance has been in progress for some time. The performance starts after dark, about nine o'clock, and lasts until past midnight. The religious character of bon-odori has largely disappeared, and today it is considered a social event to which most of the mura comes. This is the first really big celebration following New Year's, and although it is diminishing in importance, it is a crucial time for bringing villagers into close contact for a brief period.

Eighth Month

There are no festivals or holidays during the eighth month. September 1 or 2 and 11 or 12, the two-hundred and tenth and two-hundred and twentieth days after the first day of spring, are felt to be the most dangerous days for storms and typhoons. Farmers wait anxiously to pass them safely, for it is said that after the latter date there is little likeli-hood of damage to the rice crops. No special observances are held, but the days are marked by everyone in the buraku, as they are all over Japan.

Ninth Month

About the end of September is the second Buddhist service, the tsuichō-e, which is held at the house of Kurusu's Buddhist priest. First held in the buraku after World War II, it is a memorial service for those from Kurusu who were killed in the second world war. Every household which lost a member in the war has at least one person at the ceremony.

On the middle day (sha-nichi) of the autumnal equinox (higan) the buraku holds its sec-ond festival of Jichin-san. Festivities on this occasion have been on the wane during the past thirty years. Formerly wrestling was held at the Kurusu shrine on the eve of the festival, with prizes awarded the winners by the sponsor. A large fire was built before the shrine, and people gathered from all over the mura to see the matches. When the shrine building was removed to the Hachiman Shrine in Nishitani in 1916, most of these observances at the old site diminished in importance until today virtually no outsiders attend.

On October 12, the autumn athletic meet at the Yasuhara Middle School is held. On October 13 and 14, by the new calendar, the Autumn Festival of the Nishitani Hachiman Shrine is held. All the buraku, including Kurusu, which are in its jurisdiction participate. This is the third of the big festivals of the year, and everyone in Kurusu rests on the two days given over to it. (For a full account of the festival arrangements, see Chapter II.) Almost everyone in the buraku goes to the Hachiman Shrine to watch the ark of the god brought out and to see the costumed lion dancers. A number of little stalls are set up at the entrance to the shrine where souvenirs, inexpensive candies and other foods may be bought. On rainy festival days, there is a rushing business in rain coats and hats.

The festival falls between the typhoon season and the rice harvest, and people give thanks at the shrine for having passed safely through the former and ask for success in the latter. When the ark of the god is carried from the shrine down the long, steep steps, the purpose is to permit him to view the rice crops in the fields from a vantage-point before the shrine gate.

Tenth Month

There are no festivals during this month.

Eleventh Month

On November 27, a minor observance called the Offering New Rice Ceremony (niname-sai) is held at the Hachiman Shrine. A few people from Kurusu go. Late in December, from the twenty-second to the twenty-eighth of the eleventh month, is the period for marking the death day of Shinran, founder of Shinshū. The Ichimu-an, the temple name of Kurusu's priest's home, holds a two-day service called soshi ho-onko, but the buraku observes no rest day and few people attend the services. Occasionally a priest from Takamatsu is invited by the Kurusu priest to come to perform the services.

Twelfth Month

Some households in Kurusu make a little mochi for the new calendar New Year's. Since the major observances of New Year's are by the lunar calendar, every household makes a large quantity of mochi just prior to the general celebration, at the end of the twelfth month.

Household Gods

In every house but one in Kurusu there are at least two religious shrines. (The single exception is the home of the buraku Buddhist priest in which there is only the Buddhist family altar.) Both shrines are always found in the zashiki, to the left of the tokonoma, the alcove for displaying objects of art which is theoretically the highest seat of honor in the house. The Buddhist family altar (butsudan) stands in a recess next to the alcove. The Shinto god-shelf (kamidana) is ordinarily high on the wall still further to the left, so as not to be directly above the butsudan. The contrast between these two household shrines points up some of the contrasts between the two religions in which all Japanese participate.

Butsudan

The Buddhist altar is the most expensive item of furniture in a farmer's house, but its size and quality vary greatly with the financial circumstances of the household at the time it was purchased. In Kurusu, the largest and most elaborate is that of the buraku priest. This altar, which reaches from floor to ceiling and is of ornate black and gold lacquer, was installed in 1935 at a cost of 670 yen, about 270 yen for the image of Amida and 400 yen for the altar itself. The relative magnificence of the altar may be judged from the fact that at this time rice sold for 31 yen per koku (4.96 bushels), and an ordinary house cost about 1,000 yen to build. In other houses, both Shinshū and Shingon, the altars are considerably smaller than this. Some of the more modest ones contain a small scroll picturing Amida Buddha, rather than a statue of him.

Lights are burned on the altar on all Buddhist festival days and at all memorial services for the dead. Small white candles are commonly used, but in two houses in Kurusu (those of the priest and of the sawmill owner) the butsudan have been electrified. The electric light bulbs in these two altars are in small black metal lanterns.

One of the daily duties of the housewife is to place a small quantity of cooked rice in two little porcelain cups in the butsudan. Fresh fruits are also offered to the Buddha. The rice is replaced every morning, but fruit may be left for a longer period. All food placed in the butsudan is ordinarily eaten by the family, since it is the essence which has been offered. When large quantities are used in special ceremonies, they are removed and divided up among the guests before they depart. Besides the statue of the Buddha, the large number of ceremonial objects, and the piles of offerings occasionally placed in the altar, there are the memorial tablets for the dead (ihai). These are most prominently displayed during the memorial services in the home.

Kamidana

The Shinto god-shelf is an inexpensive item, although newer ones tend to be somewhat more elaborate than older varieties. In Kurusu the gods found most commonly on the kamidana are Izumo-taijin (Daikoku) and Tenshōkō-taijin (Amaterasu). These may be represented by small images or simply by talismans from their shrines. Most kamidana have a number of charms and half-forgotten mementos put there by past generations, although some houses do clean them off occasionally. In very new houses, the materials of the shrine are untreated light wood, white unglazed pottery and a glass cover. On some of them is a small bright metal mirror, replica of one of the three sacred treasures of Shinto. Old kamidana are dark with age and have no glass to protect the dusty objects on them.

Daily offerings are made to the Shinto gods, just as to the Buddha, usually tea and a little rice. At New Year's mochi is placed on the kamidana, and most houses keep fresh flowers or grasses in a small bamboo holder next to the shelf. When a funeral is being held in the house, a piece of white paper covers the face of the kamidana. A small quantity of the first rice of the harvest is cooked and placed in a cup on the shelf. Most people, on first arising, go to the butsudan and say a short prayer, but few in Kurusu pay similar respects at the kamidana.

Gods, Shrines and Temples

Buddhism

Buddhism is largely a household religion, making its principal concern those activities dealing with death and the dead. The only Buddhist rites which bring the village

together are the Bon Dance and the May third ceremony for the village war dead.   The
latter is truly religious in nature, but the former has become almost entirely a social occasion the religious overtones of which are of little importance.   Buddhist priests perform
funeral ceremonies in the home and officiate at memorial services for the dead there.
They also perform rituals and say prayers at prescribed times in the temples, but without
the presence of a congregation.   Instruction in religious matters is not a part of their duties.

The hierarchy of the Buddhist church has its influence at the buraku level.   In Japanese Buddhism, each major sect has several sub-sect divisions.   The main temple for each
sub-sect is called the honzan.   All temples of that sub-sect subordinate to it are called
matsuji (branch temples).   Thus, in Yasuhara the two Shinshū temples are branches of the
main temple of the sub-sect called Kōshō-ha in Kyōto.   Every matsuji has a number of
parishioners and maintains a death register (kakochō) for each family which "belongs" to
the temple.   In this book the death of an individual is recorded and his posthumous name
entered by the priest.   Households "belonging" to a temple are called its danke, their name
for their temple being dannaji.

The main temple makes requests of the branch temples for contributions of money
for the maintenance of its buildings and the support of its priests and their families. This,
in addition to contributions from pilgrims, accounts for the bulk of the main temple's income, for under the post-surrender land reform the temples lost much of their farm lands.
The branch temple then assesses each of its member-families according to its view of
their ability to pay.   Nowadays there frequently is trouble in collecting this money, primarily because some families question the right of the main temple to ask for money.

The branch temple requests a separate fund for its own use, the purpose of which is
for repairs and maintenance of buildings.   It asks for no donations for its priest and his
family, for he is expected to earn his living from the fees received at funerals and memorial services.   Although the ideal priest is a frugal man, by no means do all of them
observe the canon of the simple life.

A branch temple with many member-families will be quite wealthy.   Should a member-
family refuse to give subscription money to its dannaji, the priest will not officiate at any
ceremonies for that family.   No household in Kurusu has fallen under such a ban, but it
is said that it has happened occasionally in other parts of Yasuhara.

The dannaji of the seventeen Kurusu households for whom I have data are six different temples.   Twelve families are registered in the three temples in Yasuhara, seven
Shinshū and five Shingon.   Five are members of temples in other villages, three Shinshū
and two Shingon.   None of the Kurusu families belongs to the Tendai sect temple in Yasuhara, which apparently has virtually ceased to function.   The five families who retain membership in temples outside the mura seem to have been the last to arrive in Kurusu, for
people are slow to change registration from their original temple to one in the area to
which they move.   The non-mura temples in these cases are in villages only a few miles
from Yasuhara.

A charge which the lay villager occasionally levels at the Buddhist priest is that he
is today more undertaker than preacher.   Some priests resent the allegation and take pains
to demonstrate that public interest in sermons is so low that it would be useless to attempt to gather people for regular services.   The Kurusu priest recalls that before the
war his eldest son tried to assemble buraku children in his home at intervals to give them
simple lessons in Buddhism.   As an attraction he gave small gifts, but since even this   ·
failed to bring them regularly he abandoned the plan.   In the opinion of many priests, old
people in the home are best able to give such instruction.   As for the fact that only the

Small statue of Jizō-san dated 1763.

Figure of Amida Buddha in the butsudan of a wealthy home.

Buraku priest in simple robes. This man was one of my best informants.

old take a really active interest in temple services, many priests say that their failure to attract the young is simply fate (innen).

As has been pointed out, the home of the priest residing in Kurusu serves also as a minor temple called Ichimu-an. Ichimu is also the brush-name used by this man in his artistic and poetic efforts. He has had no formal religious training, but took an early interest in religious matters and became established as a local priest who serves Shinshū families throughout Yasuhara. His eldest surviving son, who is studying under him, participates in most ceremonies with his father.

There are in Kurusu two statues of Jizō, small stone images which stand along paths in the buraku. Most people have no clear idea of the nature of this deity, but on his day (the twenty-third of the sixth lunar month) some people place flowers near his statue and prayers are tied to nearby bushes. Although his origins are Buddhist, few are certain whether he is Buddhist or Shinto, nor does this vagueness as to his identity concern anyone particularly. One of the statues in Kurusu is housed in a cast-off Shinto shrine. The statue, which stands in a field, bears the date 1763 and is said to represent a yama-bushi ("mountain priest" or itinerant priest) of the area who was deified by the local people upon his death. No one attributes any special powers to either of the Jizō, nor are they known by any special names.

An interesting story is told about the Jizō now housed in the Shinto edifice. In each prefecture, some years before the surrender, there was one paddy field designated saiden (sacred field) from which the rice was offered to the great national Shinto shrine at Ise. The rice in Kurusu is of such high quality that a field in the buraku was being considered for the honor. It developed at the last moment that the field in question was the very one in which this Jizō stands, and since the judges felt that the presence of a Buddhist image rendered the rice unsuitable for presentation to the Shinto gods, a field elsewhere in Kagawa was selected. It is suggested by others that the real reason for choosing another community was simply that it was able to raise more money to influence the decision of the judges who made the selection. Whatever the cause, Kurusu's rice was never sent to Ise.

Shinto

There is a small Shinto shrine in Kurusu which has had a somewhat checkered history. Prior to 1916 it was one of the important lesser shrines of Yasuhara and was known as Kurusu-jinja. Its god was Ame-no-minaka-noshi-no-mikoto, represented by a small round stone resting within the shrine building itself. A small stone gateway (torii) stood at the foot of a short flight of steep, stone steps leading up to a small wooden shrine building in a grove of pine and bamboo. In 1916, the Nishitani Hachiman Shrine of Yasuhara was elevated from the rank of village shrine (sonsha) to that of county shrine (gōsha) and at the suggestion of the county office, a total of thirty-seven gods from small shrines throughout Yasuhara were removed to the Hachiman Shrine. It had become difficult to maintain the numerous minor shrines, primarily because each had such a small group of parishioners.

Accordingly, the shrine building and original torii of Kurusu-jinja were removed to the newly-elevated Hachiman Shrine and placed near its main building in the shrine compound. Since that time a new torii has replaced the old one in Kurusu, and on a stone pedestal on the site of the former Kurusu-jinja building is a large natural rock with the names of four gods carved on its face. The chief name is Amaterasu-o-mikami, the Sun Goddess. On the pillars of the torii are two patriotic slogans. The spot is little used except at the spring and fall festivals, and during the harvest seasons piles of straw block the entrance to the shrine.

The god worshipped at this site is Jichin-san ("protector of the land"), tutelary god of the buraku. There is considerable confusion as to his identity, however, even on the part of the village Shinto priest. Usually five divinities are named when speaking of Jichin-san: Amaterasu-o-mikami, Onamochi-no-mikoto, Uganomitama-no-kami, Sukuna-hikona-no-kami, and Haniyasu-hime-no-mikoto. According to the Shinto priest he may sometimes be Ukemochi-no-kami. Some say he was Ushi-gami-sama (Cow God), and others equate him with Kojin-sama or with Tenjin-sama. All these names are quoted, not with a view of clarifying the issue, but to demonstrate the lack of codification of Shinto on the popular level. Perhaps the consensus in the buraku is that originally he was Ushi-gami-sama (the Cow God). Forty or fifty years ago, small straw figures of cows were made by boys in the buraku and offered to this god on his festival days, but this custom has disappeared completely except for one very old man who every spring and fall makes such a figure and takes it, not to the buraku shrine, but to the former Kurusu-jinja now located in the compound of the Hachiman Shrine.

All the households in Kurusu are parishioners (ujiko) of the Hachiman Shrine in Yasu-hara. In the Shinto system there is nothing exactly paralleling the main and branch temples of Buddhism, but there are shrines in Japan generally recognized as the main shrine of a given god. For Hachiman-san (God of War) it is Tsurugaoka Hachiman-gū in Kama-kura. These main shrines do not exercise any financial control over smaller ones, nor do ujiko plan to visit them as Buddhists plan to see their main temple at least once.

Before the surrender, the Nishitani Hachiman Shrine received central government funds through the prefecture and the mura. The former contributed about forty yen annual-ly, the latter approximately one hundred yen. Most of the expenses were met with income from shrine lands and subscriptions by the ujiko, however.[2] In the immediate post-war years the shrine lost its agricultural lands and the revenue from them; in addition, sub-scriptions dropped following the surrender because the people felt that the gods had failed. The present Shinto priest of the village feels that the Occupation's insistence on the aboli-tion of feudalistic and militaristic aspects of life led the people to abandon the gods. Dur-ing the first years of the Occupation he had said nothing for fear of being accused of being anti-American, but he had held firmly to the belief that the gods must be respected. For the past two years he has been impressed by the resurgence of interest in shrine affairs, which he takes to be a sign of general reaction against the wholesale abandonment of re-ligious observances following the surrender. This striking decrease in religious activities following World War II has affected Buddhism as well as Shinto. Its importance has been overestimated, however, for there is good evidence that the decline had set in long before the war. I have the impression that a great many such trends, having been accelerated by the dislocations of war and surrender, are now alleged to be strictly post-war phenomena.

Shinto priests theoretically are given Shinto funerals, but the Hachiman priest's fam-ily is also Shinshū, and Buddhist funerals are held in their home. Both Shinto and Bud-dhist priests participate in those observances of the other religion which are held on a buraku basis, although not those on the village level. Thus, Kurusu's Buddhist priest takes his turn as sponsor for the buraku Shinto festival, as does the Hachiman priest for the Buddhist prayer services held by rotation in his buraku.

On the occasions of the spring and autumn festivals to Jichin-san, there are nineteen buraku in Yasuhara which must be visited by the priest, and his son, who will succeed him. The older man performs the services at seven of these shrines, while his son handles the other twelve. The priest, who is also a farmer, is given food at each buraku he visits and about one hundred yen in cash for his services.

Besides officiating at shrine festivals, the Shinto priest is called upon to perform cer-tain purificatory rites from time to time. A person entering the years of misfortune comes

to the shrine for yaku-barai (expelling evil) which the priest performs. He may be called
to a house to perform kama-barai, a ceremony designed to purify a newly-constructed oven,
so that fire may be lit there. More important are the occasions upon which he is called
to bless the construction of a new building.

It has become increasingly difficult for the priest to make a living from shrine income alone, and he has taken up a kind of geomancy for supplementary income. When a
house is to be built, the priest is consulted as to which direction it should face, and the
location of the unclean (kegareta) bath, toilet, kitchen and well. The plan which is drawn
up is called kasō uranai ("prospect of a house"). Care must be taken that none of these
unclean things be placed in the northeast corner (kimon, devil-gate) or the southwest corner (ura-kimon, back devil-gate) of a dwelling. Most people in Kurusu believe that a family's ill-fortune often may be traced directly to their failure to follow the advice of the individual making the kasō uranai.

"Folk" Beliefs

In Kurusu, as in all Japan, the fox (kitsune) and badger (tanuki) are believed to have
supernatural powers. As there are few foxes in this area, people say that they are not so
important in folk beliefs, and there are no Inari shrines with the characteristic fox guardi-
ans in Yasuhara or the surrounding area.

People tell how, during the war when electricity was curtailed, tanuki often came
down from the mountain in Takabatake-buraku to the east of Kurusu. They were especially
liable to do so on moonless nights or when the weather was dark and stormy. Many individuals I talked to reported seeing the lanterns of the badgers, first one moving alone, then
joined by another, until a string of bobbing lights could be seen moving in procession.
Even now tanuki lanterns are seen coming down from the mountain behind the village office
on dark nights. In the old days, it was not uncommon for farmers working late at night
to hear the badger's stomach-drumming (hara-zutsumi) on the hillsides. The conventional
representation of tanuki, regarded as a sly and licentious figure, shows him standing upright with a protruding stomach and enormous testicles. He has a suggestive grin on his
face, and carries a lantern in one hand. There are no such figures in Kurusu, but they
are often seen in gardens and in front of shops and places of business.

The most striking badger story, told widely and with relish in Kurusu, deals with
tanuki's ability to assume a variety of forms. The event described below occurred quite
recently, during the Second World War. At the time of a severe food shortage, one of
the men of nearby Takabatake-buraku told an aged female relative that she might as well
die because she could not work and earn her keep any longer. She was living with his
family at the time because she had nowhere else to go. The old woman brooded over the
rebuke and not long after hanged herself. Her death profoundly shocked the village and
the man in question, already an unpopular individual, was severely censured. One moonless night, he was on his way to a Buddhist prayer meeting in Kurusu, carrying a lantern
to light the path. As he neared his destination, the candle in his lantern went out. Stopping, he saw the ghost of the old woman, all white, rise up beside him on the road. The
man dropped the lantern and ran to the nearest house, arriving in a state of shock and
unable to speak. People say that it was a tanuki which appeared in the form of the old
woman to frighten him.

Notes

1. J. F. Embree, Suye-Mura, A Japanese Village, Chicago, 1939, 263-264.

2. Supreme Commander for the Allied Powers, Civil Information and Education Section, Religions in Japan, Tokyo, 1948, 23, bears this out. It is a mistake, however, to regard any of the shrines as entirely government supported, for the grants were seldom more than tokens of support.

Chapter IX

ASPECTS OF CHANGE

As will have been evident from the foregoing, life in Kurusu, while it exhibits many traditional features, shows also evidence of striking change. It is quite clear, for example, that ready-made consumer goods have largely replaced the products of local craftsmen; people now buy things which they once made for themselves. This includes goods such as ready-made clothing, kitchen and table utensils, some new foods, and a host of other items which may be had for cash. The local light sawmill has made it unnecessary for a man to fell and process his own lumber; it too may be sawn to order or purchased. The decline in knowledge of home remedies has come about partly because of the astonishing variety of patent medicines and other drugs dispensed by the local drug store. Since 1945 more farm families have taken advantage of the services of the licensed midwife, and adult women no longer count completely on their own skill in pre-natal care and delivery. The amount of home industry in Kurusu has decreased over the years in respect to clothing, native footgear and headgear, as well as straw ropes and mats, which formerly were manufactured by several houses in the community.

The process of change also has had a far-reaching effect on the life-cycle of the individual, on the patterns of family relationship and on the social organization of the community. The extended family, operating as a relatively independent economic unit in which a major proportion of the things required for living were made, is giving way to small families whose members purchase virtually everything they need and as much as possible of the things they desire. Furthermore, there are signs that the social life which used to center in the kinship group or local area is shifting gradually to non-kin groups, or even to nearby towns, often within easy reach by means of public transportation. In rural Japan, perhaps one of the most important changes which has affected the life-cycle of the individual has been the introduction of compulsory public education, now co-educational, for a nine-year period. Although new legislation affecting the rights of the individual in the family has been enacted over the past seven years, these legal changes seem to have had little effect in Kurusu. The hold of the extended family on individual members has weakened considerably, but this de-emphasis of extended ties seems to be related less to new laws than to broad social and economic changes such as increased mobility and the availability of a wide variety of consumer goods for cash. Movies and other forms of entertainment, now available both in the village and in nearby towns, have made serious inroads into the social life formerly centering on the activities of the family and the shrine and temple. Young people, particularly, seem to prefer being entertained rather than to adhere to the older pattern of participating in group recreational activities such as the Buddhist Bon dance. The shift is somewhat less marked among older people, but even among them not everyone takes the interest he once did in local festivals and other entertainment.

The process of national industrialization has fostered a movement away from the village in search of wage-paying work. This is, of course, closely tied to the availability of and the desire for consumer goods. The movement in search of work ranges from commuting to emigration, but whatever its form, it affects the patterns of family and community relationships. It also increases contact with the outside world and fosters a flow back from it into the community.

The sawmill does furnish day labor to some residents of Kurusu, on a full-time or part-time basis. A number of men work full-time at a dam construction project in a nearby village. Such jobs require short commuting at most. One or two men occasionally

107

leave the buraku for work which may keep them in the city for as long as six to eight months, but it is more common for such men simply to emigrate. Ordinarily they do not plan to return unless economic difficulty forces them to abandon their efforts to maintain themselves in the city. Occasionally they do come back to the village. Agricultural day labor, for which cash wages are paid, can be had locally during the busy seasons, but such jobs last for a few days at most. With both the countryside and the cities suffering from over-population and under-employment, the development of widely dispersed light industry throughout the rural areas seems to offer one of the most satisfactory temporary solutions to the basic problem of too many people on too little land.

Contact with the outside world has been aided by such products of industrialization as automobiles, trucks, bicycles, buses, radios, movies, newspapers, and road-making machinery. These facilitate not only emigration but commuting. Although the rail line which formerly connected Kurusu with the towns and city to the north was removed several years ago, it has been partially replaced by a bus line which serves the same area, making trips to the city possible, if uncomfortable. The number of bicycles in the buraku has increased greatly since the surrender, facilitating travel within the village and its environs, although they are infrequently used for the journey to the city because of the tedious uphill return trip. Radios, newspapers, and magazines are found in substantial numbers in the community and are important in informing the villagers as well as in helping mold public opinion. A few progressive farmers take advantage of agricultural publications and radio programs and often make trips to agricultural fairs in other parts of the prefecture. It is jokingly said that the most popular radio program is the weather forecast, with music a close second. The main road through the village, just across the river from Kurusu, is well serviced by the prefecture, which uses a scraper as well as manual labor to maintain the hard, graveled surface. Although it is true that the average person does not often go as far as the nearest city, a distance of about eleven miles, travel to more immediate points is not uncommon.

The increasing use of cash, and the necessity for it, have led in the last ten years to the introduction of the first purely cash crop in Kurusu; this is a reed used for making mats and sold to a local weaving establishment. It is the hope of the men who have started the crop that it will prove adaptable to upland terrace cultivation, for these areas, which are too wet for winter wheat, now lie fallow in winter. Most Kurusu farmers look upon the new crop with disfavor because of the great additional labor required in its cultivation. However, the desire for cash is great, and it is probably safe to predict that others will be planting the crop before many more seasons have passed. Animals are raised, chiefly work cows, but the profit from re-selling them and buying a calf is not great and seems actually to be incidental to the main purpose for raising the animals.

The double bond of consumer goods and wage-earning has drawn communities like Kurusu closer to the larger society of the country, and to the world. As a result, villagers are more vitally affected by economic cycles, wars and major events in far parts of the earth than they were when they had a more self-contained economy. Influences over which they have no control now affect them to an extent which formerly was not the case. The most obvious example of this type of influence is World War II.

It is not possible to present here a complete picture of the impact of the war on Kurusu or Yasuhara, but the following points should make it clear that rural Japan suffered only slightly less than the urban areas in a war in which all were involved to the fullest extent. There were, of course, shortages and tighter government controls and power shutdowns. The forests were cut off in this part of Kagawa and many of the logs rotted where they were felled because they could not be moved. Old buraku which had functioned as social units for many years were combined for political and administrative purposes, but these mergers of expediency have since been abandoned. Women wore shapeless baggy

suits in place of kimono and men dressed in olive-drab "civilian uniforms." With the surrender in August 1945, Shinto reverted to something more like its older popular form without the prop of central government support and the nationalistic trappings of pre-surrender
times. Many turned from shrine worship altogether. The Emperor himself was criticized
in the public press for all to read; even his voice had been heard on the radio calling for
an end to the war. A few Americans came through the village, speeding along the highway, and "jeep" became a word overnight. Anyone who wished to do so could go into the
city and see hundreds of uniformed foreigners there. There were men from India as well
as the British and American soldiers, both black and white. They were rough, big men,
and seemed almost the only active well-fed people in all the devastation of burned and hun-
gry Takamatsu. Radicals appeared on all sides urging the farmer to better his lot. The
land reform law was enacted and the majority of tenants who had never hoped to own their
fields finally could buy the land on which they and their families had paid high rents for
generations. The radicals seemed less appealing somehow, when a man had his own land.

But the buraku had paid heavily to learn what modern war can mean. A total of
twenty men and women left Kurusu during the course of the war, out of a total population
of less than one hundred. One couple went to Manchuria where the husband worked as an
army guard on the Manchurian Railway. They had three children there, two of whom died
in the long post-surrender repatriation process. The woman returned alone to Kurusu one
day with a small baby girl and only the clothing they wore. A year later, when he had
been given up for dead, her husband was repatriated. Two young men who had left the
buraku as civilian war workers—one to Korea, the other to Kure city in western Japan—
both returned after the surrender.

Of the sixteen other men who went into the armed forces and saw service in Formo-
sa, New Guinea, China, Manchuria and the South Pacific, only seven returned alive. The
other nine were sent back to their families—a small box of ashes wrapped in white cloth.
Three of these nine were brothers, and two others were brothers of the man who had returned from Manchuria, both killed in the closing days of the war. In all, Yasuhara lost
one hundred and eighty-five military personnel killed in the war. The death toll among
civilians who went to the cities is not known.

On July 4, 1945, when the influx of refugees from the bombed cities of Honshu had
already started to reach Yasuhara, the four cities of Shikoku were destroyed in coordinated
fire raids. The skies to the north of the village glowed until daylight, and a vast pall of
smoke rose high over the plain. The flood of refugees came. The people of Yasuhara,
like those in other villages in Kagawa, have many kinsmen in the urban centers and it was
these relatives who descended upon the village. Six of the wartime sixteen households in
Kurusu were filled almost to overflowing with the refugees. Most of them were gone within six months, but their stay is a bitter memory in Kurusu. The destitute urbanites consumed quantities of food, wore what little clothing the farmers could spare them, packed
the sleeping quarters of the house at night, and did little work. Whether or not it really
seemed so bad at the time, the unpleasant memory persists, and stories tell how the city
people complained, mocked their rural benefactors, and in the process introduced a number of new ideas, products and an increased desire for material goods. Some families
found this experience so unpleasant a strain on relationships that to this day they do not
visit one another. In one household in the buraku there were at one time twenty-one evacuees from five families which had fled the cities. The shortest stay of any one individual
was one week; most of them stayed up to four and five months.

The net effect of all the trials of World War II has been marked. During the period
in which I was in Kurusu, the Japanese Peace Treaty was negotiated, signed and ratified
and the United States and Japan implemented a mutual security pact. There was much talk
in the buraku of rearmament and the future. This was especially true of the women and

of the younger men, who felt that they would face certain draft calls in the event of the establishment of new military forces. People spoke also of the heavy tax burden such a program would entail, and of the hardships an increased tax load would mean to the farmer.
But most frequently they spoke of their desire for peace. The initial reaction to World
War II had been lukewarm in the rural areas, but with the early victories and intense
jingoistic propaganda the farmer came to support the national aspiration for expansion. But
in 1952, the people of Yasuhara appeared to be extremely reluctant to lend support to another such effort.

The disappearance of local industry and crafts and the departure of people from the
community to work in the cities have led to another type of change. New jobs have appeared to replace the old specialties, but it is apparent that the electrician, truck driver,
mechanic and white-collar worker have not replaced the older occupations in any consistent
way. With this change in the type of work it is possible to detect a general trend from
skill to non-skill, and from independent work in which some originality or at least personal craftsmanship could be expressed, to more routine operations. This does not mean
that all the new types of work are non-skilled, or that those which are disappearing are
all skilled. Even though some of the new jobs require a high degree of craftsmanship and
a high level of competence, and although some of the old ones were exceedingly routine
and without demand for skill, the over-all trend is away from craftsmanship and individual-
ity toward standardized simplified procedures.

Many of the Kurusu men possess new skills learned while in the armed services, and
some of them are now employed at the dam construction project mentioned above in their
capacities of steam drill operators, electricians, etc. The buraku must now call in a
number of specialists such as roofers, midwives, plasterers, masons and mechanics to do
jobs which formerly were performed by most adults in the community, or to service new
machines like kerosene engines, radios and bicycles. Farmers who formerly depended
upon few outsiders now seek the advice of agricultural experts at the prefectural experiment station and the men who work in the village cooperative on matters such as chemical
fertilizers, insect and weed killers, new crops and new machines.

Simultaneously with the development of economic dependence on the outer world, there
has been a shift of political power and control in the same direction. This pattern has
two aspects—on the one hand government is taking over old services that formerly were
controlled or provided by the community or the family, and it is also introducing new
services such as public health, agricultural extension and welfare. The wide variety of
Japanese government programs for agricultural areas affects Kurusu, as it does every
community in the country. Crop insurance, land tax, residence tax, postal savings, crop
requisitions, health and welfare programs, support for education, all are brought to bear
in the rural areas. The taxes are most fiercely resented, as formerly was the case with
the crop requisitions. On the other hand, many people feel that government should provide
more services, such as expanding farm credit facilities, guaranteeing more liberal insurance terms, and giving more aid to education than already is given. The increased pa-
ternalism of the central government is typified by the fact that destitute families may now
go on government relief, whereas formerly they were aided primarily by the community or
by the landlord whose land they cultivated.

There have been some political changes on the local level, but it is difficult to assess
their long-term effects. With the extension of the franchise to women in the post-war
period, all adult residents of Kurusu are able to vote for government officials at all levels
from village assembly to the National Diet. Voting turnouts are very high in Japanese
elections, but there is definitely a decline in interest in elections the further removed the
office at stake is from the local scene. The intense interest in politics on the village
level, regardless of the fact that policies are in large part determined by administrative

order from upper echelons of government, may be explained by the fact that within this apparently tight system of control the local official has considerable leeway in interpreting and implementing of orders which he is to execute.   The villagers tend to be cynical about national political parties and their wrangling, a cynicism which was in no small part responsible for the abandonment of the parties in the 1930's and the turn to the military for strength, stability and integrity in government.   There is a feeling that the Diet functions without much regard for the electorate, another reason for the relative lack of interest in the national campaigns.   Until the surrender in 1945, the history of Japanese government was one of increasing centralization, with village government firmly in the hands of a small group of politicians behind whom the landlords exercised real power.   The decentralization of administration under Occupation pressure—a move of doubtful wisdom from the point of view of finances—has not radically altered the pattern of power in Yasuhara, except insofar as the former tenants have gained a measure of economic and social independence from the landlords.   The personnel of the village office remains much the same, partially because they are professionals whose livelihood is local administration, and also because they still control the local scene sufficiently to be returned to positions of power.

The land reform, as much as any other single factor in the period since 1945, has contributed to the breakdown of formerly important social distinctions between landlord and tenant in Yasuhara.   Prior to the reform, Kurusu was a buraku of tenants; now 80 percent of its farm land is owned by those who farm it.   Although taxes are high at present, they in no way approach the 50 to 90 percent rents which obtained in this area before 1947. People constantly mention the fact that they do not now have to pay over-elaborate respect to the landlords; they say that there has been a general leveling of social distinctions in the village.   The power of the landlords is by no means broken, but it clearly has been reduced.

Older people lament the passing of morality and manners, and the tendency of older adults to despair of the succeeding generations is as marked in Yasuhara as it seems to have been always in other times and places.   Children no longer feel absolutely constrained to accept the judgment of their elders, especially in matters of marriage, but the immediate family still retains much of its hold on the individual.   This trend away from tight family control has been a long-continuing process and cannot be laid directly to the influence of the war's dislocations, however.

Kurusu, like most other rural Japanese communities, has seen vast changes within the past fifty years, changes merely accelerated by World War II and the Occupation. Change has come to be viewed as inevitable, but only in part desirable, for with inability to select those changes which are particularly desired comes the necessity for accepting a host of distasteful or threatening changes.   The central government for many years attempted with not inconsiderable success to control importation of new things, but with the surrender, such controls largely broke down.   Many villagers resent the imposition of changes by an occupying power, especially those innovations which have seemed to fly most directly in the face of tradition, such as equal inheritance, and co-education, but for the most part the farmers in Kurusu remark on the advantages to them resulting from many of the changes of the past seven years.   They remain convinced that some of the social and economic gains which they have made will be lost, and point to the current trend to illegal recovery of lands by their former owners which is now in progress.   Japan has long enjoyed a standard of living and health far higher than that of other Oriental nations, a standard which for the farmer went even higher just after 1945.   Yasuhara people fear an approaching reduction in this standard, particularly if Japan undertakes large-scale rearmament, but they will resist any such reduction as long as there appears to be any hope of maintaining at least their present level.

A striking change in values has been the decline in religious interest and participation.   In Kurusu, as throughout Japan, both Buddhism and Shinto suffered severe setbacks with the end of World War II, particularly the latter. To be sure, Buddhism seems to have been losing ground for many years as anything other than a system dedicated to funerary rites, demanding little participation and inspiring little. But the general ethical and moral collapse of the immediate post-war period served to intensify the shift from active religious life. Today there seems to be a slight tendency once more to contribute money willingly to the temples. Associated with this tendency is the revival of the Buddhist Bon dance, but as a social function sponsored by the village youth organization. However, Buddhism, though important for its rituals for death and for its memorial services, no longer assumes much importance in the daily life of any but the aged.

Shinto, whose gods were thoroughly discredited by the defeat in the war, was always two religions during the period of State Shinto. Shrine attendance and donations were virtually compulsory for a period, and it was this imposed form of Shinto, in which local gods took on national importance and shrine policy was dictated by a central government agency, which vanished almost overnight with the surrender. Popular Shinto, which existed before State Shinto and served as its base, had no compulsory features, nor has it any in the post-war period. Attendance at the shrines has risen since the low around 1945 and 1946, but like Buddhism, Shinto has suffered an over-all decline through the years. Young people regard many of its beliefs as mere superstitions, observing that they are "uncivilized" and "primitive." The festivals of Shinto, like those of Buddhism, are shorter and less elaborate than in the past, and it seems virtually certain that neither Buddhism nor Shinto will attain even their pre-war stature as vital religions in this area.

The foregoing summary of major areas of change in Kurusu and Yasuhara clearly indicates the necessity for further work in a variety of Japanese communities, as well as a program of longitudinal studies in selected mura and buraku. A study such as this one will, it is hoped, prove useful to those who would deal with problems of change in rural Japan. But its usefulness will be greatly enhanced when the study is viewed in the perspective of related studies, such as its companion in this volume.

MATSUNAGI

THE LIFE AND SOCIAL ORGANIZATION OF A
JAPANESE MOUNTAIN COMMUNITY

by

John B. Cornell

ACKNOWLEDGMENTS

I wish to thank Leslie A. White, Alexander Spoehr, Mischa Titiev, Joseph K. Yamagiwa, Robert B. Hall, and Richard K. Beardsley for their support, advice, and encouragement in my training and field research. My gratitude for their assistance goes to my colleagues in the field: Edward Norbeck, John D. Eyre, Robert E. Ward, Forrest R. Pitts, David Wheatley, David Plumer, Robert J. Smith and Toshio Noh. For the people of Matsunagi is reserved special thanks for their stoic forbearance and patient attention to my queries, especially the Ota family and Shinome Hasegawa. Finally, I would like to acknowledge my debt to the Social Science Research Council for the generous fellowship grant that made my work in Japan possible.

John B. Cornell

Ann Arbor, Michigan
September, 1955

CONTENTS

xxi

ILLUSTRATIONS

Artist's Impression of Matsunagi.......................................Facing page 113

ARTIST'S IMPRESSION
OF MATSUNAGI
AT TOP HOMMURA AND OBARA

Chapter I

INTRODUCTORY

Rugged, forbidding, apparently without life: the mountainous mass of Japan conveys this impression to the traveler approaching it from the sea, but as he nears the port of Yokohama, tiny fishing boats appears, bravely and even gaily painted, to point the way in for his ship. Volcanic mountain peaks seem to hide the communities over which they watch: the great cities and rice villages of the rich lowlands; the fishing ports along the coast and on small islands; and in the hills and mountains behind the plain, the less favored villages. Though their cities swell with the overflow population of the land, the Japanese are still predominantly rural and agricultural, scattered in small communities throughout all the islands. They cultivate tiny plots of land on the steep sides of minute islands in the coastal waters, in the narrow, irrigated coastal plains, and on slopes and eroded plateaus of hills and mountains that rise abruptly near the shore. This pattern of habitation is repeated wherever sea, plain, and mountain, in that order, rise one above the other.

Whatever the principal occupation of the Japanese rural community, some of its peasant population cultivate subsistence crops on a limited scale at least. Coastal fishing not supplemented by some farming provides a precarious living. By the same token, forestry rarely yields to agriculture even in the upland and mountain communities. Only in the higher ranges of hills or mountains is there sufficient forest industry to relegate agriculture to a secondary position in the economy. In the high alpine mountains of central Japan, inland from the Tokyo plain, such communities are found, but apparently forestry activities have only become important with the opening of modern lines of communication to these places. Before that, almost their only source of livelihood was an extremely marginal type of agriculture.[1]

The hands of Japanese farmers are gnarled with callouses from constant handling of their tools, and their feet are wrinkled and horny from daily contact with the earth. This is the mark of their almost horticultural type of cultivation. Japanese agriculture, which is fundamental to all types of economic life in the nation, is highly intensive within the confined areas it has conquered.

Geographical Setting

Matsunagi-buraku is a mountain settlement in a rather remote part of southwestern Japan known as the "Middle Provinces" (Chugoku). Of the several old provinces in this region, Bitchu is the historical and cultural milieu to which our community is most intimately related.

Present-day Okayama prefecture, which includes the old province of Bitchu, is an area best known for its rich farms and leisurely provincialism. In the northern part of the prefecture is the county (gun) of Atetsu which, because of its inaccessibility, has received the unenviable epithet "the Hokkaido of Okayama prefecture."[2] The northern part of Atetsu nearly abuts upon the crest of the central mountain range of Honshu, the principal Japanese island. North from this line the land slopes down to the Sea of Japan coast and the country of Izumo.[3] Matsunagi is situated on the rolling plateau that forms the southern part of Atetsu-gun.

Kusama-mura is a village (mura) territory of Atetsu and a minor administrative unit directly under the Okayama prefectural government.[4] Kusama consists of three smaller

114

MAP I

OLD BITCHU PROVINCE
AND THE
ATETSU COUNTY AREA

areas, called oaza, each having historical unity. Matsunagi is only one of several face-to-face settlements (buraku) in the largest of these, Oaza-Kusama.[5] Thus, Okayama prefecture, Atetsu-gun, Kusama-mura, and Oaza-Kusama, are successively smaller territorial divisions that orient Matsunagi to the greater Japanese realm.

By fast train from modern Tokyo the traveler can reach the prefectural metropolis and market center, Okayama City, in about fourteen hours. From Okayama he is best advised to continue by rail for, as in all Japan, roads are notoriously poor. At Kurashiki, ten miles to the west of Okayama on the main rail line, the Hakubi branch line begins. At first the traveler remarks on the broad, level rice paddies he sees about him. Then, as the train runs abreast of a river, the Takahashi, a gorge-like river valley abruptly begins. There follows a long succession of tunnels and bridges, until finally, two hours out of Okayama, the chuffing little engine pulls into Ikura in the narrowest part of the stream canyon.[6] Atop the precipitous mountain wall above this station is the rolling plateau of Kusama-mura. The dingy, third-class train goes on to Niimi, the chief town of the county, but to get to Kusama one must alight at Ikura, proceed on foot across the river and climb a rocky, tortuous footpath to the tableland above.

A rest stop or two is needed before reaching the top, because the path rises rapidly. After half an hour's climb, fields, houses, and finally a prefectural road appear, swallowing up the path. This is the plateau. The road rolls on through a broad, flat belt of cultivated land, sprinkled with dwellings. Except in the mornings and evenings, when those who have regular duties in the valley below are on the move, few people are met along this road. Within minutes buildings become thicker and one is in Hommura, the chief settlement of the village. Besides business establishments, there are the village office (yakuba) and the public schools here. The central Shinto shrine of the southern half of the village sits on a hill above Hommura in a splendid grove of cryptomeria. The prefectural road winds on east and north, past bypaths that lead to outlying settlements and the isolated buildings of the local Agricultural Cooperative, until again homesteads become more numerous, though still widely dispersed, and the area under cultivation expands to the limits of the level land. This is the growing merchant settlement of Obara, where Matsunagi people do much of their shopping. At the northern end of Obara is the village cattle market and the prefectural Veterinary Station, which figure importantly in cattle-raising, one of Matsunagi's major industries. Just beyond the cattle market a branch motor road strikes off to the east. A guidepost at this point announces that by turning off this way the traveler will shortly arrive in the heart of Matsunagi. The branch road runs among low, wooded hills, between which there is a relatively extensive, flat area of cultivated land and grassland. This is Kanabara, a district divided between Obara and Matsunagi. The hills that rim Kanabara converge, rimming its eastern edge with a belt of forest. Only a small saddle remains open in this mass, through which the road leads into the main settlement of Matsunagi.

Strictly speaking, Matsunagi does not lie in mountains at all, but on an elevation rising no more than 500 meters at any point. This terrain is known as the Kibi uplands.[7] Its surface is rolling and set with numerous low hills which usually bear a crown of trees. In the Okayama plain to the south the only forested areas are hilltops, but here extensive forests cover whatever land has not been put to farming.

The basic rock of Matsunagi and the immediate vicinity of Kusama is limestone, though granite prevails throughout most of this upland. Watershed forests have been maintained, so that the surface is little eroded. Still, the porous limestone makes for rapid underground run-off, which hinders the storage of water in wells or springs. Water is rather scarce and high in mineral content.

MAP II

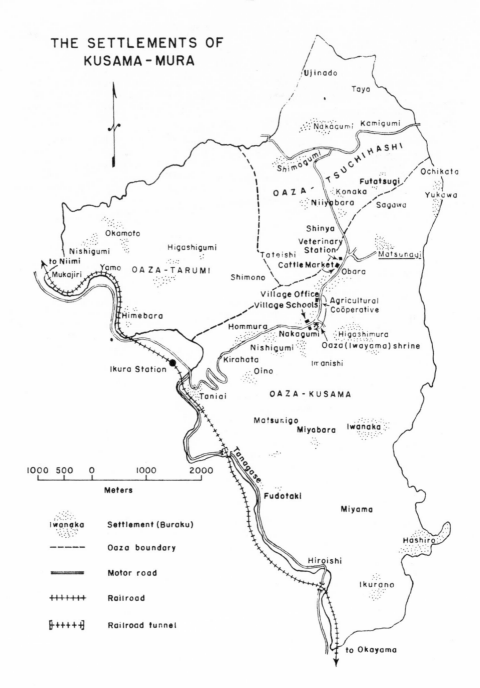

THE SETTLEMENTS OF
KUSAMA-MURA

Ujinado

Taya

Nakagumi   Kamigumi

Shimogumi

OAZA - TSUCHIHASHI

Ochikata

Futatsugi

Konaka   Yukawa

Niiyabara   Sagawa

Shinya

Okamoto

Higashigumi   Veterinary
Station   Matsunaji

Nishigumi   Tateishi   Obara

to Niimi   Cattle Market

Mukajiri   Yamo   OAZA-TARUMI   Shimono

Himebara   Village Office

Village Schools   Agricultural
Cooperative

Hommura   Higashimura

Nakagumi   Oaza (Iwayama) shrine

Nishigumi   Imanishi

Kirahata

Ikura Station   Oino

Taniai   OAZA - KUSAMA

Matsunigo   Iwanaka

Miyabara

Tanagose

Fudotaki

Miyama

Hashiro

1000 500   0   1000   2000

Meters   Hiroishi

Ikurano

Iwanaka   Settlement (Buraku)

- - - - -   Oaza boundary

————   Motor road

+++++++   Railroad

⊞+++++⊞   Railroad tunnel

to Okayama

Even in Atetsu a distinction must be made between the upland areas and those of the river and fault valleys. The plateau is geologically a peneplain. A scarp lying just north of Kusama cuts across the middle of the area from east to west in the vicinity of Niimi. We are most concerned with the drainage lines of streams that rise in this scarp and descend toward the Inland Sea. The Takahashi river on Kusama's western boundary is the chief of these; on the eastern boundary runs the Sabushi, a short, precipitous stream that joins the Takahashi at the southern tip of Kusama. The Sabushi twists snake-like between the steep-sided walls of its valley, but it is broad enough to make extensive rice paddy cultivation possible, especially in the neighborhood of Yukawa-buraku, just above which, on the lip of the plateau, stands Matsunagi.

A small, charcoal-burning bus makes daily trips between Yukawa and the railroad in the Takahashi valley, offering the only other important means of access to Matsunagi. Matsunagi people descend to this valley not infrequently on business at the rice-wine distillery or at the government tobacco warehouse.

One's impression of this mountain area is of open, cultivated zones like islands in a sea of forests and grassy wasteland, in a proportion which is completely reversed in the lowland plains. While Matsunagi and its environs do not have the great stands of forest that are found in the higher mountains of Japan, there is much good timber here. Matsunagi is considered to lie in the zone of mixed evergreen and broadleaf vegetation which covers most of southwestern Japan. In this interior zone there are more broadleafed species than on the sea coast and, for Japan, an amazing amount of slope and level grassland. Cryptomeria, the most important commercial species, is the stateliest tree of the forest, often towering over one hundred feet. Red pine is another very common species, standing in close-packed ranks of mast-like trunks on the slope and on the level ground.

Perhaps the forests once abounded in game animals such as wolf and deer, but these have long been gone. An occasional fox or badger is taken by a professional hunter, and rabbits are still numerous. Pheasants and other mountain birds are frequently seen in the woods and fields, particularly in the autumn. At this season, too, flights of ducks settle in the paddies at evening. Crows are very common and are especially brazen at harvest time. Frogs and snakes teem in the drainage areas and paddies, and the first singing of the frogs in the new year is considered to mark the onset of spring.

The weather in Matsunagi seems to be a compromise between that of the Sanindo to the north and the Sanyodo to the south. It is best characterized as temperate and wet. In common with all Japan, there is no dry season. There are sixty inches of precipitation annually, with peak periods coming in the "plum rains" of June and July and again during the typhoon season in September. Temperatures are seldom below freezing, even in the coldest month, and snow falls very rarely. Heat and humidity tend to make the summers exhausting, though in shaded places there are usually cooling breezes, and nights afford pleasant relief. The growing season is slightly more than 200 days. The dog days (doyo) of midsummer are almost perfectly cloudless, but in the winter many days are totally overcast. Nevertheless, winters are by no means as gloomy as in the Sanindo.

The soil in the uplands of Matsunagi is thin and sporadically pierced by outcroppings of rock that keep considerable sections of fields out of cultivation. Most of the soil is reddish and has a clay texture, which is characteristic of all southwestern Japan. However, it does hold water well and is considered good for upland farming. Another type, the "humus" soil, which is richer in vegetable matter, is best for rice paddy as it drains more readily than red clay, but its distribution is very limited.

MAP III

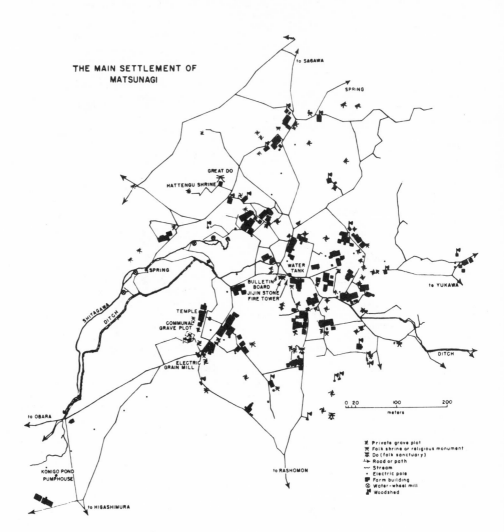

THE MAIN SETTLEMENT OF
MATSUNAGI

to SAGAWA

SPRING

GREAT DO

HATTENGU SHRINE

SPRING

WATER
TANK

to YUKAWA

BULLETIN
BOARD
JIJIN STONE
FIRE TOWER

SHIYAGAWA
DITCH

TEMPLE

COMMUNAL
GRAVE PLOT

DITCH

ELECTRIC
GRAIN MILL

0 20   100   200
meters

to OBARA

𛲟 Private grave plot
𛲟 Folk shrine or religious monument
𛲟 Do (folk sanctuary)
𛲟 Road or path
𛲟 Stream
. Electric pole
𛲟 Farm building
⊗ Water-wheel mill
𛲟 Woodshed

KONIGO POND
PUMPHOUSE

to RASHOMON

to HIGASHIMURA

Historical Prologue

This entire western end of Honshu, i.e., Chugoku, has figured in most of the important developments of Japanese history. But the inaccessibility of the Kibi plateau area seems to have delayed settlement there until comparatively late. It is believed that the earliest inhabitants of the low-lying parts of Atetsu were of Chinese or Korean extraction.[8] Archaeological remains also point to this: there are abundant passage graves and stone cists in the valleys, particularly those that converge at Niimi, which bear close resemblance to types found in Korea.[9] However, in Kusama and neighboring upland villages there are no such remains. Nothing is dated earlier than the feudal forts built during the 16th century, when battles raged here.[10] But little is known of the area before the Tokugawa feudal period (1603-1868). During most of that time the area was under the control of the daimyate at Niimi,[11] until the authority of the new national government replaced feudal power at the beginning of the Meiji era in 1868.

The first practicable transportation in the arterial Takahashi river valley appeared no earlier than around the beginning of the 17th century, when navigation, initiated in the south, was gradually extended as far as Niimi (see Map I covering this area). In the latter half of the 17th century, the products of the northern part of Bitchu province had begun to move by square-sailed, flat-bottomed river boats to the town of Tamashima on the Inland Sea. Earlier, footpath highroads for men and animals had been the only means of movement through the area, but these were intended for officials and military men rather than for transporting goods. Local people still travel between settlements along the former highroad to the south, hard by Matsunagi, which was once used by the Niimi daimyo on his regular trips to the feudal capital, but the main road has shifted to the Takahashi valley. Footpaths were not replaced by vehicular roads until Meiji times, when two-wheeled cattle carts and four-wheeled horse wagons were introduced.

At the time of World War I, a burst of expansion occurred, so that by 1920 there was bus transportation between Niimi and the town of Takahashi, halfway down river toward the sea. In the next decade automobiles very largely superseded jinrikishas for passenger traffic on the main roads. In the back country, though, the ancient two-man sedan-chair continued in use until the beginning of the last war. Fifty years ago, most country folk walked from Kusama to Okayama or Kurashiki, where railroad facilities were by then available, stopping the night along the way, probably to arrive at the railroad the second day out. Only those who could afford it hired a jinrikisha or went by boat. In 1928, completion of the railroad between Niimi and Okayama brought a rising scale of travel outside, an increase of trade both in and out of the village, and abandonment of river transportation. The final link with the outside, the prefectural road from Ikura up to the tableland of Kusama and a branch road to this from Matsunagi was built about 1930. Thereafter, carts and even automotive vehicles were able to come directly into the settlement.

No historical materials shed light on what was happening in Matsunagi itself in the eras before Meiji, although we may be sure that it has long been a mature settlement. It may well be that until the end of feudalism the only literate person here was the Buddhist priest. There are brief temple records, stating that a Buddhist temple was founded here some time between 1624 and 1644 by an itinerant preacher from nearby Nakai-mura. Oral tradition says that the settlement once had sixty households,[12] though now there are only thirty-six. It is unclear when this decline occurred, for within memory there has been little change in the size of the buraku. There are large areas of abandoned dry-fields which have returned to forest, and the remains of house foundations are scattered through the principal settlement area. Some households emigrated to Hokkaido after the beginning of the Meiji reign, but there was no large movement to that frontier. In the main, emigrating households have been replaced by newcomers, such as wartime urban evacuees, or by the creation of new branch households purely within the buraku.

CHART 1

Age Distribution in the Population of Matsunagi

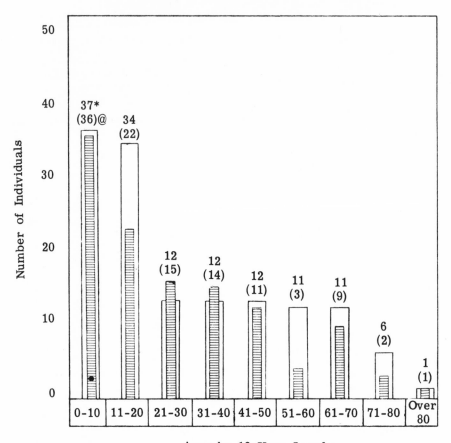

Ages by 10-Year Levels

☐ Males
🗏 Females

* Number of males
@ Number of females

Until March 1928, Matsunagi was a single administrative unit, but at that time the heads of the households decided to split into two divisions, now known as Ushiro-gumi and Mae-gumi.[13] Each of these divisions (jokai) has its own administrative machinery under the mura government, though the physical settlement itself is unchanged.

The Buraku People

In late 1951, Matsunagi had 240 inhabitants, a little over five percent of the population of the mura.[14] Of its two administrative divisions, Mae is the larger with 150 people, while Ushiro has 90. Fifty-two percent of the buraku people are under twenty years of age. The departure of young people to marry outside the buraku or to work in urban areas accounts for a spectacular drop between the age-groups ten to twenty, and twenty to thirty (see Chart 1). Then, too, the war cost the buraku several young men in the twenty to thirty group. From the age of thirty, the decline in numbers is more gradual. Still, Matsunagi people are predominantly youthful, even exceeding the national average in this respect.

The Buraku Settlement

Properly speaking, a buraku is not a definite territory but a cluster of dwellings. The forest holdings and cultivated areas of Matsunagi interlock with those of adjacent buraku and in this irregular terrain do not have an orderly distribution, but boundary points are usually recognized along paths that connect buraku.[15] Territories are generally defined by the location of homesteads rather than by land area. The main group of homesteads of Matsunagi is loosely concentrated in a hill-ranged basin, somewhat tilted toward the edge of the plateau and the river valley to the east. At two points there are gaps in the rim of this basin, permitting a clear view across the valley to the opposite highlands and to the higher ranges of hills and mountains beyond. Even in this main settlement of the buraku, buildings are set among cultivated plots which cover most of the floor of the basin, rather than on the sides of the peripheral hills. In this feature an upland buraku like Matsunagi differs strikingly from a lowland settlement, where houses are thickly clustered on the slopes of hills, not in the valuable level paddy.

A Buddhist temple, raised above the homesteads of its parish, is the most prominent local structure.[16] The road winds into the buraku beneath the temple, finally terminating in a spacious area, a sort of "public square." Here are found a public bulletin board, a flagpole, and a fire tower. Footpaths fan out toward the sides of the basin from this point, tying all the homesteads and detached structures into their network. A stream flows out of paddies nearby, passes behind the temple and disappears in a glen at the edge of the main settlement. Other than a few springs and wells, this is the only source of water in the buraku. In 1758, according to tradition, a great fire destroyed many houses, and so for fire protection a diversion ditch from the natural stream was dug meanderingly across the main settlement. During most of the year this ditch provides water at several collecting basins worn in its course by generations of use. A modern note is struck by the shafts of electric poles that rise above the rooftops, the bare wires burying themselves incongruously in the weathered roof thatch. Outside the main settlement, a few satellite homesteads of Matsunagi are scattered from the cattle market in Obara to the vicinity of the natural limestone formation of Rashomon[17] in the heart of the buraku's best forests close by.

The somber grays and browns of roofs dominate the color scheme of the buraku, broken only by the warmer hues of vegetation and crops through the changing seasons. Though dispersed,[18] homesteads tend to cluster in neighborhood groups. These are

122

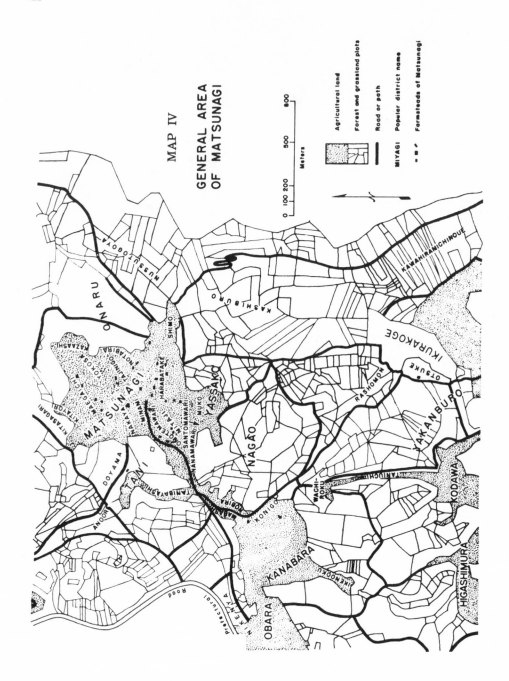

MAP IV

GENERAL AREA
OF MATSUNAGI

Meters

0   100 200   500   800

Agricultural land

Forest and grassland plots

Road or path

MIYAGI   Popular district name

Farmsteads of Matsunagi

identified by the distribution of dwellings, which often seem to the observer nothing but a mountainous bulk of roof. Other structures such as woodsheds, ash-burner sheds, or square-shaped sanctuary pavilions (do) are set apart from the homesteads on the hillsides. No part of the settlement is bare of the varied wooden, ceramic, or stone shrines and sacred objects, which are manifestations of local folk religion. Where the stream becomes a millrace as it nears the clearing of the main settlement, a handful of water-wheel mills stand. Most of them, however, are slowly moldering into ruin.

The Economic Base

Other plateau villages in the area differ hardly at all from Kusama. Some of their buraku have an almost pure sort of upland agriculture, but most are like Matsunagi, predominantly dry-field with some rice paddy. The pattern of subsistence is based upon a group of staple cereals, consisting of barleys and wheat rather than rice.

Because they are mostly farmers, the people of Matsunagi did not greatly fear the possibility of food shortage and even near-starvation that faced so many urban dwellers in the hard winters of 1945 and 1946 following the war. Certainly, conditions have never approached the state of famine that is reported of the late Tokugawa era in this area.[19] Though a number of commercially prepared foodstuffs are now used in the community, the tradition of local self-sufficiency in food probably has changed less than any other aspect of material culture in the past few decades.

The Kibi uplands are the center of Chugoku's cattle industry, one of the largest in Japan. Although in the Okayama plain there has been some use of dairy cattle, only an ox-like native breed is found in the high country. The standard practice is for each farmer to keep only one cow at a time. These animals are rarely seen outside their barns but whenever cattle market time comes around, the highland and valley paths are filled with animals being led to market. Then the favorite topic of conversation becomes pedigrees and prices on the hoof.

In Matsunagi, tobacco is the major money crop. It requires a farmer's best dry-fields but, after exacting arduous labors, puts a sizeable sum of cold cash in his pocket once a year. Forest activities, lumbering, charcoal-burning, fuel-wood gathering, also contribute heavily to the distinctive "mountain" character of this region. At each station along the railroad forest products await shipment, bundles of firewood and charcoal nearest the lowland and logs and heavy timbers farther into the interior. Most forestry at Matsunagi is of the interior type.

Notes

1. This information was obtained from Mr. Iwao Ishino of the Ohio State University, who was acquainted with such a community in Nagano prefecture through his work in the Social Research Section of S.C.A.P. in Japan.

2. Hokkaido, the northernmost of the Japanese main islands, is associated with uncivilized frontier in the minds of Japanese.

3. In common parlance this region is called Sanindo and that on the Inland Sea side of the central divide of Honshu is Sanyodo. The Sanindo is cold and cloud-covered; the Sanyodo is warm and sun-drenched. Differing in climate, these regions also differ in cultural affiliations. The Sanindo has been subjected to strong Korean influences. The Sanyodo's traditions relate it rather to the ancient province of Yamato at the eastern end of the great Inland Sea, where the first central polity in Japan was established.

4. Atetsu and other Japanese gun, unlike our counties, have no unique governmental function of their own.

5. Until the modern era in Japan began, the face-to-face community was called mura rather than buraku; this usage survives in the names of modern buraku in the vicinity of Matsunagi, e.g., Higashimura and Hommura. The oaza of today owes its integrity to the fact that in feudal Japan (until even as late as 1899) it was the village unit of government.

6. This particular place is called the Atetsu narrows; it is renowned for its scenic beauty and is a favorite tourist attraction of the prefecture.

7. See G. T. Trewartha, Japan: a Physical, Cultural, and Regional Geography (Madison, Wis., 1945), p. 546.

8. See Atetsu-gun Kyoikukai (Atetsu County Education Society), ed., Atetsu-gun Shi (History of Atetsu County), I, (Okayama, Japan, 1929), pp. 183-261.

9. The passage graves in particular are much like those erected by the Han (Chinese) colony of Lolang, or Lakliang, in northern Korea around the beginning of the Christian era. Cf. R. Fujita, Chosen Kokogaku Kenkyu (Studies in Korean Archaeology) (Kyoto, 1948), plate no. 12, and Atetsu County Education Society, loc. cit., for a comparison of the Korean and Japanese grave types.

10. Periodic wars between rival military factions marked the period between 1490 and 1600 in Japan.

11. This fief was in the hands of an undistinguished family named Seki, the first recorded lords of Niimi, from 1698 to 1868.

12. See Chapter III, where the household is separately considered.

13. The names mean respectively "back" and "front" divisions, in reference to their geographical relationship to the center of Kusama-mura. The term kumi (gumi) has a multitude of meanings, but here it should be translated "administrative association." Hereafter, this suffix (kumi) will be replaced by the word jokai (the administrative machinery of the division) to avoid linguistic confusion. The use of kumi is restricted to only one of its special meanings (see Chapter IV).

14. This survey was conducted so as to count actual residents only, excluding those few persons who are legal residents of the community but live elsewhere. Kusama has a somewhat denser population than most other purely rural villages adjacent to it. Since the beginning of Meiji, when the first, highly unreliable population figures became available, there has been a steady, though unspectacular, growth in population. This is probably also true of Matsunagi, though it is impossible to trace population change at community level. Early population materials are taken from Atetsu County Education Society, op. cit., pp. 423-450.

15. For administrative purposes territorial limits are drawn about each buraku, but these are arbitrary and often inconsistent with social facts.

16. Elevation of a (Buddhist) temple higher than the houses of its parish is quite general throughout this area and, as far as the author knows, this practice is consistent with the settlement pattern in the towns of the area, too, and even in a metropolis like Kyoto.

17. This formation, which consists of eroded bowls pierced by natural bridges or gates, is one of the most famous of several limestone curiosities in this area and attracts a considerable number of students and tourists each year.

18. In Matsunagi, homesteads are relatively more compactly grouped than in most other upland buraku in this mura.

19. War seems to have had little effect on the diet in an isolated community of Matsunagi's type even during the times of greatest scarcity. Descriptions of these earlier famines are found in Atetsu County Education Society, op. cit., pp. 293-312.

Women seated by their irori offer tea to guest in their kitchen.

A farmer returns from harrowing his rice paddy wearing straw rain garments and a bark rain hat.

An old woodsman in winter garb shoulders his ax.

Chapter II

NATIVE RESOURCES AND MATERIAL CULTURE

Geologically and topographically, the land of Matsunagi is especially well fitted to an upland type of agriculture. Indeed, the entire mura of Kusama provides one of the most extreme examples of upland cultivation in Atetsu county.[1] But even in Matsunagi, which has among the lowest levels of paddy cultivation in the mura, about 18 percent of the land is devoted to rice paddy.[2]

Conversion of dry-fields to rice paddy requires a large expenditure of labor and a favorable drainage situation, in which water from the hillsides runs into a central collecting basin. Such a condition is not often found in this elevated limestone plateau where an adequate water supply is a nagging economic problem. Instead of rice, therefore, dry-field cultivation of barley, wheat, and naked barley, collectively called mugi, is characteristic.

Patterns of Buraku Landholding

A farmer thinks of crops and land productivity in terms of field units. But fields vary exceedingly in size, and in particularly confined areas the configuration of the terrain determines their limits and shapes. Yet, Matsunagi's fields, in this level tableland, are more generally rectangular or at least more rectilinear than those on the slopes of nearby valleys or in the foothills about the Okayama plain. Slope cultivation in Japan almost invariably requires the construction of terraces for both paddy and dry-fields, but since there is little slope cultivation in this buraku, not much of the land is terraced. The largest single field in Matsunagi is about five-eighths of an acre and there are several of a quarter to half an acre. The very smallest are no more than a dozen square yards or so.

The broadest classes of landholdings are (1) farmland, (2) forest, (3) grassland, which is often classed with forest, (4) houselots, and (5) grave plots. Forest lands are the most extensive of all, whereas farmlands are the most valuable. Houselots are of value mainly because of the important buildings they hold. The division of both farm and forest land is highly atomistic; but the distribution of an owner's forest land is the more scattered.

The people of Matsunagi owe the great bulk of their livelihood to the land, and there is no sort of property that is more vital to their continued existence. When a farmer runs into hard times and debt, in his desperation he first sells some of his forests or grasslands. At the very last, and only as a final recourse, his cultivated land is sold bit by bit. Then, if all the land is lost, he and his family are forced to leave the buraku and seek a foothold elsewhere.

There are, to be sure, more than slight differences among household domains, but no one owner is a preeminent landlord of others. Nearly all own enough cultivated land for subsistence. Only three recently arrived families have no farms of their own and are dependent on rented or borrowed land. The rest are landowners, and the old, established residents among them, the hard core of buraku society, in general have the largest establishments. Furthermore, no households own much of any other type of land without a proportionate amount of tilled land; forest and grasslands amount to about two times the cultivated holdings.

Because of the poor, rocky soil of farming lands in this area, and of the over-all distribution, there are perceptible differences between the recorded area[3] and that which

127

is actually workable. According to the reckonings of the buraku people themselves,[4] the average holding is about 1.8 acres, which is above that of the whole mura.[5] Very often a household will own a good bit of land in the immediate vicinity of the homestead, including of course the land on which the homestead stands, but the greater portion of its fields in this open-field system are scattered through the buraku's farmed aza, or districts. As a rule, these holdings are not uniformly sprinkled through all this territory, but tend to cluster in a few districts, the remainder spread more widely, one or, at the most, two plots to a locality.[6]

TABLE 1

LAND OWNERSHIP IN MATSUNAGI*

	Cultivated Land		Forest Land
	Form of Holding	Area in Acres	Area in Acres
	Self-cultivated	52.8	.....
	Dry-field	42.8	.....
	Paddy	10.3	.....
	Rented	10.8	.....
Matsunagi-buraku	Dry-field	9.8	.....
	Paddy	.9	.....
	Leased	11.0	.....
	Dry-field	8.8	.....
	Paddy	2.3	.....
	Totals	63.5	110.5
	Averages per household	1.7	5.0

	Cultivated Land		Forest Land	
	Mae-gumi	Ushiro-gumi	Mae-gumi	Ushiro-gumi
Area:	(acres)	(acres)	(acres)	(acres)
Totals	38.7	24.8	68.0	61.8
Averages per household	1.7	1.1	5.2	6.9
Plots:				
Total number	453	303	....	....
Average number per household	19.7	21.6	....	....
Scale of landholding:	(acres)	(acres)	(acres)	(acres)
Largest unit	2.16	2.55	7.4	10.1
Smallest unit	.37	.84	3.7	1.5

*These figures cannot be considered completely reliable, even though they are taken from the most complete and authoritative source available, the records of the Agricultural Land Committee of the mura. Data on forest holdings have not been so compiled and are therefore less complete and up-to-date.

Land ownership itself is somewhat different from working the land, for a single household may own a good deal more land than it cultivates, the remainder being leased to tenants. Or in some instances, the land being worked may consist almost entirely of rented land. The proportion of tenanted to self-cultivated land is approximately one to four.[7] Nearly all land leases are contracted between households in the buraku. Until the end of the war, land rentals were high and paid in the produce of the fields, but such rentals in kind are now forbidden and have been replaced by a graded system of money rent.[8]

Within the territory of Matsunagi itself few changes were made by the land reform.[9] All the temple's farmed lands were redistributed; however, only two well-to-do private owners lost land, while eighteen others acquired holdings in the process.[10] Instead of keeping the temple lands intact by transferring them to the ownership of the Buddhist priest, they were divided among those households that previously worked them as tenants; the priest himself received only a minor portion of them, what he had been cultivating before the reform. In Matsunagi and in this area generally, though legally possible, it is often socially and morally impossible to separate a tenant from the land he rents so that the owner may make a new disposition of it; this is because the tenant becomes, so to speak, feudalistically identified with the plots he works himself. As a matter of fact, because of the low rentals that leased land now brings in, landowners tend to regard this use of excess land as an act of charity to other households with insufficient fields of their own, rather than as a real source of income.

Patterns of Local Agriculture

Though at every season of the year the predominant colors of the fields change, the painstakingly precise pattern of parallel rows of growing plants always seems the same. Such intensive cultivation exacts an immense amount of hand labor from the farmer, for long experience has taught him that plants must stand at certain optimum intervals in the rows and the rows must be consistently the right distance apart. Even the paths that run through the open, cultivated areas or end at the edges of fields are carefully adjusted to the intervals between plots, which are sometimes only the breadth of a human foot. Few paths are wide enough to permit passage of the two-wheeled farm carts used on the wider roads in the lowlands.

How long paddy rice has been cultivated in Matsunagi is not known, but because paddy irrigation is difficult, it probably appeared considerably after the original settlement. The cultivation of other, dry-field cereals, including dry-field rice, however, is old. In 1950, Matsunagi planted dry-field rice in only some 42 percent of the total area devoted to wet rice. So presumably as the area of paddy expanded, production of dry-field rice declined.

Though rice is the dominant crop of Japan, it is grown in the buraku only to supplement mugi and other subsistence cereals.[11] Nevertheless, it is a prestige crop. The richest households eat rice rather than barley as their basic food. Until he grows sufficient rice to feed himself, or at least to improve the taste of his barley diet, the Matsunagi farmer attempts to expand his paddy wherever water resources permit, even though he is probably not economically justified in doing so.

Paddy rice is grown in widely scattered districts of the buraku but usually under some form of irrigation. Where there is a long-necked valley, it usually contains a virtual staircase of small, terraced paddies, which are irrigated by natural run-off drainage. Where there is running water, the stream flow is diverted into paddies along the banks. But the most costly features of the local agricultural scene, aside perhaps from the terraced paddies themselves, are the irrigation ponds.

Small ponds may be privately developed but large ones require the combined efforts of several households. The buraku's largest pond is known as Kanabara pond. No one knows just when it was built, though it is probably well over one hundred years old. In 1948, an old pond called Konigo was enlarged by a cooperative group of households similar to the ownership association of Kanabara pond. Not only was the demand on human labor for this construction heavy, but expensive electrical pumping equipment has been necessary to raise water to the paddies. With its electrical installation this pond of course represents a technological step forward in rice cultivation in this area. Despite this, the pond does not yield sufficient water.

The fields of Matsunagi were long ago depleted of their virgin fertility and doubtless for many generations a constant battle has been waged to replenish the nutritive elements in the soil. Today, as one hundred years ago, buraku farmers depend for their fertilizers principally on materials available locally. The presence of large numbers of cattle affords an ample supply of cow manure, which is the most widely used natural fertilizer. Nature, moreover, has compensated for poor soil by providing abundant forests and grasslands, which yield green fertilizer, compost, and vegetable ash. Vegetable material may be leaves or twigs raked from the forest floor, small branches cut from trees, or grasses that grow in the meadows. There, too, grow purposely stunted trees, predominantly cork oak, which are pruned of all new shoots each spring. In late spring whole family groups may be seen descending from the grasslands above to the level of the fields with heavy loads of fresh-cut grasses. Leaves and branches or twigs are generally converted to compost before being applied to the fields. Other vegetable materials are burned in rude stone ash-kilns to provide potash necessary to offset the acidic condition of the soil.

Of equal importance is the use of nightsoil as fertilizer. This is removed from a tank beneath the toilet in each homestead and taken directly to the field in wooden buckets suspended from carrying poles. In the fields it is dipped from the buckets by means of a long-handled wooden dipper and dribbled along the rows of plants. Strong odors invariably announce that nightsoil is being handled. However, no one particularly minds this and, in fact, a farmer of the old school is said to find this odor pleasantly suggestive of the earth's fruitfulness. Unlike the coastal plain to the south, there are few field cisterns for storing and curing nightsoil in this area. Since they have become available, chemical fertilizers are generally mixed with this material before being used. Among the other natural fertilizers, the most important are rape seed hulls, soybean cake, and chicken manure. Although locally these fertilizers are thought to be less effective than the modern chemical ones, they are cheap and the supply is reliable.

Thus, chemical fertilizers only supplement natural ones. Superphosphate of lime, ammonium sulphate and sodium nitrate are the only chemicals now in common use. They have a particularly beneficial effect in dry-field cultivation and a great deal of the amount used locally is applied to mugi and to cash crops like tobacco or Chinese cabbage. Various chemical insecticides have also come into use in the past generation, the latest and most popular one is a compound of DDT introduced from America. Widespread application of insecticides has undoubtedly ameliorated the seriousness of insect damage to crops, but, more than this, it has replaced a body of ritual practices that were once employed to exorcise these insect pests.

Both dry-fields and the well-drained and sunnier paddies are subject to a seasonal system of multiple cropping. By limiting cultivation to the most productive land, at least two crops can be grown annually. The key crop in this seasonal rotation is one of the mugi group, which grows during the winter. After the rice harvest, suitable paddies, which otherwise would lie fallow, are also planted to this. The individual farmer follows his good judgment in selecting the summer dry-field crop, but it is often either soybeans or one of the millets. If tobacco is planted between the rows of growing barley and if

A corner of the main settlement, Matsunagi; In the left foreground is the communal grain mill, behind it the temple, and in the distance the high central mountains.

The farmer with his ox and plow prepares for winter dry-field planting.

These boys are pulling hand-plows between rows of winter grain.

buckwheat is put in after the barley has been harvested, a three-crop sequence is possible.
The rhythm of this agricultural cycle is established by the two major harvest-times, in
June and early July and in October and November. The early summer harvest and planting is the most vital pulse of this economic annual cycle, for the principal subsistence
crops are harvested and the greatest variety of crops fit into the multiple cropping system
at this time, all of which gradually builds up to a climax of activity in late June (see
Chart 2, for details of the activities of each economic season).

The Old and the New Technologies

In transforming the energy of his body and the resources of his land into the multitude
of goods he consumes or sells, the farmer of Matsunagi in the main continues to rely upon
the simple hand tools used by untold generations of his predecessors on the same land.
The most important are those used to till the land and harvest the crops. In this mountain area, hand tools are not dissimilar to those used in the coastal plain to the south.
The significant change in hand tools in all rural areas of Japan over the past one hundred
years has been the adaptation of old forms to modern factory production techniques. All
metal tools now in use in Matsunagi are factory-made, and generally are obtained by purchase at the Agricultural Cooperative of the mura.

Hoes, mattocks, and three-tined forks of various sizes and shapes are the basic farm
tools. The blades are fitted to wooden handles so that the working tip is canted, hoe-
fashion, toward the operator's hands. The three-tined fork is at first glance comparable
to the American pitchfork, but in design and in use the difference is considerable. The
tines of the Japanese fork are set at an angle like a hoe so that the fork is drawn toward
the user, not pushed away. This principle is basic to all Japanese hand tools. The Japanese fork is used to lift solid materials, such as manure or earth, but it is equally as
often used to till the soil, to break up bothersome clods. Sickles are among the most
useful tools. One type peculiar in mountain areas for cutting tough brush and small branches has a small beak near the tip of the blade. Metal tool blades are given hard use in the
rocky soil of Matsunagi and they wear out quickly. A hoe blade generally has a life ex-
pectancy of one or two years, after which the entire implement, blade and handle, must be
replaced.

The Japanese plow is particularly simple, consisting of a wooden frame equipped with
a winged iron tip, which undercuts the surface as it moves forward. In Matsunagi plows
are pulled by the household cow. A local peculiarity is the hand-plow, which the farmer
pulls by walking backwards. This type of plow is used together with the hoe and mattock
to remove weeds and break up the earth about plants.

In this area where roads have been footpaths until very recent times, the problem of
transportation was met long ago by making man a beast of burden. From childhood to old
age the people of Matsunagi bend under heavy loads on their backs, but they plod about
with apparent indifference.[12] For amorphous, bulky burdens, such as manure or green
fertilizers, the usual carrying device is the shoulder basket, a frame of heavy vines bound
with straw rope. The carrying straps of these and all other forms of pack-carriers used
here are of braided straw rope. This sort of basket is commonly used with a type of
Chinese rake when gathering green fertilizer in the forest. But the most popular type of
carrier is the wood and straw pack-board. Even when the object is only a lunch bundle,
it is not held in the arms but put in a shoulder sack of rice straw. All of these carrying
devices are made locally.

At the autumn harvest a ladder-like frame of wooden poles is erected in the dry-fields,
on which bundles of rice and other summer crops are hung to be dried before threshing.

Chart 2

The Annual Economic Cycle in Matsunagi

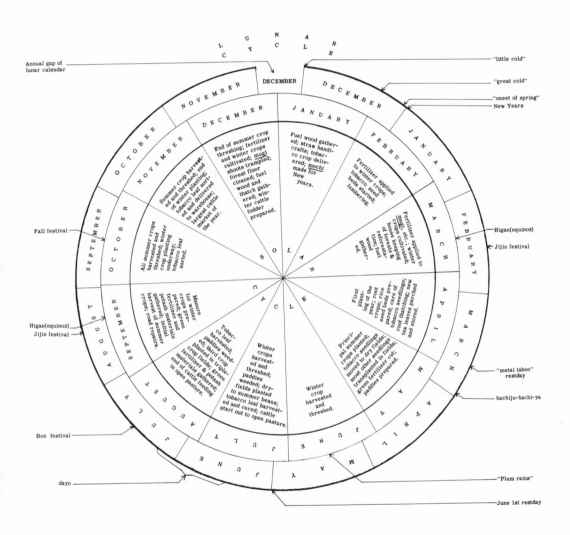

Even today some of the old methods of threshing persist. The millets may be threshed with a whirling flail of bamboo splints, rotating at the end of a long handle. More conventional are the simple pole flail and short cylindrical mallet. Until modern threshing machinery appeared, the cereals of the mugi group were threshed by beating bundles of grain over a block of wood, so that the grains would fall to the mats below. A few people without other means still use this method.

Modern machines have come into the buraku at a gradually accelerating rate in the past two or three decades. But the old machines, as well as many of the traditional tools, continue in use. Most households have a hand-powered wind-winnower (tomi) for cleaning grain. Another such machine is a rice-huller (to-usu), consisting of rotating discs set with wooden teeth. There is also a foot-powered polishing mill (daigara), an arrangement of a wooden mortar and pestle attached to a foot lever. Operating in the same manner as the to-usu, but using notched millstones instead of wooden teeth, the grinding mill (hikiusu) is especially common in this region, for it is employed to make soybean curd (tofu), a staple food. An important variation on the principle of the foot-powered daigara is the water wheel mill. The moving water wheel, by a cam device, lifts and drops pestles into two stone mortars, and by endless repetition of this movement the grain is polished. All of these machines can be made by hand locally with cheap, home-produced materials.

Kerosene has been used probably since the middle of the Meiji period, but until the internal combustion engine appeared about fifteen years ago, it was burned only in lamps. Much use is now made of kerosene in crude but sturdily built engines of Japanese design. They and power-driven threshers continue to be the most important modern machines in use today, being used by thirty-three out of the thirty-six households of the buraku. A set of communally owned machines is found in both Mae and Ushiro, but these are used to thresh only the winter grains. Private machines, though, are as a rule utilized in the autumn harvest too, the amount of fuel being the limiting factor. Fuel is rationed through the Agricultural Cooperative, on the basis of the quantity of grain to be threshed. Though kerosene is now relatively abundant, the gasoline ration, needed for priming the engine, does not suffice and so those who need more must buy it on the black market.

Electricity reached the buraku in 1923, but electric lines have not been extended to five homesteads built since then. Of those that do have electricity for lighting, most are equipped with only two or three 20-watt bulbs and larger ones may not be used without permission from the quasi-governmental company that distributes electricity. As the supply of electricity in these back-country uplands is particularly short, it is not as reliable a source of power for machinery as kerosene.[13] Not infrequently, the electric motor of the buraku's new electrified grain mill cannot be used for the whole day because of power failure, but the people accept this event fatalistically as they do many other external influences in their life. Then, too, the amount of power available is always much less than the authorized level because there are so few transformers in the local system. Only in the last few years has electricity been turned to other than lighting purposes, first in the grain mill and then in the irrigation system of Konigo pond.

The first power threshing machinery was obtained in 1935 by Mae as an association, or kumi, an organization of households to own and operate the equipment. Ushiro followed suit just after the war. The majority of these machines, though, are now owned by individual households, though neighborhood ties often obligate the owner to lend them about. The communal grain mill in Matsunagi has had a patented milling machine since 1949, and there is another owned jointly by two households. An enormous saving of time is effected by these mills, reducing the period from days, as required with water wheel mills, to minutes or a few hours. The power-driven fodder-cutter is replacing an earlier hand-operated type because of the speed and ease with which cattle feed can be cut, even though the new machine is much more expensive to buy and operate. All the power machines now in use are devoted to processing rather than cultivating agricultural products. In general, household machines have been adopted more slowly than agricultural ones. On the other hand, similar patented machines, operated by hand, such as fodder-cutters and rope-making machines, have been known since Meiji times and are therefore widely distributed.

Subsistence Crops

At the head of the list of food crops stand the three primary cereals, dry-field barley, wheat, and naked barley. Another group of lesser cereals, which forms an integral part of the agricultural pattern here, consists of three varieties of millets (see Table 2, for specific crop identifications) and buckwheat, known as zakkoku, or "miscellaneous cereals." Locally, soybean is also considered a member of this group. Rice, both dry-field and wet, ranks after these staples. A wide assortment of vegetables, including taro, sweet potato, and Irish potato, are also grown in the dry-fields. Peanuts and lily roots are usually raised in only a portion of a field; and maize, perilla, and parsley along the edge of fields. The crop list is large, but so many things are raised merely for domestic use that they represent only very tiny areas of land under cultivation. So little land of Matsunagi is tied up in rice paddies that more is available for crop diversification and may readily be turned to more intensive cultivation of any one of the plants in the present crop list, or even to an entirely new product whenever a favorable new market develops.

Cash Crops

Tobacco is the chief cash crop of the mura and buraku and in 1950 was grown on some 15 percent of the buraku fields. Temple school books in use over one hundred years ago relate that Kusama was famous for tobacco even at that time. The first local warehouse of the state's Monopoly Bureau[14] was erected at Taniai, a commercial buraku of Kusama. More recently, a warehouse has been built in Yukawa, to which the farmers of Matsunagi deliver their crop. Under the aegis of the Monopoly Bureau, the techniques of cultivation, quality of the crop, and the compensation to producers have been rigidly supervised. Each producer must receive a permit from this agency entitling him to grow tobacco. Three times during the growing period representatives inspect the crop for violations of acreage allotment and distribution of plants as well as other factors that might enable a producer to exceed his quota. In the immediate postwar years, various tricks were used to deceive these inspectors as to the size of the crop, so that the excess could be sold at high profit on the black market.

Tobacco cultivation occupies the people of Matsunagi for all but about one month out of the year. Seedbeds are prepared in the spring with great care following a rigorous time schedule. In midsummer and throughout the autumn the harvesting, curing, and sorting of leaves occupy the farmer almost continuously. In the final weeks before the tobacco is delivered, all active members of the household work late into the night sorting and preparing the leaf.[15] The most prominent variety of tobacco in Okayama prefecture is Bitchu leaf, which has been grown in Matsunagi as long as anyone can remember. This is sun-cured, being tied to straw ropes hung from a drying frame. In 1951, a new variety called "American leaf" (a kind of Virginia leaf) was first planted by a few households. It is cured in a shed in which hot air circulates through metal flues. The cost of such a shed runs high, but the return on this crop is nearly twice that of the old kind.

Most of the tobacco is grown in the area of the main settlement of Matsunagi. Since tobacco saps the nutrients of the soil very badly, it should be grown in the same field only every other year. However, because good tobacco land is limited, this rule tends to be disregarded in practice, even though most farmers are aware of the deleterious effect on the soil of continuous cropping.

TABLE 2

GROWING PERIODS OF AGRICULTURAL PRODUCTS IN MATSUNAGI

Crop Name		Growing Periods by Solar Months												
		Jan.	Feb.	Mar.	Apr.	May	June	July	Aug.	Sept.	Oct.	Nov.	Dec.	Jan.
1. CEREALS														
Mugi group	barley	—	—	—	—	—						—	—	—
	wheat	—	—	—	—	—						—	—	—
	naked barley	—	—	—	—	—						—	—	—
Rice	glutinous rice						—	—	—	—	—	—		
	non-glutinous rice					—	—	—	—	—	—	—	—	
Zakkoku group	millet					—	—	—	—	—	—			
	sorghum				—	—	—	—	—	—	—			
	Italian millet				—	—	—	—	—	—	—			
	buckwheat				—	—	—	—	—	—	—			
	soybean					—	—	—	—	—				
2. VEGETABLES														
Legumes	maize					—	—	—	—	—				
	red bean					—	—	—	—	—	—			
	pea	—	—	—	—	—						—	—	—
	cowpea					—	—	—	—	—				
	kidney bean					—	—	—	—	—				
	broad bean	—	—	—	—	—						—	—	—
	peanut					—	—	—	—	—				
Roots	white potato				—	—	—	—						
	sweet potato				—	—	—	—	—	—	—			
	taro				—	—	—	—	—	—	—			
	burdock				—	—	—	—	—	—	—	—		
	carrot				—	—	—	—	—	—	—			
	ginger	—	—	—	—	—	—	—	—	X	—	—	—	—
	giant radish								—	—	—			
	konnyaku				—	—	—	—	—	—	—			
Bulbs	lily					—	—	—	—	—	—			
	Welsh onion	—	—	—	—	—					—	—	—	—
	scallion	·	·	·	—	—	—	—	—	—	—	—	—	—
	garlic	—	—	—	—	—					—	—	—	—
Pods	chili pepper					—	—	—	—	—	—			
Fruits	eggplant					—	—	—	—					
	tomato					—	—	—						
Seeds	sesame					—	—	—	—	—	—	—		
	rape	—	—	—	—	—					—	—	—	—
Vines	cucumber					—	—	—						
	squash					—	—	—	—					
	watermelon					—	—	—	—					
	muskmelon				—	—	—	—	—	—				
	pumpkin					—	—							
	gourd				—	—	—	—	—	—				

TABLE 2—Continued

Crop Name		Growing Periods by Solar Months												
		Jan.	Feb.	Mar.	Apr.	May	June	July	Aug.	Sept.	Oct.	Nov.	Dec.	Jan.
2. VEGETABLES														
Leafs	perilla	-----	-----	-----	-----	-----	-----	-----	-----	-----	-----	-----	-----	-----
	spinach	······						······	-----	-----	-----	······	······	······
	Chinese cabbage	-----	-----	-----	-----	-----	-----				-----	-----	-----	-----
	a green	-----	-----	-----	-----	-----	-----				-----	-----	-----	-----
	lettuce	-----	-----	-----	-----	-----					-----	-----		
	cabbage						---	-----	-----	-----	-----			
	peppermint	-----	-----	-----	-----	-----	-X-	-----	-----	--X		-----	-----	-----
3. OTHER CROPS														
	tea	-----	-----	-----	-X-	-----	-----	-----	-----	-----	-----	-----	-----	-----
	tobacco		-----	-----	-----	-----	-----	---						
	shiitake	-----	-----	-----	-----	-----	-----	-----	-----	-----	-----	-----	-----	-----
4. TREES														
	mulberry				X				X					
	persimmon										X			
	citron										X			
	pear										X			
	chestnut										X			
5. WILD FOODS														
	strawberries												X	
	a berry						X							
	akebia										X			
	mushrooms										X			

1. ----- duration of growing period
2. ········ no fixed growing period
3. X   time at which harvest is taken

The crop next in commercial importance is rape, the seeds of which yield an oil widely used in cooking and formerly for lighting. Rape flowers in the spring, turning patches
of the dry-fields yellow with its blossoms. About 5 percent of the winter crop in Matsunagi is rape. All of this is processed locally in a plant operated by the Agricultural Cooperative. There the oil is expressed and the hulls returned to the producer for use as
fertilizer.

Konnyaku (Amorphophalus konjac) is a root food crop requiring at least three years'
growth to achieve maturity. The best roots are not sold until they have grown four seasons. During the winter the immature roots are removed from the soil and stored in the
warmest place in the house, on a platform over the kitchen. Consequently, when ready for
market, these roots command a high price. In 1950, Matsunagi sold some 10,000 pounds
of this product.

In the years 1949 and 1950, a great deal of chili pepper was grown in Japan for export.
The number of producers in Matsunagi was small the first year and the crop highly remun-
erative. But in 1950 nearly every household hastened to profit from it under the encouragement of local agricultural advisors. The result was tremendous overproduction, and the
price of peppers fell to less than 10 percent of the 1949 level.

In addition, Chinese cabbage and peppermint are grown for market by a few farmers
in Matsunagi. Often these are raised instead of such money crops as chili peppers or
konnyaku. Various staples, such as soybeans, rice, or barley, may be produced in such
quantities that they bring in as much or more money than any of the so-called cash crops.
Even though a farmer grows tobacco, he tries to produce at least one other money crop.
Since the war the tendency has been to diversify further the series of cash crops in order
to avoid the serious financial dislocation that failure in a single crop or in its market
might cause.

Animal Husbandry

Cattle, next to tobacco, is the most important marketed product of Matsunagi. One
reason is that pasture is always plentiful in this upland plateau. Cattle and their habits
are intimately related to the daily life of the people. The only type of cattle bred in this
region is the native horned stock, [16] which has a black coat. It is noted for its stamina,
its hard hooves, which are needed in moving over the rugged mountain paths, and for its
resistance to cold. Occasionally, an animal with a reddish coat is born. This is a re-
cessive character, resulting, it is said, from a continental Korean strain in the stock; such
animals are never bred. Matsunagi is only average in the development of its cattle industry. In late 1950, there were about thirty head of cattle in the buraku, almost one to each
household. During that year some sixteen or seventeen calves were born in the buraku.
Since Matsunagi farmers raise no stud bulls, the only animals kept to maturity are female.

Within the territory of the buraku there are two communal pastures, [17] Ikurakoge and
Onaru, as well as numerous private grazing lands. Until a generation ago a compound of
straw and wood was erected in Ikurakoge each summer, in which grazing cattle were
penned for days at a time. But now the animals are escorted to pasture only during the
daytime, returning each evening to their barns. Except for about a month in summer cattle are fed in their stalls, so that cutting fodder is one of the major activities of farm
life. During the autumn the bulk of feed is sweet potato vine; in winter and spring it is
mostly cereal straw. When fresh grasses appear in spring these may be cut and brought
in for feed but no fodder grasses are cultivated.

The local type of animal is utilized largely for draft purposes and for meat, but it may have been for manure that these animals were first introduced. Cattle breeding is popular because it is less costly in time and materials than agricultural cash industries. Each household displays deep interest and affection for its animal, even a kind of personification, particularly if the animal is a finely pedigreed cow. If the animal has the proper potentialities, its owner makes every effort to secure a high breeding qualification at the regular pedigree inspections held by the local Animal Husbandry Cooperative. Within the last year or two, artificial insemination has become the rule; this is performed in Obara either at the prefectural Veterinary Station or by a private specialist.

Twice a year, in March and November, an auction market dealing only in calves is held at the mura cattle market grounds in Obara under the sponsorship of the Animal Husbandry Cooperative. All bidding is by professional drovers (bakuro), some of whom come from a great distance. A market day is a festive occasion, to which whole families come escorting their calves for sale. Others attend merely as spectators. On this day even the precariously rocky bypaths are busy with groups of man, cow, and calf, in that order, moving toward the market. Amid the chanting of the auctioneer, the owner leads his calf onto the floor of the sale pavilion, where the bidding takes place. Most final bids are accepted by the owners. If not, the calf must be disposed of later in a private arrangement with a bakuro, which often results in a poorer price. The highest priced calves are those with the qualifications of breeding bulls, but on the average female calves are more valuable. A calf must be old enough to show its breeding when brought to market or it will not bring a top price. Markets are adjusted to the seasonal peaks of births, with the expectation that a spring-born calf will be ready for market in the autumn.

The institution of the bakuro is as old as the cattle industry here. Sometimes these men buy animals to feed themselves, but most often they act as brokers for others. Drovers are a distinct confraternity, identified with a cultural sub-pattern oriented to the cattle industry. Without being formally organized, they share a body of lore, songs, and ritual practices, most of which, however, have been abandoned in the past generation.

In Matsunagi there are few animals other than cattle. One or two breeding sows are fed for market but never kept for household consumption. A novelty is a goat kept by one household to provide milk for the owner's children. Young domestic rabbits are bought and raised to be eaten at some special occasion in the winter when fresh food is scarce, and the pelts are sold to professional tanners. Almost every household keeps a few chickens, usually no more than five or six laying hens, mostly white leghorns. Some eggs are eaten by the household, but most of them are sold to local dealers. Occasionally, a chicken is killed to provide a delicacy for some special event, but, because most people are reluctant to kill any of their own livestock, they must have some neighbor do it or simply go without. Enterprises with twenty-five or even fifty birds have been attempted in the buraku, but no stable poultry industry has developed.

Domestic cats and dogs are found in most homesteads. Dogs are more numerous; they are usually reddish-coated Japanese mongrels. Several are trained as hunters but the majority serve only as watch-dogs. Cats are motley in coat and rarely put in an appearance. They are on less intimate terms with the family, it would seem, than are the rats they are expected to hunt.

Forest Industries

In colloquial Japanese, the word yama means "mountain," but it may mean "forest" as well. Hill and mountain land are synonymous with forested land, for stands of trees are rarely, if ever, encountered in the level plains. In general, the heaviest forest growth in

A dealer in town has sent a truck in to pick up local timber.

A sawyer makes boards by the old saw and wedge method.

A sawmill operator has brought his portable machinery into a buraku forest to process lumber for market.

Lumberjack cutting logs in the forest for shipment to market.

A load of wood has just been fired in this charcoal kiln.

This man is wearing a pack-carrier over his shoulders to bring logs out of the forest.

Kusama is away from the prefectural road and the center of the mura. Situated as it is at the edge of the plateau, Matsunagi is far enough removed to be one of the more forested buraku of the mura. Though as a rule it is the lowest and flattest parts of the plateau that are cultivated, even in these areas trees appear. In Kanabara new growths of pine stand along the main road in addition to stands on the surrounding hills. In the more level areas fairly thick groves have been allowed to grow. Clearing forest and preparing fields is an enormous task, particularly uninviting from the view of distance from the homestead and the limited size of each area one could by his own resources bring under cultivation.[18] Like the rest of the county, the forests of Matsunagi have been cut over more than once. Some large cryptomeria trees which remain in places of a sacred nature may be as much as two hundred years old. Today such trees are apparently far fewer than a century ago, when the massive beams and pillars of the oldest houses were cut. A national plan of reforestation, which breaks down eventually into village segments, has been developed since the war, but so far its enforcements have not been very effective.[19] Replanting generally occurs in the slack work season of spring, and thinning of trees and removing foreign species from homogeneous stands are done at this time also.

Despite the buraku's wealth in forests, a disproportionately small amount of the economic activity of each household in the annual work cycle involves forestry. Lumbering is the most important activity in point of commercial value. A little over twenty years ago the power-driven sawmill was introduced, making possible great economy and speed in the processing of lumber. Though most cut lumber is still shipped unmilled, lumber for local consumption is almost entirely made by commercially operated, mobile sawmills. Each is owned by an entrepreneur from the area, who hires three or four operators. These sawmills move about the mura, cutting lumber wherever timber land can be leased, and incidentally cutting up logs for local householders. In a busy lumbering year, usually during winter and spring, at least one mill appears in every buraku.

The traditional method of making boards is still employed, particularly where roads are too poor to permit the entrance of milling machinery. This is the technique of the sawyer (kobiki), a specialist whose profession once had its own ritual and work songs.[20] The tools of the sawyer are the broad ax, the large saw, and the wedge. Before these tools were known, boards were hewn from logs by adze only; puncheon boards from that era are still to be seen in place on a few buildings in the buraku. Actually, there are three professional specialties subsumed by the term kobiki: (1) one who fells trees and cuts them into logs, a "lumberjack," (2) one who saws flat boards out of a single log, and (3) one who cuts and shapes building timbers with ax or adze. Of the three, the greatest skill is required in the latter specialty, but it is the second type of skill that has been most outmoded by the mechanical advance of the sawmill.

Aided by technological improvements, lumbering also absorbs more labor than any other forest activity. Working in teams of two or three, lumberjacks fell trees by hand-ax and saw. Stripped branches, useless for lumber, are left for the landowner. Most lumbering operators, largely the same men who own the portable sawmills, are residents of Kusama; they usually hire a crew of buraku men to cut the timber they have purchased in the vicinity.

The period from August to October is optimum for cutting logs which are to be used in local construction, but the general run of commercial timber, destined for shipment to urban areas, is cut nearly the year around. If there is a good deal of timber to be removed, one team is hired to fell the trees and strip the bark and another to carry the logs out of the forest to a point, usually near the grain mill, where they can be trucked out. Logs are carried out of the forest on the shoulders with aid of a forked stick. Like the lumberjacks, these carriers are usually local people. A large log may require three or four workers, each with a shoulder under it, grunting in unison to maintain the pace on the narrow paths. Where paths are sufficiently wide, a small homemade, two-wheeled truck may be used instead. In Matsunagi, operations are on a relatively small scale and few forest tracts are so remote as to require expensive special equipment to get the timber out.

No one in Matsunagi is engaged in gathering fuel wood commercially. For domestic consumption, fuel is collected independently by each household, largely between the end of the autumn harvest and New Year's. It is prepared in two forms: split-wood and kindling. Living trees may be cut for fuel but not before the dead trees have been cleaned out and fallen twigs and branches collected. The brushwood which is used as kindling is tied in bundles and left in the forest to be picked up as needed. Cork oak and red pine provide most of the larger fuel, and the bulk of kindling consists of dried pine twigs. At irregular intervals of years, woodlands in the large common pastures are redistributed among the households entitled to their use. Only trees of suitable age may be cut in the plot assigned to each household, the younger growth being left for the next user.

Charcoal is one of the chief forest products of the county, and Matsunagi shares in this regional industry on a modest scale. There are currently only four part-time charcoal burners in the buraku, but during the war as many as nine producers were active.[21]

Their packed-earth kilns, which are located in the very tracts from which the charcoal wood is cut, are constructed by the operator's household with occasional assistance of hired labor. A kiln is elliptical, built on a rough log frame and varying in size according to the area of forest to be burned. Most charcoal is made of pine or cork oak, and, as in lumbering, only the wood in the tract to be burned is purchased by the operator, the price being based on the quality of the trees and the probable volume of wood.[22] Rarely do charcoal burners of Matsunagi operate far from home, for during the five days or so that the wood burns, the operator must be able to come and go at any hour.

Finished charcoal is packed in containers of pampas grass (Miscanthus sinensis) which are made in the household, mostly by old men. There is a cooperative association of charcoal burners in the mura, but it has little function except to inspect the finished charcoal in order to maintain its quality. The charcoal burner, alone or with the help of neighbors or relatives, leases woodland and disposes of his goods to dealers in nearby towns. The market for charcoal is seasonal, but burners in Matsunagi continue to operate their kilns through the summer, storing the product until colder weather. Although charcoal burning does not require high capitalization, it is costly in time and demands considerable experience and skill. It is, however, one trade that a man with no technical training and little property can attempt with the prospect of earning a modest livelihood.

The forests provide a long list of useful products, most of which bring some income to the people of Matsunagi. The bark of the cork oak, though the supply is erratic, is the chief product of that tree. The bark is generally peeled by the owner of the trees or by local people who lease such trees. Some people tap their own trees for pine resins, but this industry is not well developed. On the other hand, varnish trees (Rhus verniciflua), which occur here and there in moderate numbers, are nearly always tapped for their sap. These trees are leased to professional collectors who handle the operation. Also, in the early mornings of autumn most people go to their forests to gather mushrooms, some of which they consume themselves but most of which they sell to buyers who carry them to urban markets.[23]

Prominent Local Handicrafts

Only two of the craft trades common throughout the nation (exclusive of the distinctively "mountain" skills called kobiki) are represented among occupations in Matsunagi:

carpentry and cooperage. Carpentry involves more skill and knowledge than any other
craft trade and commands most respect in the buraku. While the carpenters of Matsunagi
operate independently, they can easily join forces because they share a highly stereotyped
body of skills. The carpenter, like other craftsmen, prefers to work close to home, in
his own buraku, if possible. Like the sawyer, he uses a number of tools peculiar to his
special handicraft. Among the most useful of these are saws, which are cruder and lighter
than ours; he lays more emphasis on planes and adzes rather than on hammers and screw
devices. Though rude by the standards of American building, the carpenter's craft produces a carefully mortised structure having great durability. Carpentry is also an informal confraternity sharing work ritual as well as common skills.

As the most prominent of the local trades, carpentry is outstanding among the forms
of apprenticeship in the buraku. A single master, if he is exceptionally skilled and experienced, may have as many as seven apprentices at once. But most masters have no
more than two, the eldest in point of service being called "older brother apprentice" and
the others "younger brother apprentice." Between these grows a bond of friendship like
that between classmates or even between siblings, so that in later years they are inclined
to turn to each other first for assistance in their trade. A carpenter wishing to apprentice
his son is likely to ask his former "older brother apprentice" to take the youth. The apprentice spends much of his time with his master, even living as a member of the household during the seasons of greatest activity.

If the master lives at some distance from the apprentice's home, the latter will probably see his own household mates only at festivals and during the height of the harvest
seasons. The apprentice pays for his keep by helping with domestic chores, though it is
improbable that he will help in the master's fields. A beginner may receive 10 percent of
the master's daily wage, which is increased as the student learns until it probably reaches
50 or 60 percent. There are various arrangements, some of which are so ungenerous that
the apprentice receives nothing but his keep while working on the master's jobs. A popular master with many apprentices can afford to be less open-handed. At the end of each
year of apprenticeship, that is lunar new year, the apprentice may give his master a money
gratuity or a bottle of sake, if relations between the two are amicable. At the end of the
term, a similar sort of gift is in order, and the master may respond by presenting his
student with a set of tools. Usually, though, the apprentice has to buy his own equipment
piece by piece during his training period.

Other common handicrafts, the sawyer's craft, stonecutting, plastering, cooperage,
follow the same apprenticeship pattern with only slight modifications. The sawyer, too,
needs a period of training, but it is generally much shorter than the carpenter's; indeed,
nowadays this skill has so declined that there are almost no apprentices in training. The
cooper makes most of the wooden tubs and buckets used in the buraku. He, too, is self-
employed and, like other craftsmen, is called to each new job by word of mouth. At work,
a cooper spreads straw matting on the ground of the houseyard and, seated, shapes wood
and bamboo into his product. Even more than in carpentry, the tools of cooperage are
made to shape pieces to fit together exactly, for nail and screw fasteners are seldom used.
Nevertheless, this craft is not as exacting as the carpenter's, nor does it involve work
ritual. A subsidiary form of cooperage is bamboo-working, making such things as water
pipes and flooring.

The stonemason, roof-thatcher, and plasterer are craft workers who are auxiliary to
the carpenter. Like a carpenter's, their labor is better paid than unskilled forestry work,
the day wage of a plasterer being high—above five hundred yen. The mason cuts and fits
together the rough stones of a building foundation. He usually works alone, quarrying and
shaping local rock to suit his needs. The roof-thatcher usually builds and repairs the
elaborate straw roofs of larger farm buildings. Two or three journeyman specialists work

Heads of neighbor households feed grain bundles into a thresher.

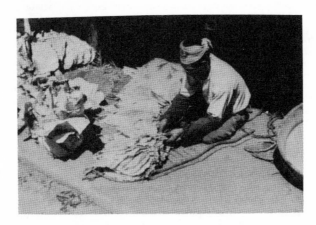

This man is tying fresh-cut tobacco leaves to a straw rope for sun curing.

Schoolboys take their household cows to pasture at Ikurakoge in late afternoon.

together, being assisted in the preparation of thatching materials by the people of the
household and their neighbors. A craftsman assembles prepared bundles of grasses to
form the roof and then trims the edges with a sickle, his most important tool. If a new
roof is to be built, he also constructs the lattice frame on which it rests. The roof-
thatcher is sometimes required to perform ritual in connection with his work, but this is
so simple that no more than a layman's knowledge is needed.

The plasterer builds the earthen walls of the building as his contribution in construction. He first weaves a lattice of vines and saplings, over which several layers of clayey
mud are daubed. He mixes his materials of the native earth, adding a binder of chopped
straw. In addition the plasterer, not the roof-thatcher, is called on to lay tile roofs and
in recent years has turned to building items of cement for household use.

Any structure in the native architectural style can be simply built within a few weeks,
though the actual period from start to finish may be many months. A craftsman must
periodically interrupt work to take care of his own farm, and usually each stage in building is carried out piecemeal, as funds become available.

A building sequence starts in the forest, where the sawyer fells a number of large
hardwood trees and shapes them into pillars and beams. Other timbers are cut into boards
and gradually all preparations for the raising near completion. Meanwhile, a mason chips
local limestone into foundation posts on the site. The next step is to bring the pillars and
beams from the forest to the site, which is done by the people of the household concerned,
assisted by neighbors and relatives. Much the same group raises the framework under the
watchful eye of the carpenter, who has prepared the beams so they will fit together neatly
and require a minimum of nails. Within the space of a single day, however large the
structure, the frame is up. In the case of something important like a main house or a
godown, just before sunset the carpenter, the sawyer, and other hired specialists perform
a dedication ceremony. Ritual, however, has a very minor place in the ordinary run of
construction.[24]

Roofing is the next to last step, the carpenter being employed to build a frame only
for tile roofs. After a plasterer or thatcher has put on the roof, the walls finally go up.
For this purpose a pole scaffolding is raised about the building, from which the plasterer
works. The walls eventually are two or three inches thick and solid enough for decades
to come. If the building is to contain living quarters, the carpenter finishes it off inside,
putting in ceilings, tracks for sliding panels, and wall alcoves. Otherwise, interiors are
left in the rough state. There may be special structures, such as cattle stalls, a toilet,
or a bath, set into the building, which will demand a good deal of additional carpentry
work. As a rule, all of the basic materials, even for a main house or godown, are obtained locally.

Clothing

A great many different sorts of clothing are used in Matsunagi, but they fall into two
general categories: the old, native forms and the new, Western ones. Most of the old
forms of clothing are still in use even though they are passing out of favor. However, the
popularity of locally made articles of wear, such as straw rain-capes and rain skirts as
well as oil paper umbrellas and winter straw footgear, is strong despite the flood of
Western apparel appearing in the past few years. Hand-woven garments of home-grown
cotton disappeared in early Meiji times, but the styles of earlier eras persist in store-
bought clothes.[25] The untailored kimono still is the basic native garment. But more and
more these are being restricted to formal and leisure-time house wear. Some are short
but most kimonos extend to the ankles. A cloth thong or band is worn about the waist to

hold the kimono to the body. But whether in the old or in the new style, clothing tends to be worn in several layers for warmth. Consequently, it is the number of garments worn rather than the type that changes from season to season.

Wardrobes are very small indeed, though women have more clothes than men. Younger men, especially, wear far more Western than native clothes. During work they almost always have on some combination of trousers and coat or shirt, much of these having been obtained in the rationing of surplus military clothing after the war. Only old men wear native dress for work, but married men of all ages have formal, crested kimonos and slit skirts for occasions like a wedding or a funeral. Men's summer clothing is extremely simple, generally short pants with or without a shirt. In hot weather, men usually wear a towel as a head band. Though these garments soon become soiled with sweat, they are changed infrequently. The number and variety of suits and coats a man owns is a clue to his household's economic position. Only the very best educated and richest people have morning or frock coats for formal wear, which are shared by all the men of a household. Two to four dark, awkwardly-cut Western suits for dress and, in some instances, a drab-colored overcoat or two are the best clothes of the younger men.

Typical of a woman's work garments are a kimono, long or short, with a pair of bloomer-like trousers (mompei). When doing housework, women wear short aprons or white cotton smocks to protect their clothing. In winter extra linings or cotton padding are sewn into kimonos for warmth. A sleeveless, padded vest is very common. Work clothing is of coarse cloth, usually a somber, dirty blue; better kimonos are of silk but usually of only the poorer grades. Women often drape a cheap towel or kerchief about the head while working. Upon returning from the fields, most women simply remove their mompei, without changing to a different kimono for house wear. The majority have no more than ten to twenty kimonos all told, both for work and dress.[26] In summer, they wear either Western skirt and blouse or a one-piece dress. But even in the warm season, formal occasions may demand native attire. In general, young women's kimonos have small, flamboyant patterns, but the designs on those of older women are large and somber. Though it is difficult these days to replace youthful kimonos with those of colors suitable to one's age, to avoid public ridicule a woman of fifty dares not wear kimonos of a pattern suited to a girl of twenty.

Children's clothing does not differ essentially from the mixture of native and Western styles worn by adults. In infancy, tiny kimonos are usually worn, but the play and school clothes of older children are makeshift and largely of Western type. The first formal suit a child gets is his school uniform, navy-blue tunic and trousers for boys and sailor skirt and blouse for girls, but this may not come until adolescence. Boys get their first complete Western suits and overcoats after graduation from school but acquire almost no native dress until marriage or later. Girls, though, begin to buy good kimonos from about the age of sixteen, when they start collecting a trousseau.

Japanese are accustomed from babyhood to go with hands and feet uncovered even in cold weather. Neither the Japanese split-toed sock (tabi) nor Western style stockings are used in everyday life in Matsunagi. The homemade straw sandal (zori) is still very popular but is yielding to a manufactured rubber sneaker. The native clog, or geta, is used mostly in traveling outside the buraku, and more by women than men. Most dress footgear is cheap canvas exercise shoes, since leather shoes are too expensive to be owned except by the more prosperous men.

Nearly all cloth garments are bought ready-made and, if not, they are made by local seamstresses, since few women have time to do more than mend their old clothes. For ordinary clothes, it is actually reckoned cheaper to buy ready-made garments. Work clothing soon becomes worn and tattered, but it is frugally mended until it falls apart.

Body Ornamentation and Personal Care

Besides the ornamental effect in clothing itself, bodily adornment is practically unknown in Matsunagi. Jewelry is almost never worn, primarily because no one can afford it, except one or two women who wear plain finger rings for no other reason than they "like to." One recent buraku bride admitted to wearing a wedding band because she had read it symbolized marriage, but such ornamentation is unusual.

Among cosmetics, camellia oil for the hair is the most familiar. Even this is not applied every day, never by most men, whose heads are shaven.[27] Young men may wear their hair long but use pomade only when they are going outside the buraku. Modern town-bred girls are accustomed to use lip-rouge and face powder, but a buraku girl would be ridiculed were she to use such cosmetics in everyday life. Only at weddings and at New Year's is their wearing clearly sanctioned. Paradoxically, though, it is said that both sexes may use cologne to complete the toilet on a dress occasion.

Young men are the only ones who patronize barbershops. A man's hair is usually cut with hair-clippers by another man or by his wife. Children's hair is cut by the father, whereas women occasionally trim their own. Cut hair is generally thrown into the path, where it is trampled by passing feet and eventually disintegrates.[28] Men shave infrequently, only once in several days.

Among girls and young women permanent waves are becoming popular but are still not common. Most women's hair is worn in a bun at the back, but, except for a bride or a little girl at New Year's, the hair is never dressed with the gewgaws or flowers which are usually associated with Japanese coiffures.

Financial Affairs and the Role of Money in Buraku Life

Like most people in this country, Matsunagi men and women like to keep their money matters pretty much to themselves, though even in matters of total income neighbors are rather well informed about each other's financial condition. They are quite aware of the value of money and how to use it. It is, however, a breach of etiquette to inquire about specific sums, particularly those which are involved in gifts. The Japanese associate money with the merchant class and since the farmer traditionally ranks above the merchant, contact with money besmirches his peasant standing. The sense of degradation connected with the use of money is still one of the important ideological features of Japanese culture. Matsunagi people are not completely at ease with money; they prefer converting it into some tangible goods to letting it accumulate.

Most farmers have no accurate idea of the money they receive and so they guess at it as best they can.[29] However, in paying the national income tax it is perilous willfully to dissimulate one's true income since such primary sources as tobacco, cattle, and many lesser cash crops are part of the public record and cannot be concealed. Income from those crops for which no record is available is figured by the amount of land planted to each crop, but this method yields only a broad approximation. In 1950, the average gross income per household in Matsunagi was 146,000 yen, somewhat higher than the upland average though apparently no more than the average in the coastal plain (see Chart 3, for sources of income).

We have already observed that the bulk of money income is derived from tobacco. Of the cash available to an average household, something between 70 and 80 percent comes from this source. The sale of a calf usually brings in an additional 10 to 20 percent of the total, and the rest is received from miscellaneous sources, principally cash crops other than tobacco.

Another source of income, which also illustrates the increasing extent of money use, can be seen in the fact that nearly every household has received money in compensation for the labor of one or more of its members. In a number of households at least one member devotes himself to wage earning as his principal occupation.[30] Regular salaries are the most stable forms of income and quite desirable. Specialized work of a less continuous nature, such as carpentry or lumbering, also involves a recognized daily wage. Even casual farm work for hire has its tacitly recognized rate of pay.[31] Regular salaries go a good deal higher than the cumulative income of day wages; on an annual basis the average salary is even slightly above the average farmer's income. But day wages vary a good deal according to the skill of the craftsman or type of job.

No one fact is more central to the economy of the modern buraku than that income all but fails to cover expenditures. Thus, under normal conditions the farmer feels he cannot afford to part with any of his own products unless reasonably sure of receiving some commensurate return, a reciprocal gift or enhanced standing in the community. Nor can he afford to pass up a promising opportunity to make money. An average household spends about 7,000 yen a month and even impecunious ones spend between 2,000 and 3,000 yen. If the household is large, this amount rises to about 10,000. A rule of thumb is about 1,000 yen a month per active individual. Some months see more outgo than others, especially the month of lunar New Year, when expenditures may be two or three times the average. Money must be husbanded to make it last between peak periods of income, which usually follow the two major harvests.

Among the regularly recurring items of expense, none is more demanding than the constant need of clothing. This is particularly true of work clothing. The average rate of expenditure for clothing is thought to be about 1,000 yen per person per year, but one large and rather extravagant household spends in the neighborhood of 750 yen per person a month. On the other hand, food costs are relatively low, since so much is raised locally. Though the people are acutely price conscious and aware of the hazards of financial insecurity, few make any attempt to budget their expenses and many scarcely give thought to the level of their total expenditures, simply buying or refraining as they have money on hand.

Taxation is one of the major financial burdens of most households. Where possible, the taxpayer shades income estimates in his favor. Even though the pressure of national income taxes has increased since the war, people are still more conscious of local mura levies such as a property and a head tax. Income taxes are paid through a collection association in each administrative division of the buraku. The primary national and mura taxes together consume about 5 percent of total estimated income in an average household, but taxes may run as high as one-third of the total cash income. Substantial delinquencies occur in the national levies, but are rare in mura taxes. On the whole, more complaints are expressed about the cost of consumer commodities than about the level of taxation.

Money is also much used in gift-giving. Once, probably not more than a few decades ago, all gifts were made in kind, of which rice was the most common. In wartime the government discouraged gifts of any scarce foodstuff and consequently it became necessary to turn to money. Now money constitutes the bulk of gifts, especially where they are routine and clearly stipulated. There is a general effort to keep the amount small, below one hundred yen and even as little as ten yen in many cases. The relative abundance and greater convenience of handling money make it quite likely that it will continue to be preferred in gift-giving.[32]

In times of prosperity debt is of little consequence. And since the beginning of the war, the ko, a form of mutual lending association,[33] has not been operative in Matsunagi, but there is some small-scale indebtedness, most of which does not involve interest

JOHN B. CORNELL

CHART 3

Comparison of Primary Sources of Household Income

in Matsunagi*

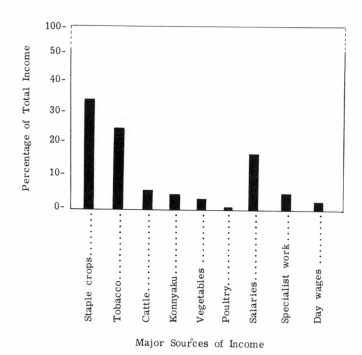

Major Sources of Income

*This material is abstracted from income tax returns filed by thirty-one socially distinct households for the tax year 1950; the actual number of returns involved is thirty-seven. Items consumed domestically but for tax purposes converted to money values by the taxpayer have been combined with cash income in these data. So, as nearly as the people can estimate, this represents the real income of the entire group of reporting households.

CHART 4

Annual Cycles of Money Income and Outgo in Matsunagi

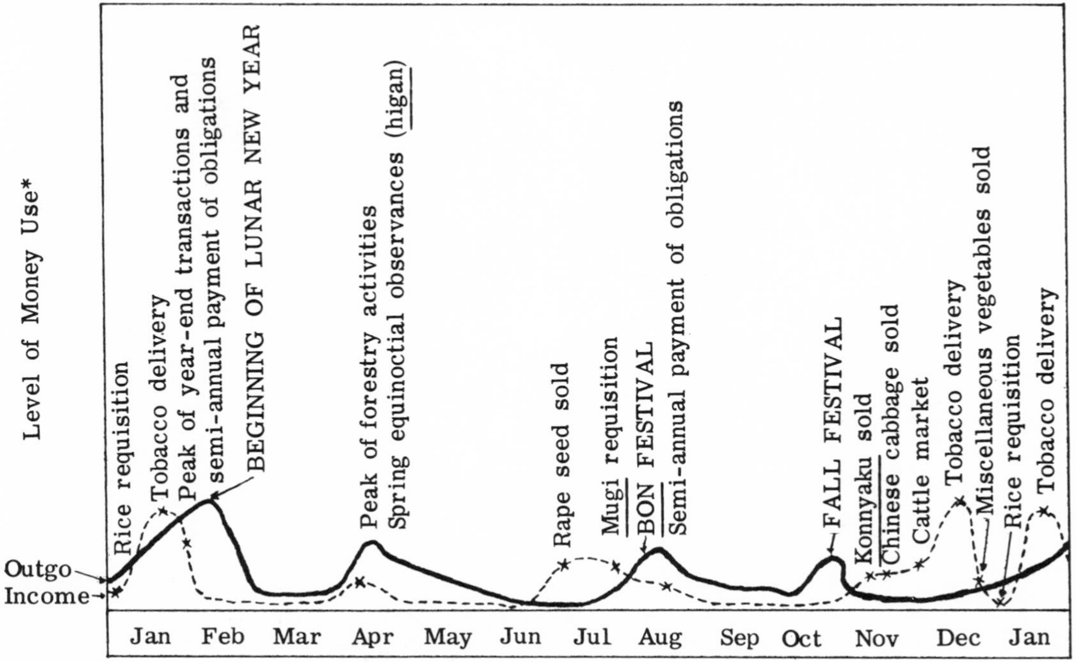

Level of Money Use*

Outgo
Income

Time Duration in Solar Months

*The vertical axis shows only approximate relationships, not absolute
levels, in the cycles of money use.

because it is made on a personal basis within the community.[34] The only other important source of ready cash is the Agricultural Cooperative, which serves as a local bank. Only three of Matsunagi's households have such loans and the amounts are insignificant.

Savings in the form of deposits with the Agricultural Cooperative or postal savings or insurance are very much in vogue. Inflation has all but eliminated the value of prewar life insurance. But a good many households have recently taken out new postal life insurance based upon the inflated yen, which is primarily intended to assist in educating a child or in marrying off a daughter. There are only two or three large commercial life insurance policies in the buraku; all were taken out after the war largely as an investment of surplus funds. Such policies are expected to provide for the policy-holder's children and perhaps leave enough to make possible a grand tour of the famous places of Japan for himself at the age of sixty-one. Still, as one man intimated, holders of insurance fundamentally doubt the wisdom of this long-term savings and think perhaps they would be safer if their money were readily available as deposit money.

Most savings represent not so much accumulations of wealth as simply caches of money to be drawn on as needed during the periods between peaks of income. Today the money saved during and after the war has been spent or dissipated by inflation and there is almost no incentive to save. Most households keep their funds in short-term accounts with the Agricultural Cooperative, for only three or four months or a year. A large sum received, for example from a tobacco crop, is left in such an account for a few months to draw interest.[35] Every household belonging to the Agricultural Cooperative owns at least one share in it, but such shares are more tokens of membership responsibility than savings of any real value.

Physical Welfare and Patterns of Work

The people of the buraku are boastful of their vigor and good health. Dysentery was once a scourge, but most of the contagion that has broken out recently can be classed as intestinal fever and is attributable to parasites spread by water contamination or poor sanitation. Contagion of this sort today is readily restricted to a buraku area through the modern medical practices of the mura Health Clinic in Yukawa.[36] However, most present-day illnesses are chronic intestinal disorders.

The buraku farmer does not regard his children as mere domestic laborers of course, but in the tight schedule of the annual cycle of work a sizeable labor force of healthy offspring is a decided advantage to any household. Before the advent of modern medical care, infant and child mortality rates were high. As a consequence, it was often necessary to resort to adoption to obtain an heir. Some of the older residents recall that many of their siblings failed to live beyond childhood. Modern medicine has, however, considerably reduced this mortality rate, without lessening the desire for large families.

Birth control is practically unknown. In most families children are born throughout the child-bearing years of the mother. As a result, family groups in Matsunagi are large, larger than in communities in the plain or in the fishing areas. The average number of living children in thirty-seven nuclear families runs between four and five. People consider five children an optimum number. Nevertheless, as many as eleven children have been born to a single family.

With only slightly over three working members on the average per household, those with much farm land and forest must apply themselves throughout the entire year with almost the same diligence as at the harvests. The household musters its full force of able-bodied individuals whenever the agricultural season injects a sense of desperate

A traditional hikiusu huller has been borrowed from a neighbor to hull a little rice
for immediate use.

This octogenarian spends her
day in the house making straw
articles for home use and
for sale.

Working on a common home-
made loom, this retired old-
ster is making straw mat containers for charcoal.

urgency into the work. When work is not so pressing, the usual work team is the youngest conjugal pair in the household, the first son and his wife. To this basic team other
individuals are added as need arises and lighter secondary tasks, on the order of wood-
gathering or rope-making, are assigned to less active members, usually the old.

Though work may be put off in the slack season, so that all but the most hard-pressed
may nap for an hour or two on midsummer afternoons, there is no avoiding work if the
household is to survive. From the beginning of the harvest in June until the end of the.
autumn harvest in December a consistently high pace is maintained. There are almost no
prescribed rest days during the entire year. Only white-collar workers expect to have
their Sundays off, which only frees them for tasks at home.

In setting the pace of farm work there are a few well-known standards, but statements
such as that an individual should be able to hoe about one-quarter acre or plow half an
acre a day are rarely fulfilled in practice. Responsibility is usually divided among the
work group only when harvesting or planting but it is undifferentiated in cultivating or
weeding. When harvesting grains, some individuals cut the crop and others tie cut stalks
into bundles. Plowing with a cow is done by active men only; most hand-weeding is done
by women. In general, machinery is handled by young men. Within the limits of their
strength, women work no less hard than men. Whatever may be the working-age individual's main employment, whether he works in an office or attends school, he is expected
to lend a hand in the fields when at home, particularly at times of peak farm activity.

Diet and Nutrition

Most households of the buraku produce enough basic foods to keep themselves alive
and in health, even though they must surrender a part of their cereal production to the
government to be redistributed through a rationing system.[37] In 1951, food rationing was
still important in maintaining. an adequate nutritional level. Rationed foodstuffs are sold
at low fixed prices through a complex mechanism of quota computation, in which the number of persons is balanced against the productive capacity of each household. Only two
well-to-do households do not receive a staple ration at some time during the year. The
heaviest periods of rationing come in the last month or two before each of the major
harvests, and a few nearly landless households must obtain a ration almost the entire year
around.

The buraku has passed through unusual times in the past ten years. But there are
now signs that the people are turning to their old accustomed means of supplying themselves with necessities: buying from the surpluses of others rather than depending on government food rationing. If the household does not raise a substantial quantity of its own
food, the difference must be bought on the black market. If the household cannot meet
these prices, which are about twice the controlled figures, it must do without or depend
on the charity of some neighbor who has a surplus. So important is the rice-eating tradition that all other cereals are prorated both officially and popularly in terms of rice. The
basic ration per day of one active individual is calculated at about half a liter of rice or
the equivalent, which invariably means a greater volume, of some other cereal.[38]

Japanese divide their foods primarily into two classes: gohan, the staple, and o-kazu,
the relish. Though these upland people, like their countrymen in the plain, feel that rice
is indispensable to the diet if one is to perform hard farm labor, very seldom do they
consume rice all by itself. As a rule, either barley or naked barley gohan is the heart
of the meal. If the supply is adequate, as much as one-third may be rice. But many
consistently eat nothing but mugi. The millets, buckwheat, as well as wheat, are less
commonly eaten than the barleys though probably no less than rice. These are used as

flour in preparing special dishes or as a glutinous dough cake (mochi) to break the monotony of the regular boiled grain diet.

Relish (o-kazu) may include a very wide variety of foods, but for the most part these
are vegetables. During the summer, fresh vegetables are eaten, whereas in the cold season only prepared or stored vegetables are procurable. The great bulk of the out-of-
season vegetables is starchy, consisting mostly of such root crops as Irish potatoes, sweet
potatoes, and taro. In the most routine meals pickled giant radish (daikon) or Chinese
cabbage (hakusai) or perhaps a little soybean paste (miso) is always served. Protein is
not plentiful in this diet; most of it is derived from the soybean. Though there are undoubtedly some protein elements in the staple cereals and the starchy foods, only a few
foods, like miso, are considered to be sources of protein. Eggs are generally reserved
for special occasions. Because of the difficulties of transportation, fish is only occasionally brought into the buraku, and what there is usually is salted or otherwise preserved.
Therefore, routine meals never include fish. Beef or pork, too, are almost unknown.
Sometimes rabbits or chickens are slaughtered for food, but most meat must be purchased
from outside suppliers, who do not appear often and are too expensive to patronize many
times a year.

Among the relatively few imported foods available, dairy products are least popular;
officials are hard put to get children to drink the supplemental milk ration served at
school. Fresh fruits may be bought in season at local stores, but the fruit that is brought
into these mountains is generally of poor quality. The persimmon is the only important
domestic fruit, and the most plentiful variety of this is dried until it sugars and is used
as a confection rather than being eaten fresh. Though there is a sugar ration (in 1951,
amounting to two-thirds of a pound per person each month), most households use considerably less than their allotment. Although children may be given candy as a special treat
from time to time, this and other commercial confections have no regular place in the
diet.

Judging from these facts, nutritional balance in Matsunagi would seem to be totally inadequate, particularly in protein. But as a matter of fact no important dietary deficiency
or resulting pathology has been found in this area. The people of the community are
notably healthy and fertile.

Notes

1. In 1921, Kusama and neighboring Toyonaga-mura had by far the least area in paddy of
   any mura in the county, though in their territorial extent they equal or surpass other
   mura of the region.

2. Because of the difficulty in getting accurate statistics in this area, most statistical material is approximate rather than exact.

3. Since the early Meiji period there has been a land register (tochi daicho) for the oaza
   and the mura in the village office, in which each plot of land, regardless of size or
   type, is identified and the ownership attested.

4. Material on landholding is taken from an unpublished report drawn up by buraku officials of the Agricultural Land Reform. For a summary report of this reform, see
   Raper and others, op. cit., Pt. IV, Chap. 1.

5. The average holding for the whole mura is 1.5 acres per household.

6. For some idea of this distribution, see Map IV, above, in which a similar minute division of forest plots is illustrated. The aza are areas indicated by names on the map. Of the general Japanese landholding pattern, Trewartha writes, ". . . the tiny Japanese farm is composed of several little unfenced parcels, scattered [in different aza] in many directions at varying distances from the village in which the agriculturalist lives. It may take him as long as an hour to walk from one of his scattered fields to another. This 'open-field' system of unfenced, dispersed plots, which exists also in China and in parts of Europe, is the result of several factors. Chief of these are centuries of renting, buying, bartering, and inheriting; the farmer's desire for a diversity of crops; and the antiquated methods of irrigation. Each of these parcels of land is further subdivided into little fields of various sizes and shapes." Trewartha, op. cit., pp. 190-200.

7. There is a slight discrepancy between the amount of land worked under tenancy and that rented out to tenants (Table 4) because in both cases some of the land involves households which are residents of other buraku and whose landholdings do not figure in the summaries for Matsunagi.

8. The Land Reform Law of 1946 instituted this system on a nation-wide basis. Lease contracts are now (as of 1951) required in all tenancy arrangements, the actual contract terms being worked out within the framework of this system. There is a legal maximum on rentals nowadays, but no land in Matsunagi is productive enough to bring the top rental.

9. To be classed as an absentee landlord and therefore ineligible to own land, one had to reside outside the mura. Land owned within the precincts of Matsunagi by persons residing in other buraku of Kusama was not taken away by the reform.

10. In all, 5.9 acres changed hands. Of this, half an acre was grassland, which in such mountain areas seems also to have fallen under the provisions of the reform.

11. Japan specializes in rice to an extraordinarily high degree. In 1937, rice occupied 39 to 40 percent of the total crop area. Cf. Trewartha, op. cit., p. 213.

12. People say that loads up to 165 pounds can be carried by men in level terrain; when there are slopes to be climbed, this weight is cut in half.

13. Japan has one of the highest percentages of homes wired for electricity in the world, but it has suffered from an especially acute shortage of electric power since the war. The shortage has made necessary regular conservation days on which all power is cut off during the daylight hours. In the mountains, too, inclement weather results in damage to facilities that cannot be quickly repaired. However, the situation here contrasts with nation-wide practice, wherein most farm power is supplied by electricity. Cf. Raper and others, op. cit., p. 29.

14. Not until 1900 was tobacco production in Atetsu regulated by the state, at which time the Monopoly Bureau of the national government was established. Since the war, it has become the "Monopoly Corporation."

15. All tobacco grown in Japan is of the same species; Nicotiana tabacum. There are three major groupings of native types, all of which are either true variants or hybrids of local variants. While no exact data are available, it is thought that tobacco was introduced to Japan by the Portuguese in the late 16th century. Tobacco was probably first cultivated in the vicinity of Nagasaki about 1605. Cf. Kokumin Hyakka Daijiten (People's Encyclopedia), VIII (Tokyo, 1935), pp. 12866-12871 (article on "Tobacco," in Japanese).

16. There are no milch cows in the mura since there is neither an outside market nor a place for milk in the local diet.

17. The communal pasture is a feature of this cattle country but it is by no means common in Kusama; the only other such area is in Oaza-Tsuchihashi, another division of the mura. The most famous pastures are in Chiya-mura in the northern part of the county, where grazing lands are much more extensive than in Kusama.

18. Trewartha pertinently observes: "The fact that more than half of the country [Japan], though occupied for milleniums, is still in forest is explained by the preponderance of hill land and mountains unsuited to widespread agricultural utilization. But while a greater area of fertile arable plains would undoubtedly make for greater prosperity, it must not be assumed that because this rugged land cannot be cropped it is without economic value. It is not only a source of timber, but of charcoal, wood fuel, wood pulp, and various foods, such as nuts, fruit and bamboo shoots." Op. cit., p. 62.

19. The Forestry Cooperative of the mura indicates what areas should be reforested under the plan and provides seedlings for replanting. The rest is up to the landowner. During the war little heed was given to the consequences of unrestricted cutting. While the war years do not seem to have been particularly destructive of Matsunagi's forests, postwar demand for lumber, particularly since the outbreak of fighting in Korea in 1950, encouraged excessive cutting. In the spring of 1951, nearly every household with forest land sold some of its timber to take advantage of the high prices then prevailing.

20. These are barely known today, having gone out of use during the past generation like those of the bakuro.

21. Most of this charcoal now goes to the Okayama and Kobe-Osaka areas. It seems that wartime government controls on charcoal production were less severe than those instituted at the end of the war, when most of the producers abandoned this enterprise. But by 1951, the number of charcoal burners had begun to increase again slightly, after controls had been relaxed.

22. An experienced eye can estimate the volume with sufficient accuracy. The unit of measure is the saya, which is obtained for any log by squaring the diameter of the smallest end.

23. In the spring of 1950, many households in the mura began growing a cultivated mushroom known as shiitake. Each grower prepares several hundred host logs and the mushroom spores are planted in them, the first growth appearing about a year after planting. As is the case with so many recently introduced cash crops, the authorities stress the value of shiitake for the export market.

24. For further information on the social aspects of construction, see the discussion of communal assistance in Chap. IV.

25. Formerly, sumptuary laws prohibited farmers from wearing anything but the poorest cotton garments, but with the onset of Meiji such restrictions were abandoned and even good silk kimonos became part of the peasant wardrobe.

26. An urban woman of average means will have perhaps 30 to 40 kimonos, none of which is as poor as the work kimonos of Matsunagi.

27. The close-cropped type of tonsure buraku men prefer is known as "chestnut burr head" because the hair resembles the outer husk of the chestnut.

28. This practice is said to have arisen out of the belief that feet treading on the hair strengthens the head on which it grew.

29. These past few years the buraku people have had to itemize their incomes in order to file an income tax return. Since 1947, a reform tax law which puts stress on a national income tax has been in effect. The national system of taxation is now much like the American one.

30. For further details see the discussion of labor specialization in Chap. IV, p. 190.

31. Most day wages range between one hundred and two hundred yen, but the base is about one hundred and fifty yen, or what farm labor gets. These days hired labor is very hard to get, chiefly because of the high level of forestry activity; consequently, forestry wages largely determine those of other casual labor.

32. The social aspects of gift-giving are discussed in Chap. IV.

33. See J. F. Embree, Suye Mura (Chicago, 1939), pp. 138-147, for a detailed description of the operation of such economic ko.

34. However, there is reputedly one formal loan outstanding made by a usurer of nearby Higashimura. Details on such matters are not well known even to residents of the buraku, for even more than in matters of income, people seek to keep the facts of their indebtedness as secret as possible.

35. For most of rural Japan, the post-office has long been the only banking institution, though these days in Kusama the Agricultural Cooperative is taking over its banking function by popular preference.

36. This was built in 1931 as a contagion control clinic for Kusama and adjacent Toyonaga-mura. It is easily reached from the buraku over the rocky but rather short descent to the Sabushi river valley below. Or, if an emergency arises, the clinic's licensed doctor will call at the house. The clinic provides beds, modern medicines and simple operations and is staffed by trained nurses and midwives. It is sponsored by the mura and is closely tied to the local health insurance program, to which almost all households of the mura belong. In the past year or so most of the series of new antibiotics, for example, penicillin and streptomycin, have become available through the clinic.

37. This rationing system, which has prevailed since early in the war, is controlled by a local committee on foodstuffs. Supplies of rationed items for distribution in the mura are provided from a central government storehouse in Niimi.

38. One active adult is expected to consume about 72 liters of rice per year. The commonly accepted unit of measure is the bag (hyo). The average meal consists of a go (.18 liter) or two, which is to the buraku people a rather modest amount and also somewhat more than the official ration. It is the impression of familiar units, like the rice bowl, that counts in estimating the quantities of this sort, not a precise measure. This estimate can of course only approximate actual conditions, since intake varies so much with sex, age, and availability of food.

Chapter III

HOUSEHOLD ORGANIZATION, HOUSING, AND DOMESTIC LIFE

The homestead clusters of Matsunagi squat on the sloping floor of the main buraku settlement like ponderous, shaggy, primeval creatures. Essentially, the homestead is a main house facing a dooryard, about which the auxiliary structures of the farm are grouped. The typical farm group includes a main house, a barn, a godown, a bathhouse and toilet, and, removed at some distance, a woodshed. In the past two years, a tobacco-curing shed has been added to a few homestead groups.

"Homestead" refers to the physical residence of a household. The "household" is the group sharing a common abode, following the same daily routine, and supporting itself with common economic resources, principally land and tools. Therefore, it is the economic base of the community.

The household group has social preeminence too. The point cannot be made too forcefully that this is the most pervasive element in buraku life. It sets the conditions of social organization, interpersonal relations, and even temperament. The material in this and the chapters to follow points to concrete conclusions as to the degree and kind of effect on a restricted folk society of Matsunagi's type resulting from this emphasis on household. As an initial step, the household itself needs to be examined.

Legal households in Matsunagi are more numerous than those which are socially functional.[1] Each of ten distinct households consists of a single group of parents and their children; the rest have in addition one or more grandparents and perhaps a first son and his family. A typical household includes three biological generations,[2] and averages over six persons, the range of membership being from one to thirteen.

Household Residence Ties Versus Descent Ties

"Family," as it is used here, agrees with "household" insofar as both imply common residence. The residential family is either nuclear (conjugal) or extended. The latter is usually a composite of nuclear families headed by lineal male heirs.[3] Though for the most part the membership of both the unilocal family and the household is identical, unrelated individuals occasionally become residents, either temporary or permanent, and usually participate in household life without reference to membership in any descent group. Even when a new resident is a close kinsman, his place in the household may disagree with his family relationship. The family, then, is organized by ties of descent, while the household exists from the fact of a number of people living together. That the household is set up along family lines, means that both also have, in Japan, an unequivocally hierarchical structure. Still, for the purposes of our analysis, "family" and "household" should be considered sociologically separate groups.

The features of the general kinship system are all represented at its focal point, the unilocal family. First, let us consider the rule of descent, which in Matsunagi consistently follows through first-born males, unless there is no male heir, in which case the oldest daughter continues the line. By tradition, a household head should relinquish his authority to his heir at the age of sixty-one and go into relatively inactive retirement, but this practice is rarely found in rural communities, certainly not in Matsunagi. Here, there is no perceptible lessening of activity at any specified age, and many old men continue to be consulted on household problems until death.

159

Inheritance affords continuity to the household as descent does to the family lineage. As age comes on the incumbent head of the household, an informal decision may be made to transfer property to the heir.   This is done merely by registering the fact at the yaku-ba.[4] People feel that discarding the rule of primogeniture would seriously weaken the ability of the household to survive and to protect its dependent members, particularly since few households have more resources than they need for their own support.[5] Conflicts over inheritance are infrequent because all members of the group understand the need for a single head to represent them all, combining in himself both the leadership of the family and of the household.

Yet, if a man remarries and has children while the children of his first marriage are small, the new wife may wish her offspring to succeed in spite of the prior right of the husband's eldest son.   One recourse the husband has is to take his wife off and set up a new establishment, leaving the old one to his original heir.   Primogeniture may also be overruled by a quarrel, forcing either the eldest son or his father from the household and requiring that a new heir be named.   Should there be bad relations between a man and his son-in-law, who has been brought into the household as a successor in the absence of male heirs, the same thing may happen.   On the father's departure, the eldest daughter and the son-in-law, her husband, receive the property.

To maintain descent through males it is always highly desirable that sons be born. Failing this, the normal recourse is adoption, which can be easily arranged by registering at the yakuba.   Nor is any ceremony necessarily connected with this event.   Adoptive ties can also be quickly dissolved upon agreement of the interested parties.   Adoption in Japan is such a flexible device that there are no particular limitations of sex, age, or previous relationship among its requisite conditions.

However, most cases of adoption in Matsunagi involve nephews and nieces.   A conjugal pair without any surviving children usually look to the siblings of the husband or wife for a child that can be spared for adoption.   Usually one of the parental siblings has more children than he needs.   A blood tie is considered more desirable than no relationship at all because it is easier and more economical to arrange an adoption between close relatives.   No one receives money or property, for to yield an extra child to some childless relative is a charitable obligation.   If a young child is adopted, he may be left in his natal household until he is of age to marry and inherit, but if he has many brothers and sisters, his parents probably will want the adoptive parents to take him as soon as possible.   Still, children available for adoption are not so numerous that a family will take an extra child for insurance just because all its children are girls or because the apparent heir is sickly.   Moreover, parents feel that an adopted child can never completely replace their own flesh and blood in their affections.

Although adoptive individuals fit into the established relationships of the family, adoption does not necessarily mean that an heir so created becomes concomitantly a part of the household group.   Since adoption is both a legal and a social act, it does not always involve a reorientation of the living pattern in a household or an actual shift of residence. For example, take these actual cases.   A man adopts his younger brother as heir but they continue in the same relative positions in their natal household.   A lone woman adopts a girl whom she agrees to let live and work in the household of her birth until marriage, when the girl and her husband will come to live with the adoptive parent.   Again, a childless man adopts his niece and her husband as a conjugal pair, thereby avoiding the problem of obtaining a spouse for his heir, and all three continue to reside in the same household, as before.   Adoption at an early age typically means a change of residence, or a realignment of family relationships, or both.   Adoption of an adult, especially if married, is less likely to make an important change in his life until he inherits.

One other noteworthy form of adoption is that of bringing an adult male into the household by marrying him to a daughter in case there are no sons. Having only daughters means that the eldest daughter and her husband must live in her parental home. The husband, then, is a yoshi, or "adopted husband"; but, like any adopted son, he also becomes in time the legal property-owner and household head.

Marriage is seldom affected by degree of kinship or by place of residence. In fact, buraku residence does not force any particular limitation on one's choice of a mate. Few families have close blood kinsmen in the buraku and so avoidance of prohibited degrees of kin is not a problem. Even marriages of first cousins occur occasionally. There is no objection, either, to the marriage of a stepbrother and sister who have been raised in the same household, provided they are not legally registered as siblings.[6]

In Matsunagi, very few cases of such marriage practices as the junior sororate and the levirate are known, though in Japan these are rather common means of preserving relationships between families when a spouse has died. However, bride exchange is sometimes found. This takes place when each of two households is willing to marry a daughter to a son of the other. Such an arrangement simplifies the marriage negotiations, which can be done by one mediary for each household. A not unusual phenomenon of arranged marriages is intermarriage of two families through two or even three generations; most often this involves first cousins, but nearly as frequently, a generation, or even two, is skipped between such intermarriages.

Household Social Structure

Respect for elders and submission to male prerogative are principles of familial behavior.[7] The dominant male of the household, whatever may be his connection with the family lineage, is the nominal household head. The property may have come to him because he is married to the lineal heir, but it is he whose name and person represent the people living in his homestead in all larger social contacts. Thus, male prerogative is paramount in household life, from the new-born boy baby to the aged, retired household head on his deathbed. But age, too, has its rights to which even sex prerogatives must at times yield. A man listens to his old mother's advice as long as she is still vigorous and conversant with household affairs. Within the same sex, an older woman takes precedence over her son's wife, and in form does so until death, although as the younger woman becomes accepted into and better acquainted with the household, she usually assumes the dominant feminine role. Though belonging to the general Japanese pattern, the unsophisticated people of Matsunagi do not consciously couch familial relationships in the classic terms of filial piety and duty to family lineage.

In ordinary usage Matsunagi people do not employ personal names very often, either in direct address or in reference.[8] Instead, a relative is called by the same word used for him by the other members of his own household. Interpersonal behavior in both "family" and "household" contexts may be designated by similar sets of relationship terms.[9] The most frequent terms of address in both refer to relationships in the extended family.

Whereas the unilocal family, i.e., that part of the lineal descent group sharing a common residence, is organized terminologically as an extended family, the household is composed of a series of complementary roles, each assigned to one or more specific individuals of the family. Usually, in an average household, this series consists of nine distinct classifications:

1. Old Man.......... the aged, retired or inactive, former household head

2. Old Woman....... the old, largely inactive mother or mother-in-law of the household head

3. House Head ...... the mature, active household head

4. House Mistress... the housewife and mother of the children of the household head

5. Eldest Son .... the eldest son and heir of the household head, who takes an active part in household work

6. Young Wife....... the wife of the eldest son and most subordinate adult member of the household

7. Younger Son...... the younger, work-age son(s) of the household head, who does not inherit and therefore must eventually leave the household

8. Girl .... the adolescent or grown but unmarried daughter(s) of the household head

9. Child .... the school or pre-school age child(ren) of the household head or of his eldest son

The division of work and responsibility in the household is made on the basis of these roles.[10]

That these household roles are not the same as familial relationships is shown by fitting family members of equal status into roles which are unequal in family hierarchy. To illustrate, in one buraku household an elder daughter becomes de facto House Mistress on the death of her mother, while the eldest son (a younger sibling) is still a child. Her husband, an adopted spouse, sometimes acts as House Head, but her aged father is still very active and retains this role in most household functions. When the eldest son at length is married but continues to live in his father's house, his wife becomes a Young Wife, while his older sister continues to act as House Mistress and therefore remains superior. The eldest son, who even after full maturity does not relinquish this junior status, should by all conventions succeed to the headship, but because of outside interests he is content to let his old father and his sister take dominant roles. Or again, the younger brother of this aged householder returns from a life spent in the city to live out his remaining years in his brother's household. Both of these brothers occupy the position of Old Man, still the younger is supernumerary; even though he is a member of the family, he really fails to fit into the pattern of conventional roles. In another local household, an unrelated young girl is brought into the household to be married to a son. She becomes a Girl (in the household) for the interim until marriage. Her actual or potential kin relationship to the family is subordinate to her household role.[11]

A major feature of terminological usage in the household is a modified teknonymy (addressing a person by the term for his relationsip to a different person, exemplified in the U.S. by addressing one's wife as "Mother"), which also demonstrates the existence of this construct of roles. In this, age and generation differences are disregarded if they conflict with the way in which relationships appear to the youngest group of siblings in the household, that is, the Children. In an actual case, a niece and her uncle marry brother and sister; the niece normally calls her uncle "older brother" (i.e., the husband of the "older sister" in her household) so that to the children the terminology will appear consistent with their household roles, which put them in the same generation. In another instance, the seven year old sister of a small boy's father is called "older sister," not "aunt," out of regard for the similarity of their statuses as Children in the same household. A change in status relationship to the household brings a change in manner of naming. When this girl leaves the household in marriage, she is thereafter called "aunt." As a married adult of another household, she is called by a term consistent with her actual blood relationship to the nephew.

The Homestead

The central play and work area of a homestead group is the dooryard, its hard-packed earthen floor tamped by many generations of feet. Here crops are threshed and dried on mats, washing is done, tools are kept, cows are sunned, children play, and building timbers are shaped. The dooryard is a litter of tubs, old mats, tools, and other miscellany much of the time, except when a real effort is made to put things in order just before lunar New Year's. Generally, the dull wood, earth and thatch of the buildings are left in unallayed drabness. To enter a house one usually comes into the dooryard first; though some have rough-hewn steps leading into it, no homestead, save the temple, has a true gate entrance.

The typical farmhouse in Matsunagi is in its customary features like farm dwellings in many other parts of Japan; the main house is built according to a single, fixed architectural standard, and the design and method of building the other structures of the homestead are the same, except in details.

The antiquity of a house can be seen in its huge beams, sagging frame and over-all massiveness of construction. Though no one knows the exact ages of all the houses, at least ten are thought to be over one hundred years old. The newer the house the smaller its beams, for by Meiji times there was a dearth of great trees. A main house that is not kept in repair eventually begins to lean on its pillars and must be braced lest it collapse altogether.

Houses are equilateral boxes, though in many cases out-buildings are so juxtaposed against the house that, except for individual peaked roofs of thatch, they seem all one building.[12] The most splendid old houses have the thickest thatch and an air of bucolic elegance which even their worm-eaten floors and weathered storm doors cannot erase. The conventional house has a ridge ornament of thatch tufts, called "box-ridge," which is distinctive to the area,[13] and carved wooden panels in the smoke-holes at either end of the roof. The roof of a main house is particularly wide and extends two or three feet out over the dooryard for shelter against rain. More than two-thirds of the side facing the yard is flanked by a wooden veranda or walk, set beneath the broad eaves. The remaining third is occupied by the kitchen doorway and wall. The back of the veranda is closed by sliding paper-covered panels (shoji) rather than solid wall. About the middle of this side, splitting the veranda in two, there is a toilet, which is built at the same level as the veranda, enclosed by a hip-high parapet, and floored with lathes of split bamboo. Often there is an open urinal at ground level in front of the toilet enclosure for convenience when coming directly from the fields.

The interior of the house, which is the scene of most life activities, is basically a single-story structure of five rooms, though most houses have a vestigial second-story room that serves as storage space. Save for the kitchen, all rooms are floored with reed mats (tatami).[14] Between the rooms the only partitions are sliding panels, either of wood or of wood frames covered with paper like those at the back of the veranda. These may be quickly removed from their tracks, thus combining all rooms into a single large one. Mat-covered rooms have wooden ceilings, which hide the stark, black beams of the house. Built into the walls of the rooms are wooden cupboards for storing bedding and alcoves for household ritual activities. The rooms in which guests are formally received are closest

CHART 5

A Typical Homestead Group

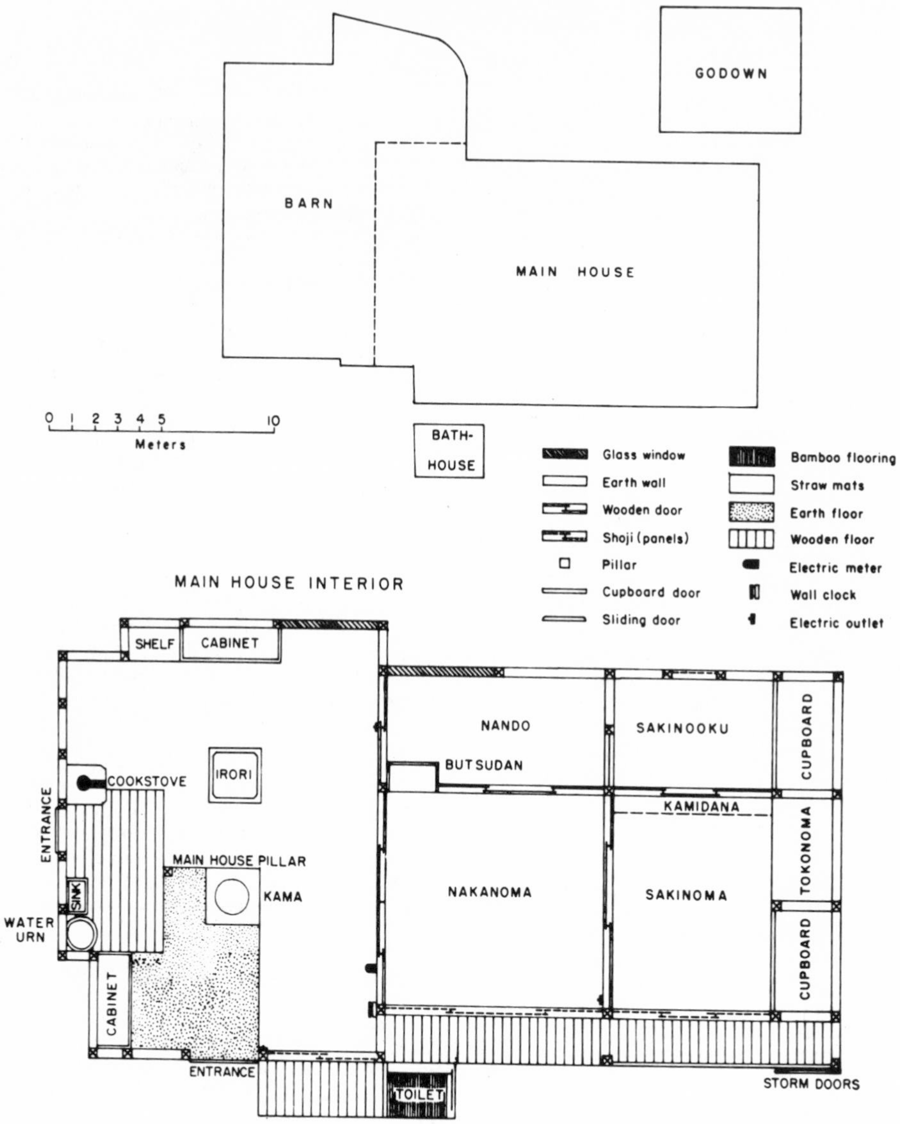

GODOWN

BARN

MAIN HOUSE

0 1 2 3 4 5   10
Meters

BATH-HOUSE

	Glass window		Bamboo flooring
	Earth wall		Straw mats
	Wooden door		Earth floor
	Shoji (panels)		Wooden floor
	Pillar		Electric meter
	Cupboard door		Wall clock
	Sliding door		Electric outlet

MAIN HOUSE INTERIOR

SHELF   CABINET

ENTRANCE

COOKSTOVE   IRORI

NANDO   SAKINOOKU

BUTSUDAN

CUPBOARD

KAMIDANA

MAIN HOUSE PILLAR

KAMA

NAKANOMA   SAKINOMA

TOKONOMA

WATER URN

SINK

CABINET

CUPBOARD

ENTRANCE

TOILET

STORM DOORS

to the dooryard. The middle-room (nakanoma) is most used in everyday living, for sleeping and for storing clothes. The head-room (sakinoma) is the principal parlor, where the most formal entertainment of guests takes place. Here are found the god-alcove (tokonoma) and the god-shelf (kamidana), where deities of household, family and nation are worshipped. Behind these rooms are the inner sleeping-room (nando) where the parental couple sleeps and birth occurs, and the outer sleeping room (sakino-oku), which may be either a sleeping place or a storeroom.

The kitchen occupies perhaps a third of the area of the house and is actually several rooms in one. Most of the kitchen space at the end and back of the house is devoted to food preparation and storage, to a cabinet, dishes, cooking tubs, a cook-stove, sink, water urn, and a variety of kitchen utensils. Most of the kitchen floor is raised to the level of the veranda, except for an earth-floored entry (doma). The kitchen platform is made like the veranda, but most of it is covered with coarse straw mats. Amidst this matting is an open hearth box (irori) and a pothook above it for use in cooking and heating water. An earthen oven (kama) and a fuel box are located at the back of the doma. The kitchen has no ceiling, so smoke from the irori passes up into the beams and out through the smoke-holes at the ends of the roof. The beams above are caked with soot, which incessantly showers down upon the entire kitchen. The main pillar, standing near the center of the kitchen, is a heavy squared timber, the largest of the house, to which is attached the shrine of the chief kitchen deity. Over the house beams of the kitchen, poles are laid to form a drying platform, on which farm crops such as konnyaku are stored in winter. Sometimes there are earth-lined pits covered with board lids beside the irori, in which other root crops are stored against the winter cold.

When people have come up in the world, they seek to express their affluence by adding extra touches of elegance to the homestead. An obvious sign of wealth and position is the guest-apartment (hanarezashiki),[15] which is normally separate from the main house. Elaborations like tile eaves, built with less slope than the thatch roof above to permit more light to enter, are also quite common. Instead of paper-covered window panels, too, glass windows that admit more light are now rather general. But the two most luxurious houses of the settlement have tile roofs and white-plastered outside walls decorated with elaborate motifs in blue.

In the godown, the second ranking structure of most house groups, family heirlooms, good clothing, formal dining equipment, seed grain and a variety of other valuables are stored. To protect such treasures from fire and the ravages of rats, all godowns have tile roofs and rodent-proof rooms. A few of these are finely decorated with a finish of white plaster and a colored family crest. A barn, resembling a house in construction, sometimes is converted to a dwelling if a main house is beyond a household's means. A bathhouse and a second toilet are combined into a separate structure in the dooryard or back of the house by the most well-to-do.

It is common practice to squeeze as many structures as possible into whatever building space is available, so that it is often difficult for the uninitiated to decide how many separate homesteads there are. The only exception to this crowding is the woodshed, which must be situated at some distance from the other buildings so that accidental combustion of fuel will not result in a general conflagration.

The Routine of Household Life

Food preparation and eating are probably the most important functions of daily household life and they directly concern every member of the group. Cooking and other culinary activities are performed at the back of the kitchen, where the necessary equipment is kept. One woman, usually the House Mistress, attends to all food preparation. Cleaning the staple grains is usually done by the Household Head or by a grown son, but carrying the grain back and forth to the mill is a woman's task. The cook takes care of washing the vegetables at one of the places where water flows through the buraku, usually in the ditch across the main settlement. What little refuse there is in food preparation is left beside the ditch or stream to rot.

The kitchen is expected to be one of the darkest and least clean parts of the house. The cook works directly on the floor, without even a low Japanese table for support. If dough is to be cut, a broad kneading board laid on the floor provides a surface. Bamboo baskets, pottery bowls, metal steamers and wooden tubs comprise nearly all the kitchen containers. All kitchens have several good steel knives and metal spoons, which are cheap. But the most common utensils are bamboo chopsticks and wooden paddles for handling cooked grains. The fire in the irori burns most of the time and so the cook-stove is stoked from it before preparing a meal. To fry foods in oil, the cook hangs a pan over the irori on the pothook; for steaming or boiling grains or stew, she uses a metal vessel on the stove. On hands and knees, she attends to her pots and feeds fuel, a stick at a time, into the flames. Supplies such as soy sauce, dried squid, or pickled relish, are kept in the cabinet at the back of the room. Dishes are washed in the sink simply by rinsing them, but even this perfunctory treatment is given at most only once a day and usually only once in two or three days.

Cooking techniques include boiling, steaming, frying, toasting and even baking. One does come to the conclusion, however, that frying and boiling predominate in Matsunagi, since so many of the foodstuffs are root vegetables, which are most conveniently prepared in these ways. For pickling such foods as giant radish and Chinese cabbage, vats of brine are made ready soon after the autumn harvest; pickling in soybean paste, a longer process taking as much as two or three years, is also quite popular. In addition to the ordinary fare of noodle dishes (soba and udon) and various vegetables fried in batter (tempura), a rice and relish dish soured with vinegar (sushi) is a great favorite. If a special dish is served, it is likely to be one of these. Next to gohan, the boiled grain staple, no food is more widely consumed than mochi, a steamed dough of rice or millet that has been beaten into a glutinous mass. Mochi with sweet bean jam inside is called dango; with a covering of jam on the outside, it is o-hagi. Most mochi is made into small cakes or strips, which are dried and put away to be toasted at the irori as needed. Several months' supply of mochi is made just before lunar New Year's because water of that cold season is said to preserve the grain best.[16]

Fish and meat, fresh or canned, are among the least common foods, although fish is usually served at important holidays. As a substitute for fish, which is of poor quality even when available, tofu is regularly made in the household; soybeans are ground to a viscuous liquid on a rotary quern and this curdles into the cheese-like curd. This may be eaten alone, toasted, or in winter frozen to improve its taste. Unlike Japanese cookery in general, there is little emphasis on soups in Matsunagi, except among the more affluent households. Another characteristic in this area that has a direct bearing on everyday eating is that each household gathers and dries tea from its own plants in the spring of the year.

Everyday food is very simple and highly monotonous. The meal is built about two, perhaps three, bowls of gohan. From the beginning of the winter-crop harvest in June until the close of the autumn harvest in December, there are four mealtimes each day, while during the other six months there are only three. Typical menus under the four-meal schedule are:

1. Breakfast: hot boiled grain (gohan), pickled giant radish or Chinese cabbage, and tea.

2. Lunch: cold, leftover gohan, pickled radish or cabbage, or a pat of bean paste (miso), and tea.

3. Tea: cold, leftover gohan, pickled vegetable or a pat of miso, and tea.

4. Supper: in place of boiled grain, some sort of hot noodle dish with relish, or soup of miso with gohan, and tea.

The evening meal, thus, is the only one that offers relief from monotony; all others must be simple because there is no time for extensive preparation. Before the evening meal, the House Mistress leaves the fields somewhat ahead of the others in order to have time to make noodles and cook them with some sort of vegetable relish. On ceremonial days, or if there are guests in the house, a special dish of this sort is always served at the end of the day.

The entire household tries to be present at meals, and even in summer, when a fire is infrequently lighted in the irori, meals are taken about this hearth. Mealtimes are very important in setting the rhythm of household routine. Closely corresponding to status hierarchy, the oldest man sits toward the guest room, which is the position of the honored guest; the humblest position is directly opposite and is reserved for the cook. In general, women sit with their backs to the rear of the kitchen and men with their backs to the outside door. The children take places wherever there is an opening in the group.

Each individual, with the exception of young children, keeps his rice bowl, relish plate and chopsticks in a wooden eating box (zembako) between meals; eating dishes are rested on the cover of this box in lieu of table and left in it unwashed after eating. Usually, the senior members of the household are served first, but there is really no fixed order for this. Food is consumed with much noise and in great haste, a second and even a third bowl of gohan being taken by men. Still, there is no gustatory pleasure in the usual meal, only the satisfaction of energy needs. The diner pours tea into his empty rice bowl from a metal teapot kept warm on the coals of the irori, to rinse out his bowl as he washes down his food. This act ends the meal. In seasons of heavy work there is no loitering in the kitchen for conversation.

But there is more opportunity for group conversation during the meal than at any other time of the day. Therefore, whenever need arises, talk turns to important household or family matters over the food. This group discussion constitutes a genuine household council, in which the course of household affairs is set.[17] The prerogatives of each member of the group in this discussion differ somewhat, though all but the barest newcomer have the opportunity to express their opinions. Children are ignored in such talks, if they are present at all. The household head casts the deciding vote, unless he yields to the more mature judgment of his aged parent; but the final outcome also reflects the opinions of the whole group. Problems such as marrying off a daughter require more consideration, and feminine influence may outweigh men's in this.

The House Mistress of necessity spends more of her time in the homestead than all but the aged members of the household. If there are old people at home, she will be able to help with the outdoor work to a greater extent, but someone must always be on hand to guard against thieves.[18] The mistress assigns junior members of the group the household chores, which commonly include bringing water from a nearby well or collecting basin.[19] Fetching water is time-consuming because two, or even three, times a day it entails several staggering trips from the well with a pair of brimming buckets hung from a carrying

TABLE 3

A TYPICAL DAY'S SCHEDULE IN A MATSUNAGI HOUSEHOLD*

Hour	Activities
5:00 A.M.	Young Wife rises, kindles fire in the irori and starts to boil gohan. House Mistress rises and assists in preparation of breakfast. After the women, the men arise and prepare to eat breakfast. Everyone listens to early-risers program on radio for half an hour.
6:00	Breakfast finished, Young Wife and House Mistress accompany men to the fields to work. Old Woman and Old Man remain behind to tend house. Old Man begins his daily chores; feeds cow, looks for eggs, brings in wood. Children arise and are served breakfast by Old Woman.
7:00	One of the Children goes for water while the others help Old Woman or play. Old Woman prepares school lunches. Old Woman offers tea to ancestors at the buddha shelf.
8:00	Children depart for school. Old Man takes up where he left off, weaving a pair of straw sandals at his seat near the irori. Old Woman tidies up after breakfast, sweeps kitchen floor about the irori, and from time to time adds fuel to the irori fire. Pre-school Children play about the house and dooryard with neighbor age-mates.
9:00	Workers in the fields take a few minutes' break to smoke or talk.
10:00	Mail carrier comes by with postcard notice from the yakuba.
11:00	Old Woman prepares lunch, using leftover gohan from breakfast. All workers return from the fields to eat and converse together; as soon as meal is over, they go back to the fields.
12:00 M.	Old Woman tidies up the lunch equipment, and returns to sewing and watching the young Children. Old Man turns back to his straw handicrafts.
1:00 P.M.	Clothing peddler comes by; he is invited in for a cup of tea at the irori, but Old Woman tells him household is well supplied with clothes.
2:00	Children return from school.
3:00	Old Woman prepares cold gohan for tea. Workers come back from the fields; the whole household eats this meal together, including school-age Children. Meal eaten, workers depart at once for the fields, teen-age Children going along to help. Old Woman, assisted by older children, puts eating equipment away and sweeps floor around the irori. Young Children resume their play.
4:00	Old Woman and Old Man by this time have gone back to their other work.
5:00	Pre-adolescent Children are sent for bath water at the concrete tank by the public bulletin board, and drinking water from the spring. Oldest girl Child begins to heat bath water. Workers in the fields take a rest break and the men smoke.
6:00	House Mistress returns to the house to make warm gohan and soup for the evening meal.
7:00	Old Man enters bath with a young Child.

TABLE 3—Continued

Hour	Activities
8:00	Other workers leave the fields and, after reaching the house, the men enter the bath in order of age, the older Children going in after them.
	Evening meal is served and the household members sit together for this; the radio is turned on for news and perhaps a variety program; the group as usual takes this opportunity to talk over mutual problems.
	House Mistress and Young Wife put away meal equipment and ready grain to be cooked for breakfast.
	Men turn to making straw sandals and other straw articles.
	Children read the newspaper, magazines, or play.
	All listen to the radio while thus occupied.
	Old Woman enters the bath with a young Child.
9:00	House Mistress takes her turn at the bath and finally Young Wife bathes.
	House Mistress and Young Wife take up family mending and sewing.
	Children and old people go to bed.
10:00	Men go to bed.
	House Mistress and, finally, Young Wife retire, after the latter extinguishes fire in the irori.

*No actual household in Matsunagi conforms exactly to this schedule on any day of the year, but this might fall during the late autumn harvest (even though one would expect tobacco sorting to occupy everyone for several hours after sunset at this time). Note that this schedule is organized in terms of the nine household roles, the names for which are underlined.

pole. When possible, girls or young women are sent on this errand, but in cold weather boys or young men must be dispatched. Though men or boys are charged with keeping fuel in the house, it is generally a young girl or young woman who fires the household bath before the rest come in from the fields. For those too young or too old for farm work there is usually an infant to be tended.

Household chores are only incidentally a means of disciplining and training the young; the assistance children render their household is of serious economic importance. When there is important work to be done about the homestead, manpower is diverted from the fields to this temporary project. But this diversion is not done without good reason. Most improvements about the homestead devolve upon men. Regardless of the arduous tasks women may perform in farming, heavy construction work like lifting foundation stones, raising the frame of a building, or preparing the thatch for a new roof, is rarely expected of them. Small repairs about the place are handled by the House Head or by one of his sons without the assistance of neighbors or craftsmen. In sum, no individual in the household, even though he is regularly employed outside the buraku, is without some responsibility directly connected with the operation of his homestead.

During the day the House Mistress or some other woman left at home to tend the house takes advantage of gaps in the schedule of other work to do the laundry, but only as often as is absolutely necessary. Washing is done in a low tub in the dooryard and usually consists of ordinary or work clothes, since good clothes are not worn enough to need much cleaning. Clothes are hung to dry on a bamboo pole beneath the eaves of the front of the house, adding to the disarray of the dooryard area.

It is a source of embarrassment to most housekeepers that so much dust and soot accumulate in the living quarters of the house, though doubtless this attitude has grown as a result of recent government propaganda on sanitation.[20] The custom is to set aside one day a year for a general housecleaning with all active members of the household participating. The young men climb into the house beams and sweep the irori soot with brooms, while women clean the lower beams with shorter brooms on bamboo poles. Tatami mats are beaten outdoors, and the earth beneath the floor of the house is swept clean. Men clean the irori pothook. The general kitchen area is swept and its mats are beaten. Women take care of most of the tasks at or near floor level, men assisting only with the heavy, dangerous work. As this housecleaning usually comes just before the beginning of summer, floors and mats are sprayed with insecticide and sometimes a covering of lime is strewn over the earth beneath the floors.

Housecleaning may extend to tidying up the dooryard, especially if it happens just before New Year's, but on the whole only the most obvious dirt is removed. Worn-out straw mats in the kitchen are usually replaced at New Year's and repapering of the shoji is done once then and again later in the year. The responsibility for maintaining a modicum of neatness in the house each day rests with the House Mistress, though she may delegate a younger woman or child to assist. Two or three times a day, generally about mealtime, the kitchen is swept with a small straw broom; other rooms are swept out only about once a week.

Privacy in all aspects of house life is difficult to achieve by our standards because of the fact that the entire house is shared by all persons of the household. In bathing, elimination, changing clothes, or sexual relations, there is no effective barrier against the eyes and ears of others. Still, people do not expose themselves naked before each other but remove only their outer clothing. A semi-clothed body of either sex does not attract overt interest.[21] Instead of privacy, feigning unawareness of others is so ingenuously cultivated that it is convincing.

Men, old women, and children tend to use the front toilet of the house, in which only the lower part of the body is concealed. Although this arrangement would not seem to provide much privacy, it is proper etiquette to ignore the person in the toilet as though he were completely shut off to outside view. A man may micturate within a few feet of a woman, but she will rigorously avoid speaking to him until he is through. Adults always use a toilet, even though it may be inconvenient to reach. Women, until they reach old age, are expected to be more circumspect than other members of the household and so they invariably use an enclosed toilet.

Upon rising, hands and face are washed in a metal or plastic wash basin in the dooryard and dried on a thin Japanese towel. At the same time one may brush his teeth with tooth-brush and powder as he has been taught in school, though only the young and the better educated do this regularly. Wash basins and tooth-brushes are kept in the bathhouse, the brushes in a notched bamboo log hung from the wall. Thereafter, ablutions are rare until the evening bath. However, those returning from the fields during the day normally wash their feet in a tub of warm water provided in the dooryard before mounting to floor level in order to remove field dirt.

The native bath, a tub set over a brick or stone firebox, is usually situated in a separate bathhouse.[22] These days most tubs are of iron rather than of wood, which was once universal, and several have cement and tile platforms about the top. Recently, one bath was built entirely of tile. Baths are not usually shared between households, except in some few instances where relatives have none of their own. Heating the water takes half an hour or more of firing. By the time the workers have returned from the fields, the bath is ready. The Old Man enters first, to be followed by the other men of the household in order of age. Although the order may vary greatly, the Old Woman usually bathes next, then the House Mistress with the Young Wife last. Children are wedged in wherever convenient, and the very young ones are always accompanied by an adult. The body is washed before entering the tub, often in plain view of others, for many baths are not fully enclosed; the bath water is unchanged from first to last and at the end tends to lose much of its relaxing warmth. Leaving the bath, one puts on a padded robe (tanzen) in winter or a light kimono (yukata) in summer, both of which are worn during the evening and for sleeping. [23]

In regular sleeping arrangements, the only concession to privacy is to the youngest conjugal pair. At the marriage of the eldest son, the older parental pair relinquishes the use of the nando for sleeping and moves into the nakanoma. And the aged couple then moves into the sakinoma. However, neither of these front guest rooms are closed off for sleeping like the nando. The youngest child generally sleeps with its parents, while older children sleep in the nakanoma with the grandparents. Other adults range themselves in the guest rooms wherever there is space.

In the tatami-covered rooms of the house, heat is provided by earth-lined fire-boxes (kotatsu) set into the floor, in which coals frugally saved from the irori are burned. These fire-boxes are especially important in keeping warm during sleep, for the heavy comforters are laid over a frame covering the kotatsu so as to conduct heat to the pallets placed about it. When many guests are being entertained, to warm the hands small charcoal braziers (hibachi) of metal, ceramic, or wood are placed about instead of a kotatsu. Lighting is now nearly always by electric bulb; one hangs near the irori, one in the nakanoma and one in the nando. These lights on long cords may be moved from room to room wherever needed.

In the evening, after bathing and eating, there is not often time for relaxation and amusement. There is nearly always some task to keep adults busy till bedtime. For the women the principal evening duty is sewing, or more often mending of work and school clothes. The masculine counterpart is making sandals, rain-capes, mats, or any of a variety of straw items used about the farm. Household members sit about the irori on winter evenings working and talking. Sometimes the radio is turned on or younger persons read. In their spare time, men play native games like chess or simplified go. Visiting is rare in the evening, though young men may go to a friend's house after supper. Girls, however, are never allowed to do so. Bedtime comes early, unless the household must work very late preparing tobacco leaf for delivery. Often there is no time after eating for anything but to retire.

The household maintains ritual relations with a group of deities which are intended to secure and maintain its welfare. These deities are largely of Shinto origin. Several tutelary shrines are standard features of any house. In the sakinoma, the tokonoma serves as the shrine of the national Sun Goddess, Amaterasu, and of two other major deities, which, however, vary from household to household. Their representations are nothing more than wall scrolls with the name of the deity inscribed in Chinese characters. In the same room is the god-shelf fastened to the wall somewhat above head level, on which rest various votive paper wands (gohei). Both tokonoma and god-shelf are repositories for a number of miscellaneous deities which the household has adopted for personal reasons rather than because of convention. In the kitchen, inside or near the cupboard, is a shrine to the paired deities, Daikoku and Ebesu, who are the bringers of good fortune and largesse; the shrine itself may be a simple plaster plaque or a miniature building containing statuettes of these gods. A shelf on the main pillar of the house is the shrine of Rokusama, [24] the deity of the oven. The oven in Japan is regarded as a vital part of the house and, in fact, is the symbol of an independent household.

Household shrines in general may be decorated with simple wooden or bamboo vases containing branches of 'sacred sakaki (Eurya ochnacea) or similar shrubs. Even in the spring and summer, decorative flowers as such are rare in the house, but when the house-keeper has time to do so, she usually places some in the tokonoma. It also may have a decorative straw rope suspended across it, left there from New Year's. The god-shelf is used for keeping wooden or paper talismans, souvenirs of some healing rite or a pilgrim-age to a celebrated shrine. Such pilgrim's souvenirs are also fastened to the ceiling or wall of the sakinoma, as a means of advertising one's travels and piety. During the year, offerings and prayers should be made to all the household deities on the 1st, the 15th, and the 28th of each lunar month. A bit of gohan or something else from the regular fare is left in a small ceramic dish at each shrine, but in many households the practice is no longer observed.

Buddhism is another sort of religious tradition in the household, and it is centered on the buddha shelf (butsudan). This is merely a recessed box in a wooden, sometimes rich-ly worked cabinet set into the wall of the nakanoma. It contains the ancestral tablets (ihai), before each of which stands a small offertory dish. At breakfast one of the old people, or if they cannot, the House Mistress puts a little tea in this. The actual graves, however, are often far from the house and are neglected most of the year.

The oldest household residents are customarily responsible for all domestic religious offerings, less because they are in a position to act as representatives of the group than that their religious interest is strongest. Still, the daily round of household activities allows for only a mechanical and perfunctory observance of ritual relations between the people of the household and the supernatural beings who are thought to share this abode with them.

Notes

1. There are in fact thirty-nine legal households, two of which reside in Obara and have no social intercourse with Matsunagi. In another instance two brothers have set up separate households under law, but continue to live in one social group under the same roof.

2. A generation level is not the same thing as an age level, since age discrepancies be-tween siblings or between spouses may be so great that they are associated with dis-tinct age levels, i.e., biological generations, yet in the household are regarded as members of the same generation.

3. According to Murdock, the nuclear family "consists typically of a married man and woman with their offspring. . ." The extended family "includes two or more nuclear families united by consanguineal bonds such as those between parent and child or be-tween two siblings." G. P. Murdock, Social Structure (New York, 1949), pp. 1, 23.

4. Since the war, each nuclear (conjugal) family has been obliged by law to be registered as an independent household, but this has had no effect on the composition of residence groups. Under direction of the Occupation, inheritance laws were changed to provide equitable division of property among all offspring, lineal relatives, and the spouse. However, in Kusama neither the reform of registration nor of inheritance seems to have taken place.

5. Raper and his co-workers report similar findings in thirteen widely scattered villages. See op. cit., p. 212.

6. While there are no explicit rules of incest in Matsunagi other than restriction on marriages between members of a nuclear family, marriage probably never occurs between genealogical relatives closer than first cousin.

7. Sansom points out that "the central point of Confucian doctrine is the cult of the family. . . . The highest, almost the only duty of a man, is his duty to his parents, . . . [But the Japanese] while respecting its [Confucianism's] traditions, [were able] to conform its teaching to their needs." G. B. Sansom, Japan: a Short Cultural History (New York, 1943), pp. 113-114.

8. The avoidance of personal names is a common phenomenon in Japan, which may be ascribed to a feeling that use of such names implies an unseemly intimacy. Names are uttered by the parent in addressing his children, between siblings, or between playmates, but rarely are used outside the household.

9. Japanese kinship terminology is bilateral in extension but unilineal in emphasis; that is, it emphasizes the patrilineage (direct line of the father) at the expense of collateral relatives, such as father's brother, father's father's brother, etc. Like our own system, it tends to combine under relatively few terms all relatives except those directly in line with ego, most of whom belong to his family group. Only within the patrilineage are generation differences and age differences in generation, in addition to the primary, or familial, relationships, recognized.

10. The names used here are selected to show age and sex in household role. Terms like "Old Man," "Young Wife," etc., are not kinship terms, which would vary with the speaker, but are used uniformly by household members as well as outsiders in indirect address and designate the person's role in the household.

11. These illustrations are genuine though, indeed, not all commonplace.

12. See Chart 5, which is a diagram of a typical homestead group and interior plan of its main house.

13. The pattern of ridge ornaments differs so strikingly from place to place in Japan that it identifies each locality. The author does not recall having seen another ridge ornament exactly like the Kusama style elsewhere in Japan.

14. These padded mats are universally used in native construction. The standard dimensions of the mat, approximately three feet by six, is the unit by which sizes of rooms and of houses are determined. The reader should not confuse these reed mats with others of straw, used in the kitchen.

15. This is often called nikai, which refers to the fact that most such guest rooms are on the second floor of a barn or stable. It should be noted that such rooms, too, are always covered with reed mats.

16. All of these dishes are well known throughout Japan.

17. Raper and his colleagues observe that in modern rural communities "important questions involving family members are commonly decided by a family [household] council." Op. cit., p. 209.

18. When the whole household must be absent to work in the fields, the house may be left with only an unbarred door to stop intruders. A house watcher (rusuban) became

especially necessary after the war, when many black marketeers roamed the area buying up, or stealing, scarce foodstuffs. If it is necessary to leave the house unguard-
ed, someone of the household may try to work nearby, or, if nothing else, a neighbor
may be depended upon to keep an eye on the house.

19. Drinking water is obtained at a spring pool near the stream and millrace. At the
point where the man-made ditch enters the main buraku settlement area there is another pool, which is closer and therefore used more often in winter. For non-potable
water there is an adequate supply in a concrete tank near the center of this area.
Several collecting basins along the ditch are also used, each one designated by a de-
scriptive name, e.g., one called do because it is near a sanctuary pavilion (do).

20. A national sanitation law requiring each household to clean its homestead once a year
is on the books and formerly yakuba officials made an inspection following a special
housecleaning week in spring. But since the war, this practice has fallen into disuse,
so that now a notice urging a complete housecleaning is the only official step taken to
enforce the law.

21. Girls and women usually conceal themselves behind a panel or wall momentarily, but
other members of the household are less chary of being seen. Much of this modesty
is probably a consequence of public education in Occidental propriety, in vogue in
Japanese schooling since the Meiji era.

22. The authorities of the Japanese Folk Studies Institute (Minzokugaku Kenkyusho) consider detached bathhouses more ancient than baths set into the main house. See
K. Yanagida, ed., Minzokugaku Jiten (Japanese Folklore Dictionary) (Tokyo, 1951),
p. 509.

23. Some do not bother changing clothes after the bath because they own so few garments.
As a rule, whether they are called tanzen or yakuta, the lounging and sleeping garments are nothing more than old, worn-out work kimonos.

24. Local people do not differentiate between the deity of the oven and other deities found
in the same part of the kitchen. Although they sometimes speak of the kama god as
distinct from Rokusama, there is no separate shrine exclusively for a kama god. In
organized Shinto, Rokusama is thought to be two individuals, one male and one female,
who are mated and therefore popularly regarded as one.

Chapter IV

BURAKU SOCIAL ORGANIZATION AND COMMUNITY LIFE

All through life there are reminders that one is part of the buraku. In relations with outsiders the sense of belonging to one locale is especially acute. This feeling takes root from the fact that at school the children clean their classrooms by buraku groups and, in the young people's association of the mura, individuals participate with their buraku fellows in events such as dancing at Bon and the annual school field meet.

In adulthood, one is often called by his family name qualified by the home place name as far as the edge of the mura, since otherwise it may be difficult to determine which family of the same surname in the area is meant. Or outsiders may simply address him as "the gentleman from Matsunagi" when more explicit identification is unnecessary or his name is unknown. Within the oaza, the buraku name is a means of identification, but only the oaza name is used when one goes elsewhere in the mura and the mura name outside.

Buraku unity today, though, is more psychological than social. One feels no serious qualms in carrying tales in criticism of people in other buraku, as he would of his own neighbors. Nor is there any larger sense of loyalty that prevents drawing invidious comparisons between other buraku and one's own. Matsunagi people are not reticent to claim that Higashimura is a hotbed of dissension among its households. In Higashimura, people opine that Matsunagi has always been notorious for its drinking and quarreling and general lack of reverence for the gods. But in the practical give and take of internal affairs, this community feeling is largely submerged in interests of more limited scope.

Formal Political Structure

The buraku is constructed of both social and political elements. By "political" we mean endowed with some legal function, whether explicitly covered by law or arising from administrative expediency created by the mura government. The political aspect of the community is represented by the two divisions, Mae and Ushiro, which are termed jokai, or "community meeting." Sometimes it is difficult to decide whether a specific function of local government pertains to a jokai or to the whole buraku, for they are not always sharply separated.

The head of a jokai[1] is named by vote of his peers every two years, but it is customary to have an incumbent serve at least two terms.[2] He presides at meetings of the associated households and in himself combines a large number and variety of official duties. He is the chief liaison official with the yakuba and may also maintain liaison with the Agricultural Cooperative. His other responsibilities are to seek information on economic production, to transmit instructions on such administrative matters as writing tenancy contracts or filing income tax returns, and to collect mura taxes. He sees that yakuba notices get to all households and is responsible for putting up on the bulletin board the many posters and public announcements that come through the yakuba from the prefectural and national governments. An active man expects to serve in this, or in some less onerous post, at some time in his life. Some other experienced or eminent local men also serve in posts representing two or more buraku, usually as members of one of the administrative committees of the mura.

Nearly all public offices are regarded as necessary but unpleasant duties rather than as positions of leadership and prestige, so they fall by default to those of respected and

175

176

CHART 6

The Political (Administrative) Structure of Matsunagi

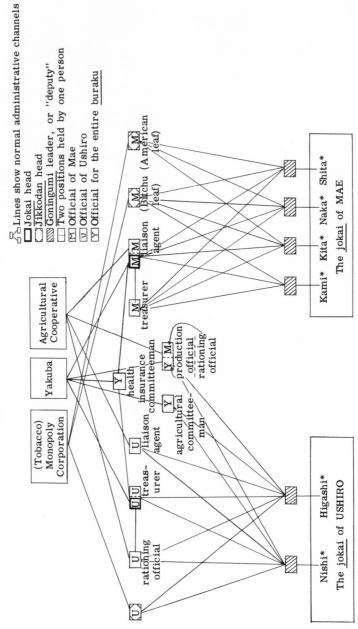

⌐Lines show normal administrative channels
☐ Jokai head
◯ Jikkodan head
▨ Goningumi leader, or "deputy"
⊟ Two positions held by one person
Ⓜ Official of Mae
Ⓤ Official of Ushiro
Ⓨ Official for the entire buraku

* A goningumi or equivalent group.

177

FIGURE 1

The Political (Administrative) Subdivisions of Matsunagi*

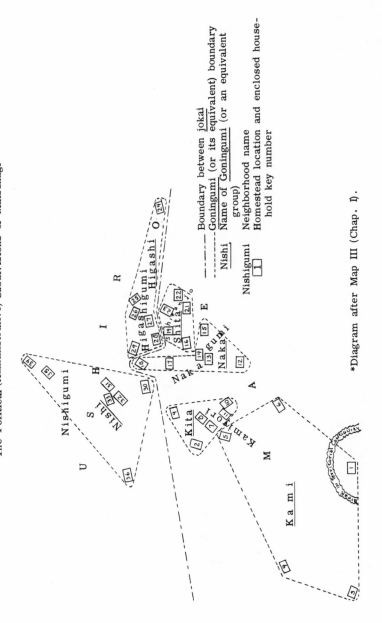

*Diagram after Map III (Chap. I).

trusted reputation but not especially high status. Young men in their early twenties know
with certainty that by age rotation they will soon have to serve in their first public office.
Often this is as leader of one of the political subdivisions of the jokai, or goningumi
(literally: "5-man group").[3] A goningumi leader stands between the jokai head and the
individual household. For example, in collecting mura taxes, notices are delivered from
jokai head to goningumi leader to individual household head, and tax money is collected
along the same channel. After a term or two in this office, one gains enough experience
to assume a more responsible job such as liaison agent with the Agricultural Cooperative
or rationing official.

All purely community offices are selected by nomination rather than by competitive
election. Before the jokai meeting at which nominations are to be made, household heads
privately consider who are available and one of them casually approaches individuals about
serving. The formal selection, though done by ballot, is merely part of the form that
since the war has come to be regarded as democratic procedure.

Jokai meetings transact communal business, which is usually related to yakuba administration or is a farming matter emanating from the Agricultural Cooperative. These
meetings are attended by each household head or his eldest son and are held in the "public
hall" in Mae, and in private homes in Ushiro. The tone of these meetings is not one of
sociability, since the jokai is an arbitrary territorial association, differing in composition
from other, social, or voluntary, associations. In meetings of a jokai, each household
has but one voice, regardless of its wealth, position, or size.

Sources of Buraku Unity

Its roots in the past help to fortify the buraku's unity in the present. Of these, one
of the most vital in Matsunagi is the cult of its tutelary deity (ujigami). Every resident,
no matter how young or humble, is a fellow of the community under the protection of the
ujigami; however, his sense of belonging to this cult group may not be especially strong.
In Matsunagi, two especially named trustees, one from each jokai, represent their constituents in cult affairs at the oaza shrine. They are also deputized to participate in celebrations of other local and national feast days at this shrine, thus freeing other household
heads from fulfilling these shrine duties themselves.

Another source of unity is the Buddhist temple in Matsunagi, which has a relationship
to the community parallel to that of the ujigami cult and its shrine. The temple parish
(danke) embraces all households which at some time have turned to the temple priest, or
bonze, to honor their dead, in effect, the whole community. The temple buildings, its
lands, and its outlying sanctuaries, all belong to the people of the parish. Like the oaza
shrine, the temple has its lay trustees, two from each jokai, who serve out of a sense of
community obligation rather than for prestige. They, like their counterparts of the ujigami
cult, are men of stronger than average belief who visit the temple at the great Buddhist
festivals to worship the Buddhas there and to remember the bonze for his services on be-
half of the parish. They also administer temple properties, taking charge of repairs and
selling timber from its forests to raise funds.

Until they were discarded in the past generation, the greatest ceremonial functions of
the whole community during the year were the festivals of Sanjo, Jijin, Hattengu, and the
"community prayers" (muragito). These and other non-cyclic rites or festival occasions[4]
brought together at least one man from each household in what for the most part was a
common religious purpose. Since the end of the war, though, ceremonial gatherings of
the entire buraku have become very rare indeed.

At one time also, events bringing together the buraku or the people of one jokai for public works were rather common, but these events, too, are exceptional today. One of the few recent instances of community enterprise occurred in 1948, when the motor road was extended into the center of the main buraku settlement with the cooperation of all households. Work was coordinated by men named to procure supplies. Each evening, the workers relaxed for a few drinks of sake before leaving for home, and on completion of the project a special theatrical performance was presented in the temple by local talent for the entertainment of all residents. Normally, some road repairs are carried out every year, but such cooperative effort utilizes the labor only of those few households having land in the area served by the road. In every case of cooperative work, however large the group involved, each household contributes an equal share of the money and labor needed.

Because of the constantly lessening enthusiasm for gatherings of the whole buraku, large-scale communal activities are now very infrequent. This turn of affairs strengthens the impression that the important setting of household life is not so much the community as it is that particular part of the community in which a household is situated.

The Residence Factor in Buraku Kin Groupings

Within the buraku relationships between all residents are largely defined by the households to which they belong. Household groups other than one's own are identified as either "relatives" or "non-relatives." In-buraku bonds of affinity and consanguinity, which with those outside the community make up the kindred, are established through marriage, adoption, or even immigration of blood relatives.

In predominantly economic relations, such as construction, threshing, or roof-thatching, non-relatives are usually called with the same regularity as those who are considered "relatives." But, unlike non-relatives, kinsmen also have ritual obligations to fulfill in the familiar crises of death, marriage, birth, and important stages in the career of each family and household head. Furthermore, they are formally called upon to reiterate the links between them at specified times during the annual ceremonial cycle, for example, at Bon and New Year.

Sometimes people distinguish "near" kin from distant kin when discussing definite ceremonial responsibilities to the lineage. "Near" kin usually include children of the family who have left the household, including siblings of the incumbent household head, and similar relatives of the natal household of one's mother and wife. In a funeral procession, for instance, the closest male relative of the deceased carries a ritual umbrella over the bier. But though this person is most likely to be a child of the dead, he may be a sibling, or a more distant relative, without disturbing the highly stereotyped funeral ritual. In other ceremonial events pertaining to the lineage, such as a celebration at a birth or a wedding, the nearness of the kinsmen who should be invited is not specified, nor are there any patterned differences in the treatment accorded one sort of relative as opposed to another. The number of relatives a household can afford to entertain is the usual deciding factor in inviting kindred to such affairs.

Though the lineal kin may be designated the "large [multi-local] family,"[5] an analysis of behavior patterns does not substantiate that these kinsmen are a sufficiently distinct group to warrant setting them apart from other kindred. By this is meant that the treatment of kin not resident in the household depends on frequency of contact more than on their type of relationship, except that some intimacy is expected between very close kindred wherever they live.

Local consanguineal groupings are occasionally formed when a junior son, or collateral, of a mature household sets up his own establishment in the community. This relationship produces a stem-branch (honkebunke) group of related households. Although a stem-branch tie depends initially upon blood, the vigor of this bond tends to fade, unless from time to time it is reinforced by intermarriage or adoption. In Matsunagi, kin groups of this sort, traditionally a constellation of a stem and two or three branch households, are weakly developed.[6] Unless it is a close neighbor to its stem house, a branch household usually relies on adjacent households for most economic assistance.

Social groupings based primarily on bonds of common residence are more fruitful to examine than those based on consanguinity and affinity, because residence factors give rise to the most active groupings in buraku social life.

Though nearly all households live in a neighborhood cluster, some neighbors demonstrate such affinity for each other that they come to be identified by the community and in their own minds as special intimates, or shinrui.[7] Households which do not have such relationships are either so well-to-do and so well equipped that they do not need to depend on their neighbors or are so unpopular that they are left to themselves. A group of neighbors are shinrui, not simply because they are near each other, but also because their behavior resembles that of blood kin. Shinrui is essentially an extension of the concept of kinship to neighbors or other households of the community, but not, it should be emphasized, to individuals as such. This sort of kin tie is functionally as important in Matsunagi and its environs as the stem-branch relationship is said to be elsewhere.[8]

How does such an extension of kinship develop? The reason may be formal, such as a relationship between one household and an outside individual, which prescribes a subsequent kin tie with his household; or informal, as when frequent casual cooperation between two households leads to the gradual emergence and definition of this tie. Persons of some sophistication see this relationship only as "acting like a relative," not as true kinship, but there is clearly very little practical distinction to be made.[9]

Most formal shinrui connections stem from an obligation incurred when someone acts as a go-between in arranging a marriage. A couple must remember their go-between in some way each New Year and present him with an especially handsome gift when he reaches his critical forty-second and sixty-first birthdays. For his part, the go-between gives the first offspring of this couple a new kimono or a gift of money when the child is introduced to its circle of relatives. Or an intermediary in such economic affairs as selling a piece of forest land may become a shinrui if he is not one already.[10] By becoming a godparent to a child of another household, a man also establishes a bond strong enough to be called kinship. In all these circumstances the expression of kinship between households centers on an individual who has been instrumental in cementing the bond. In the long run, the relationship does not prevail beyond the death of this individual.

Continuous informal association results, not in prescribed obligations, as between spouses and their go-between, but in spontaneous mutual indebtedness. Nor is this tie bounded by the life span of one man; it may endure as many generations as the households survive. The strength of this relationship is directly proportional to the distances between the households, whereas in a shinrui connection through an individual, it is not. Because the spatial relationship is a strong determinant and because neighborhood clusters of several households are characteristic of the settlement pattern, a household frequently reckons its in-buraku "relatives" as a group of nearby households. Some of these neighbor ties are very weak, some very strong; some may always be recognized as shinrui, some only when recognition is stipulated and unavoidable. Weakening of the ties may result from a decline in common economic interests; or because in countless inconspicuous ways a new generation is losing interest in maintaining the old pattern of obligations; or even because personality differences interfere with the harmony of the relationship.

Ties are strengthened by routine interdependent activities. For purposes of illustration, let us cite an actual case history of shinrui relations. Household number 16 (Figure 2) owns a large array of specialist tools, such as are used by a carpenter or a sawyer. This household freely lends these tools about to its neighbors, particularly to its shinrui. One of these shinrui, number 17, decides to build a new barn. At the same time the latter requests the assistance of households number 15 and 16, his intimate neighbors, in felling and shaping logs in the forest, carrying the finished beams to the homestead, and clearing the building site preliminary to raising the frame. Householder number 17 has a great deal of grassland, which provides him with far more thatching grass than he needs. So he readily furnishes enough to number 16 to finish his roof repairs when the latter runs short. Again, in purchasing new equipment too expensive for one household to bear alone, a combination of these three shinrui, numbers 15, 16, and 17, pool their resources and buy a power-driven fodder-cutter, which they use jointly.

Added to such routine shinrui relations are situations involving the more prescribed patterns of family ceremonial activities, which are uniquely a function of kinship. After death, the shinrui, as well as any local blood relatives, are called in to help plan the funeral and prepare the body for burial. Relatives invited to attend a party at the first birthday of a son nearly always include shinrui, such as a go-between and close neighbors. As a rule, where ritual affairs of the lineage are concerned, a household has as much to do with its shinrui as with its other local kinsmen.

"Neighborhood" Foci in Buraku Life

Territorial aggregations of households in both jokai have names, though they may not always be used. Such aggregations are the units we call "neighborhood," but it is their territorial rather than social unity that people explicitly recognize in names like Kamiyori, Shitanjo, and Nishigumi. Because these are based on mature distributions of households, they are the most stable factor in this society.

Evidence that buraku life breaks down into neighborhoods is found in the play of children. Children are nearly always at play during the daylight hours somewhere in a bit of open, unused space, along a path or in a dooryard. But it is soon apparent that children normally play in groups corresponding to the cluster of homesteads in which they live. It is the activities of younger, pre-school children that most clearly define these play areas, of which there are four important ones in the buraku.[11] In each area there are one or two places habitually used for play, most often near the center of the homestead cluster, where the children gather spontaneously. These intimacies of childhood carry on into adulthood and may constitute lasting friendships, especially if throughout life the individuals continue to reside in the same households.

The importance of neighborhood associations is also emphasized by the fact that inadvertently people often call a political goningumi by the same name as one of the neighborhoods, even though through changing household alignments they no longer coincide. In fact, most people are not conscious that there are both political and social (neighborhood) implications in the name they use for such a settlement cluster.

The outstanding characteristic of the important associations of the buraku is spatial contiguity, which reflects that the close contacts of living together, as in the neighborhood, develop close personal ties.

The goningumi of Matsunagi today appear to have been formed spontaneously out of associations of limited groups of neighbors in various parts of the community. Early in this century, it is said, tobacco producers were organized into such associations to

182

FIGURE 2

Contrasting Kin Groupings in Matsunagi*

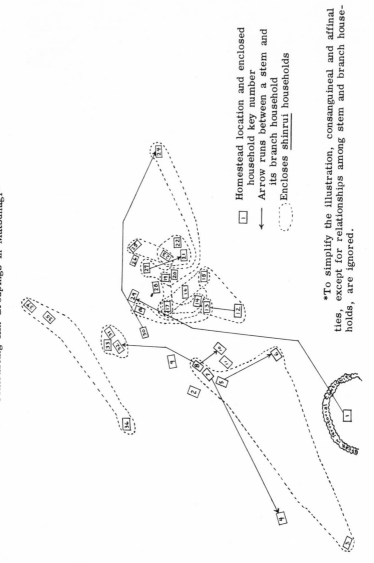

☐ — Homestead location and enclosed
     household key number
→ — Arrow runs between a stem and
     its branch household
⬭ — Encloses shinrui households

*To simplify the illustration, consanguineal and affinal
ties, except for relationships among stem and branch households, are ignored.

facilitate production and sale of their crop, and on these groups the political alignments of households are probably based. These are undoubtedly continuations of earlier territorial groupings of the same name with similar functions (see p. 205, fn. 3).

Because their purpose is the formal one of administration, composition of goningumi is more permanent and arbitrary than is typical of communal associations. Distant, outlying households are assigned to their nearest goningumi, although they may have little or nothing in common with the group, or are in fact outcasts. In contrast, a neighborhood, though geographically unified, lacks definite boundaries, and those who live on the peripheries, between neighborhoods, divide their social allegiance between two such groups. For example, a man serves as the leader of a goningumi situated in one neighborhood, but in economic and social relations his household belongs to an adjacent neighborhood.

In short, a neighborhood should be understood only as the focus, not the encompassment, of neighbor relations.

Voluntary Household Associations

Voluntary household associations are called kumi. The term may be applied to any organization of individuals or households, in which all have equal status as members. But in most instances a kumi is a voluntary organization of households having one particular function,[12] and we shall use the word only to denote this (see Chart 7).

Whereas affiliation with a goningumi is mandatory if membership in the community is to be maintained, most local associations are formed on a voluntary basis. Still, differences in functional vigor among contemporary goningumi may be explained by the fact that even such a fixed political association is primarily responsive to immediate social factors, which cause it to flourish or wane as any kumi does. Thus, goningumi in Ushiro seem once to have been vigorous and then gradually to have been supplanted by an undivided jokai unit; but in Mae, which is larger and therefore more unwieldy, goningumi subdivisions are still needed for effective liaison between the jokai head and its households. Although functionally it is useful to describe goningumi and jokai as political groupings only, their compositions to a large extent represent spontaneous alignments of households which are convenient for other social purposes as well.

This responsiveness to total social context is even more true of other kinds of household associations. Factors such as distribution of households, size of group, and the existence of other impinging associations produce change as well as stability among them. When another association has the same constituents as a goningumi, both sorts of groupings are stronger because of this reinforcement. Indeed, highly coextensive associations of this sort are concrete evidence that the households concerned make up a functional neighborhood.

The composition of a voluntary association also fluctuates as households join, leave or recombine, even though the association itself continues to exist in approximately the same form. Sometimes a single household changes its affiliation from one group to another; sometimes the entire structure of an association may require reorganization, as when several households purchase their own threshing machinery and withdraw from their communal threshing kumi. The gap created by their departure can be filled only by making new and different alignments of the remaining users of the communal machines.

Economic associations of households in Matsunagi are of two types: those based on some piece of common property, such as the open common pasture which is used equally by all members; and those in which the labor of all members is cooperatively organized.

CHART 7

Household Associations (Kumi) in Matsunagi

Only kumi whose composition is stable over a period of time (not constantly fluctuating, as a roof repair kumi) are shown in this chart. The kumi are listed by their commonly accepted names or, if they have none, by numbers. These numbers, as well as the key numbers for households, are arranged in geographically contiguous sequence through the settlement area. Within the physical limitations of the graphic technique used, the chart illustrates the fact that, by and large, neighbors become members of the same kumi.

Households by Key Number*	Irrig. Ponds		Common Land		Water Wheel Mills					Threshing Machinery		Tobacco Growers		Threshing Work						
	Kanabara	Konigo	Ikurakoge	Onaru	I	II	III	IV	V	Mae	Ushiro	Mae	Ushiro	I	II	III	IV	V	VI	VII
1																				
2																				
3	X**		X		X					X		X		X						
4																				
5			X		X					X		X		X						
6	X	X	X							X				X						
7			X				X			X		X		X						
8	X	X				X				X		X								
9	X					X				X										
10			X							X										
11																				
12									X	X		X				X				
13			X			X				X		X				X				
14	X		X				X	X		X		X				X				
15			X							X		X								
16			X			X				X		X								
17			X			X				X		X		X						
18		X	X	X					X	X		X			X					
19	X		X	X	X					X		X		X						
20																				
21			X	X		X				X		X					X			
22		X	X	X						X		X					X			
23			X	X					X	X		X					X			
24			X	X	X						X		X				X			
25	X		X								X		X				X			
26	X		X								X		X				X			
27	X		X	X			X				X		X				X			
28			X	X				X			X									
29			X	X				X			X		X							
30			X				X				X		X							X
31	X		X				X				X		X						X	
32	X		X				X				X		X						X	
33	X		X				X				X		X						X	
34								X			X									X
35											X									X
36											X		X							X

CHART 7—Continued

Households by Key Number	Economic Kumi									Ceremonial Kumi							
	Electrified	Mochi-making								Kojin					Funeral		
	Grain Mill														Mae		Ushiro
		I	II	III	IV	V	VI	VII	VIII	I	II	III	IV	V	"A"	"B"	
1	X									X					X		
2															X		
3		X								X					X		
4		X								X					X		
5	X	X								X					X		
6		X								X					X		
7	X	X								X					X		
8			X							X					X		
9	X									X					X		
10										X					X		
11															X		
12	X			X							X				X		
13	X			X							X				X		
14	X			X											X		
15	X			X							X					X	
16					X											X	
17					X											X	
18	X		X								X					X	
19	X					X				X						X	
20																X	
21	X				X						X					X	
22						X										X	
23	X						X				X						X
24						X					X						X
25	X				X							X					X
26					X							X					X
27						X					X						X
28						X					X						X
29											X						X
30				X									X				X
31						X											X
32						X											X
33						X											X
34	X							X						X			X
35	X							X						X			X
36	X								X								X

*These numbers refer to the diagram of the buraku settlement in Chapter IV, Figure 1.

**X represents a kumi membership of the household whose key number stands in the left-hand column.

Other kumi combine these two functions; though united by common property, the members may also share their labor force.

The economic kumi which own buraku irrigation ponds meet once a year, just before the lunar New Year's, to settle accounts connected with operating their joint properties and to discuss repairs or improvements. In addition to maintaining their pond, the owners of Konigo Pond assist each other in preparing the paddies for flooding in late spring. One man is asked to serve as leader (sewa-nin), to call meetings, pay bills, and in general be responsible for supervising the property. This office is customary in property-owning kumi and has an indefinite term.

The kumi of the great common, Ikurakoge, meets about every two years, always in the early part of the first lunar month. This occasion is marked by several hours of boisterous drinking, after one man from each household has met in the common to draw lots for pieces of woodland from which fuel may be cut. The sewa-nin of the group sees to cutting and selling enough standing timber or fuel wood from the common to defray the expenses of this drinking party; and he divides the area into plots, prepares the notched wooden lots, and supervises the drawing. All kumi members have an equal chance at the plots of woodland, though inevitably some draw sparser plots than others.[13] The other important common, Onaru, is organized in similar fashion.

Kumi owning threshing machinery, which is the only kind of farm machine owned by kumi or more than two or three households each, are new.[14] It is thus interesting to note that their membership corresponds to the modern jokai divisions, with the exclusion of a few landless newcomers and recluse households, whereas the pond and common kumi, dating from pre-Meiji times, do not. The organizations arrange allotments of rationed kerosene and gasoline to operate the machines. Though there is no chief kumi official, a jokai head presides at meetings held in June. If a household buys its own machines, it becomes inactive in its kumi but does not ask that its equity in the equipment be returned. It may however dispose of its right to someone who is without access to such equipment, if other members have no objection.

The associations which actually join forces to do threshing are differently constituted from those that own the machines and through which fuel is distributed. These groupings in the main follow the outlines of goningumi, but where the goningumi are weak, the kumi usually comprise groups of shinrui. The machines are used jointly by each work kumi and then passed on to the next adjacent group. The real importance of these kumi lies in the intensity of social contact that working together brings. A household that drops out of its work kumi may ally itself with one or two others to purchase and operate non-kumi machines, but for the most part having one's own machines requires that threshing be done without outside help.[15]

Save for one or two water wheel mills that are still in use, kumi ownership of these properties represents relationships that are no longer functional. Instead, most households now belong to the association of the electrified communal grain mill. This kumi meets twice a year to settle accounts for the amount of electricity each member has used. In the meantime, each household takes its turn at the mill according to a fixed roster. When repairs are needed, the leader summons the membership, and each one furnishes an equal share of materials and labor required.

Another kind of distinction that should be made within this list of kumi is that of the stimulus which leads to forming an association. The range of stimuli extends from official recognition of the goningumi by the yakuba to spontaneous arrangements for working together, as illustrated by the threshing work kumi. The tobacco growers in both jokai have been encouraged by the government's Monopoly Corporation to set up their own organizations (jikkodan). Each of these has its own head, who usually makes use of goningumi leaders instead of attempting to contact tobacco growers himself. The leaders circulate notices of inspection of growing tobacco and delivery dates. Most meetings come irregularly, when the Monopoly officials have some especially important information to impart to the growers. And, in January, after the crop has been delivered, a jikkodan may hold a party celebrating the end of the tobacco year.

At this period, too, most households join with others in making mochi, which is part of the preparation for the New Year holiday. Relatives, including close neighbors, may lend help at this time to someone who is short-handed, but the commonest and the most patterned form of labor pooling is by kumi, composed of neighbors who are not necessarily shinrui. Normally the help of a man and his wife is expected from each household of the kumi. Labor exchange kumi of this type are fluid and responsive to changing conditions, and they may easily be dissolved if, for example, there is a quarrel among the group.

In mochi-making both parents and their children move from house to house as operations proceed. Preparations begin early in the morning, when rice is put on to steam; soon after sunrise the kumi helpers arrive. Able-bodied men are needed to pound the steamed rice dough into glutinous mochi. Four or five men stand about a wooden mortar, each in succession striking a blow with his long-handed mallet. Shortly, the mochi dough is sticky enough to work and is lifted steaming to a work board around which the women of the kumi are seated; they roll and shape the mochi into cakes. Oldsters and children carry the cakes to a set of shelves where the mochi is cured by drying. As a part of the day's festivities, the host is sure to serve some special dish, like Chinese noodles or tofu soup.

Construction and roof-repair, two other frequent forms of work cooperation, require that a householder summon some of his neighbors and all of his local relatives, including shinrui, to help. But, while one is obligated to appear if at all possible, the system is flexible enough to permit substitutions. Such lack of definite composition is typical of much of the mutual assistance occurring in the buraku. When help is needed, one turns first to those who are tied to him by existing blood or affinal relationships, to close neighborhood relations, or to those having given or received assistance previously. Each household habitually cooperates with certain other households, which in turn cooperate with still others. These loosely organized work associations, then, are successively interlocking. It may be necessary to lend a hand at each of two separate and simultaneous thatchings because of obligations to both. Such labor exchange patterns, based chiefly on contiguity of residence, may in this context be regarded as uncrystallized kumi.

The kumi idea looms so large in buraku social organization that it is somewhat surprising to find that only two kinds of ritual or ceremonial kumi are now active: funeral kumi and Kojin kumi.

The importance of a funeral kumi consists of cooperative assistance in preparing for the death rites. Were it not for this banding together, few households could afford to stage a proper Buddhist funeral. Both buraku jokai have their funeral kumi, which in Ushiro is a single unit and in Mae is divided in two approximately equal parts.

If, for example, a death occurs in "A" division of Mae, all funeral preparations involving work at the homestead of the deceased are performed by the people of "A." This means preparing food for the family and attending relatives, serving the funeral feast, and arranging the house for the actual rites. One or two persons are designated to make paper paraphernalia, i.e., colored cut-outs of Buddhist swastikas and other forms to be pasted on the coffin, on the bier, and on its umbrella-like canopy. A group of men constructs objects of bamboo and wood needed during the rites. A few women sew the special white garments in which the body is buried. Duties outside the homestead and outside the buraku are the responsibility of the households of "B" division. These tasks require active men who can dig the grave, build the coffin, call the outside relatives, notify the temple bonze, and procure a death certificate. The households of "A" send two persons each, usually a man and his wife, while only one man need be furnished from each household of "B" division. After the coffin is in the grave, all duties are transferred from the kumi to relatives of the deceased.

Though normally the obligations of funeral kumi last only during the day of death, until the funeral takes place, in extreme emergencies, such as a demise in the middle of the harvest season, all who can spare a worker help to bring in the crops of the household in mourning.

Most buraku households belong to Kojin associations, but of these only two are still active. Each kumi is based on common ownership of a shrine dedicated to Kojin, the farmer's guardian deity, and unites a spatially contiguous group of households. Only the active kumi celebrate the annual Kojin festivals, one of the member households rotating as host each year. Essentially, these festivals are family gatherings, like mochi-making, and children in particular are expected to attend. The host and his shinrui in the kumi prepare food and drink to serve to the group. An adult from each household first briefly visits the Kojin shrine, often accompanied by his children, and the rest of the day until well into the night is spent in eating, drinking, and singing.

Determinants of Household Rank

The social organization of the buraku shows no class differences. There are minor inequalities of status or rank, but these fluctuate with the economic fortunes of each household. Because stem-branch household relationships are unimportant in Matsunagi, dominance of the stem over its branches is not a particularly significant source of inequality, as it often is elsewhere in Japan. All that an active stem-branch relation in Matsunagi implies is that the branch is more obligated to cooperate with the stem in out-of-the-ordinary functions such as mochi-making, roof-thatching, and the Kojin festival than any other of its relatives and neighbors.

The antiquity of a household does affect its social position provided age is accompanied by at least an average amount of wealth in land and buildings. This much may be said: those households which are the most prominent are among those longest resident in the community. But there is no true class exalted by age alone. Of five new households which immigrated in the past twenty years or so, three are headed by men who grew up in Matsunagi. Another household was attracted here by distant kinship with an old, established resident. Newcomers do not easily establish themselves without the sponsorship of kinsmen already in residence. If the newcomer is a former member of one of the local households, there is no obstacle to his settling in these familiar grounds, provided he can support himself. Usually, though, he must depend on his kinsmen or on the generosity of some other old resident for land to work and on which to live. Immigrant households join a goningumi at once and may also have informal work relations with their neighbors, but membership in any of the organized labor exchange kumi is slow to come. The newcomer may never be able to break into one of the Kojin associations, but he does have the advantage of belonging to a funeral kumi from the very outset.

Some households are set below others because of bias against their ancestry inspired by old Japanese religious beliefs concerning purity of the blood. However, these households do not form a depressed social class in Matsunagi, because they are few in number and not all connected in the same degree to the opprobrious factors behind this inferiority.

But the religious basis of their ranking does appear to isolate them more than would other factors, say, lack of property or inferior occupation.

A household of the pariah group called hinin[16] is linked administratively with the buraku, though its closest contacts are really in Obara. Before the war, people of this type could not even attend meetings of the jokai, let alone join any of the voluntary associations of the buraku. Nowadays, a representative of this hinin household may attend jokai meetings that concern it, and the household works cooperatively with buraku people when and where it has the same economic interests. But these pariahs have never been regarded as ujiko, or residents, of the community. And they have always married within their own group since they settled here in Meiji times.

Households in which leprosy is known to have occurred may also be set apart from the rest.[17] Though no cases of leprosy have been reported in Matsunagi since early Meiji, recent deaths from haemophilic conditions in two such households are taken as a sign of continued contamination of the blood. Their stigma takes the form of a marriage restriction, which forces them, like the pariahs, to marry close relatives. First-cousin marriage is frequent in these families. Except for this, they are unqualified residents of the community, though even when prosperous such households seem to enjoy less influence than otherwise might be expected.

Wealth is a primary determinant of household rank, but prestige gained through possession of economic resources ebbs at a much slower rate than wealth itself. Success in the basic profession of farming is attributed as much to ownership of fertile fields and an ample supply of labor as to individual ability. The household which has a cho (2.45 acres) or more of land is considered well-off. It is not by direct economic means that a household rises to social prominence, but because its greater resources enable it to loan equipment to others, guarantee debts, or to make public donations, such as mats to cover the floor of a public building. It is most able to build up ties of obligation by letting a propertyless immigrant work a plot of land rent-free, or by allowing others to use some of its expensive power-driven machines without compensation. Because favors establish a sense of debt in the recipient, these favors must somehow be repaid, usually in the form of labor, which is especially valuable to a farmer with many fields to work. Money permits the purchase of new machines and of course makes possible more years in school. Money also makes possible more active participation in mura affairs; only the scion of a better-than-average family may hope to serve as village councillor, school principal, or mayor.

But disparity in economic position is not so vast as to form a distinct cleavage between landlords and tenants. People with greater resources simply have to struggle less desperately to acquire subsistence, though in sum they may work harder in all their economic activities than their poorer compatriots. Popular leaders and innovators are representatives of high-ranking households for they can spare more time for public service without seriously handicapping themselves. Also, since improvements in agriculture and in living conditions are costly to make, a novelty, such as a tile-lined bathhouse, can be instituted only by a man whose enlightened ideas are supported by the substantial resources of his household.

Though farming is the primary buraku occupation, no particular stigma attaches to other common vocations. Paradoxically, despite the fact that in Japan the merchant's calling has always been held in low esteem, even some of the highly respected and monied households in Matsunagi engage in peddling as a supplemental occupation. The advantages of this money-making enterprise seem to outweigh its social disadvantages. However, with the exception of certain executive posts in the mura, such as head of the Agricultural Cooperative, or postmaster, all the working members of a typical highly-placed household devote themselves to farming.

A Matsunagi farmer, like his U.S. counterpart, must be a jack-of-all-trades, capable of carrying out the numerous tasks associated with farming. A first son is coached to follow his father as the chief farmer of the household, while younger sons customarily learn some additional specialty. Young men still living at home often seek work with a lumbering contractor in the winter slack season because the resources of their own households alone are insufficient to keep them gainfully employed. It is a point of pride among sons of wealthier families that they are not forced, through economic necessity, to turn to wage-earning in this way.

A variety of wage-earning specialties are represented in Matsunagi.[18] Among crafts, carpentry is the most respected and cooperage ranks second. Matsunagi's sawyers rank next in prestige; lumberjacks, requiring even less training and experience, in general belong to the least distinguished households. Clog (geta)-making is atypical of the usual pattern of craft specialties in this area and it is represented in the buraku only by a postwar refugee from the city.[19] The Buddhist priesthood, too, is in its economic aspects a wage specialty, but it lacks the social prestige usually associated with educated professions.

Salaried workers form an easily defined group since their time is pretty largely taken up by the work for which they are paid. There are four salaried occupations in the buraku, and only Matsunagi's two postmen, whose duties keep them out-of-doors, fail to qualify as white-collar workers. Indoor salaried jobs are rated respectable and perhaps even more desirable than farming. Farm labor is the least popular sort of regular wage-earning, and in Matsunagi employment of this sort is limited to women who do not have enough work or land of their own to keep busy. Of course, several others perform such unskilled tasks from time to time, but they are not identified with this form of labor.

An exact line between primarily farmers and workers in other categories is difficult to draw since a number of people who rightly consider themselves full-time farmers have casual secondary occupations. Nor are occupational distinctions rigidly defined. Thirty-eight people, by actual count, spend so much time at non-agricultural callings that the community thinks of them as professional specialists. Folks say of them, "Oh, he peddles," or "He of the yakuba," or "School Principal Ueda."

A household may also be judged by the behavior of its leading members. A man who is thought droll or who dances and sings well may be personally popular but not necessarily of high status. A woman is not admired who rules her own household shrewishly and officiously and strives to enhance its position at the expense of others. But such personality factors have only a moderate effect on the standing of the individual's household. Still, the prestige of a man who serves the interests of the whole community more than those of his own household raises his household above others that would otherwise rank equally. Such a man is usually acknowledged a buraku leader.

One who is respected and looked to for guidance usually has a better than average education, which means something more than the minimal six years of elementary school. The advantage of education is most striking in the case of college graduates, who are seated in the most honored positions at gatherings and are frequently selected to speak for the buraku in its relationships with the outside. Leadership among young men inclines toward those with upper school training because it is felt that the ideas of an educated person are sounder than older, conventional ones. Since among the best educated religious feeling is least strong, much of the growing indifference to all religion can be attributed to these leaders and their households. In contrast, those who are well known for their piety are today largely ignored.

The ultimate goal of every household in its relations with the rest of the community is to gain a position of respect and trust; as a social unit its aim is to achieve more property

and productivity. These objectives are sometimes contradictory. The dilemma in buraku
life for an individual, therefore, is the choice between community-mindedness and private-
interest.

Buraku Sodalities

Households are the primary units of buraku social structure; kumi and other associations of households are its major structural features; and sodalities[20] are divisions that'
cut through the social group by age levels, intersecting both household and kumi aggregations. The important status changes in the life of an individual offer the best basis for
defining age strata, of which the following six-fold series seems most fruitful.

    I. Infancy........................... from birth until four or five, when young
                                         children begin playing together

   II. Pre-school Childhood .... until children start to school at six

  III. Childhood .... the school years, until graduation from mid-
                                        dle school at about fifteen

  IV. Youth............................. early maturity and first regular work, until
                                        marriage in the early twenties

   V. Maturity .... the years of marriage, child-rearing, and
                                        greatest productive work, until about sixty

  VI. Old Age .... from the age of declining vigor and decreas-
                                        ing activity until death

Though none, with the possible exception of group IV, is an organized age-grade whose
membership is determined by passage rites and is compulsory at its age level, the existence of age groups at the active stages of life, i.e., III through V, is more positively
confirmed by their correlation with the bulk of age-mate sodalities. Matsunagi's sodalities
are, therefore, considered by successive age levels.

The first two age levels have no attributive sodalities, for at these ages the socializa-
tion process is only just begun. However, the whole of age level III was embraced until
1950 by a short-lived group, the Buddhist Children's Society (literally, Bathhouse Society,
o-furokai). It met once a month at the temple to hear tales of the Buddha and learn
sutras from the bonze; finally died from lack of interest.

Elementary school students comprise a loosely organized sodality, the main purpose of
which is self-improvement and public service. About twice a month they meet under school
sponsorship as the Free Speech Society (jiyu happyo-kai). The members demonstrate their
talents in things learned at school, and their performances are criticized by the group. The
society has a local chairman and vice-chairman, apparently chosen more for their leadership ability than for their social standing. Occasionally these children undertake some
service to the buraku, such as making a night fire-patrol or beautifying public places with
flowers. Both sexes participate about equally in meeting, but other activities are limited
mostly to boys.

Middle school students have a less active organization the principal function of which
is to be of service to the community in delivering newspapers and school notices. Its officers, a boy and a girl, are regularly the most popular individuals. Occasionally, middle

192

CHART 8

Changing Sodalities in Matsunagi*

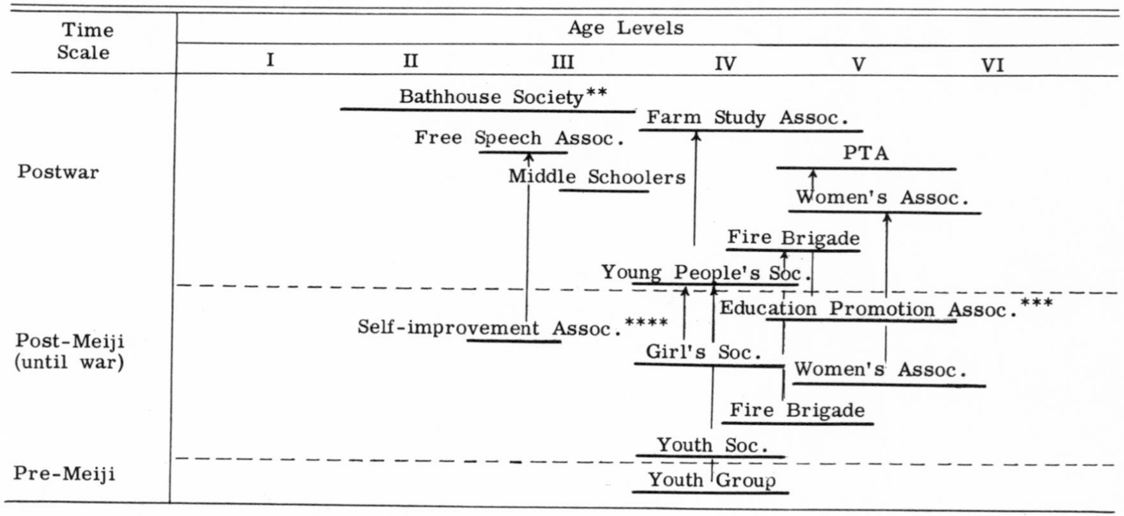

*Correlation of individual age with sodality membership is not exact. Neither does time scale illustrate the exact time relationship of each sodality to the others; all sodalities in a single era are, for practical purposes, contemporaneous. Arrows indicate continuity or change in the form of sodalities. The age levels (indicated by Roman numerals) are defined on p. 191.

**   indicates inclusive ages of individuals belonging to a sodality.

***Prewar parent-teacher organization.

****Prewar elementary students group.

school students gather in the "public hall" to play cards or chess during a rainy afternoon. But, on the whole, the activities of this group are extremely few.

Until the Meiji era, it was normal for a youth about ready to start work to enter the young men's group (wakashugumi). This association, known by various names in Japan, periodically met to spend the night in the house of some sympathetic man. There the members amused themselves, and from there they set forth on secret visits to the maidens of the community. The close companionship of this youth house and these nocturnal exploits accounted for much of the persistent strength of age-mate ties. The extinction of the "young men's group" organization and related practices is probably an important factor in the relative weakness of such ties today in Matsunagi. These days, a new member of the Young People's Society (seinendan), which is descended from the old wakashugumi, is formally introduced to his fellows at a meeting after the beginning of the year. After an exchange of bows, everyone drinks sake provided by equal assessment. Before the war, girls of this age belonged to a separate Girl's Society (joshi seinendan), which, like the men's group, was a mura-sponsored organization divided into buraku chapters.

Postwar social reforms have placed all young people in the same association, regardless of sex. The head of the local Young People's Society is a man, but nominally one of his assistants is a girl. Upon the head devolves much of the group responsibility; he is usually the only local person joining in the routine affairs of the larger mura organization. Almost all persons of this age join, but meetings are not regular. Service to the community is the keynote of its activities in the buraku, where the group has erected road markers, cleaned streams and assisted in handling equipment for local movie entertainment.

Interest in the Young People's Society is declining rapidly. In its place a new voluntary association, the Agricultural Study Society (nogyo kenkyu-kai) was formed in 1950. Besides the youths of the Young People's Society, it also includes several young married men. Its purpose is the study of modern agricultural science and its application to buraku farming. With official encouragement a whole hierarchy of such agricultural societies has appeared in Japan since the war, patterned on the American 4-H clubs.

Those persons who live outside for a time to continue their education or professional training do not normally belong to the youth sodalities of the buraku, nor do they of themselves constitute an organized group. Upper school students, for example, may see a good deal of each other at school in town, but this association is wholly informal.

The next stage of sodality membership comes with full maturity, when the young men join Matsunagi's fire brigade (shobodan), a part of a larger mura brigade. Mostly, the fire brigade is composed of those young married men who have left the Young People's Society. They are furnished uniforms and equipment by the mura, and meet once a year with fire fighters from other parts of the mura for an equipment inspection and a drinking party at the expense of the yakuba. The local fire brigade also serves the community by making nightly fire patrols just before the new year, when people are careless of fire, or by providing protection against thieves when many houses are left unwatched during a theatrical performance.

All mature women, i.e., housewives, belong to the Women's Society (fujin-kai), though by no means all are active in it. This is also a mura organization with buraku chapters, and in Matsunagi meetings by jokai units are held each month, unless the press of work interferes, to consider problems of household and family life. Few women other than two officers selected in each jokai attend the semi-annual general meetings for the mura. It is partly the demands of work and partly their husbands' objections that keep women away. Locally, the Women's Society also donates public services, such as sponsoring a movie during the Bon period.[21]

Since the war, a parent-teacher organization has come into being. This closely imi-
tates the American P.T.A. in form but actually has roots in a prewar native organization.
In 1950, it became the P.T.A. Association (pi-chii-ei-kai) with buraku chapters for both
its elementary and middle school divisions. The parents of students of both schools are
members, but, as in all semi-official sodalities, officers are chosen to take the burden
off the others in outside contacts, especially with school officials. The primary function
of the organization, like that of the corresponding prewar group, is to raise money for
needed school equipment. Except among the more public-spirited households, though, there
is little local interest in it.

Gift-giving Relations in Buraku· Life

Gift-giving is fundamentally a question of studied reciprocity. Most gift-giving does
not involve simultaneous exchange; one accepts a gift with the expectation that he will give
back the same amount when situations are reversed. The bond of indebtedness or obligation that results from gift-giving is governed by the requirement that insofar as possible
repayment must be an exact measure of the debt. The various forms of reciprocal gift-
giving are a particularly important factor inside the buraku in drawing together its social
elements.

Gift exchange is by and large a function of households, not individuals. When two or
three weeks after birth, the child is introduced to its relatives and shinrui, each guest at
this natal party brings a money gift, and very close relatives and the parents' go-between
bring new kimonos for the baby. The real significance of these gifts is to congratulate the
infant's household, so they are all subject to later reciprocation.

The most extravagant presentations are occasioned by a wedding; the betrothal gift
(yuino) is the most elaborate of these. In contrast, personal gifts to a bride or groom
from close relatives or friends, which are customary, are not carefully evaluated with a
view to making a return gift of equal scale. A record is kept of all gifts received by a
household. By consulting this record, it is at once clear how large a present must be
when the time comes to make repayment.

Today, a giver needs a rather special incentive to proffer gifts of rice or store-bought
goods rather than money. For example, gifts of rice survive in the form of discs of
mochi (kagami-mochi) when visiting outside relatives to see a performance of the celebrated
Bitchu mime (kagura). There are fewer gifts of clothing now than formerly; even natal
kimonos are presented only to the first-born in each conjugal family. Also, the custom of
offering a good kimono of the deceased to the temple bonze after a funeral has disappeared.

Most gifts of felicitation or sympathy, two of the most important categories, are in the
nature of token presentations. On the whole, congratulatory gifts are of greater intrinsic
value than those of sympathy. The largest funerary gifts (o-kuyami) are brought by close
relatives of the dead, who contribute a few hundred yen and a measure (one sho) of polished rice. Most o-kuyami are small sums of money, twenty to thirty yen each. Token
gifts of money (o-mimai) are also offered in event of illness or if some calamity like fire
strikes a relative or neighbor. When someone is sick, the money may be accompanied by
a special dish to please the palate of the invalid.

On the other hand, gratuities (o-rei) meant as return for a service usually have the
force of economic payment when a similar service is not possible in return. With few ex-
ceptions such payments are made in money. It is considered more delicate to pay with a
gratuity for such non-commercial services as given by the bonze, a Shinto ritualist, or the
intermediary who negotiates the sale of a piece of land; the customary amount is handed

over sight unseen, which avoids the distasteful problem of discussing money arrangements. A Shinto ritualist usually receives his gratuity once his ritual is completed, but the bonze may not be given anything for ancestral rites at Bon until the following New Year's. In addition to a fixed honorarium, a hairdresser attending the bride at a wedding is given a gratuity, about half again as much as her basic fee. A man living at the foot of the Kusama plateau but working in the yakuba above keeps his bicycle at a homestead near the top of the slope so he can ride to work once he reaches the tableland; he gives this Matsunagi household a gratuity for this favor. The land on which the communal grain mill stands is owned by two local households, which receive a supply of mugi twice a year from the mill's owners in appreciation for use of this land. Such periodic gratuities fall by custom at New Year's, or Bon, or both.

Buraku Ties of Hospitality

Most social gatherings in the community are situations requiring hospitality, and every visitor, however impromptu his call, is a potential guest (see Table 4). What is the nature of this hospitality? In what ways are guests entertained? First of all, hospitality is a relationship between a household group and other households or outside individuals. Secondly, it focuses on serving refreshments, widely varying in kind and cost of preparation. Thirdly, when the occasion is sufficiently important to have entertainment, it is provided by the guests themselves, who sing and dance. The latter type of guests are never unexpected visitors; they are entertained either to acknowledge previous economic assistance, to observe some family ceremonial event, or to fulfill obligations shared equally with all members of an association.

There is little visiting in the buraku without specific purpose, in most cases some practical or business matter. While a total stranger or an unknown peddler is not usually offered anything, a familiar itinerant merchant is invited to sit a moment in the kitchen or step to the hearth to warm himself and have some tea. If the household is at a meal, a casual visitor is given tea but not normally invited to partake of the food.

Most callers announce themselves at the kitchen door by a shouted greeting "excuse me," but do not enter the doma, or kitchen foyer, until someone's head is quizzically thrust from behind the nearest panel or an answering shout is heard from inside. In the summer, however, a caller may be received on the veranda rather than in the dark kitchen. Often it is the housewife who receives him. But if he is to be invited to sit with the group about the irori, the household head, if present, will proffer the invitation. Having mounted the kitchen platform, the caller greets those present with a low bow executed on hands and knees and a few mumbled commonplaces. In warm weather a strip of reed matting may be spread at the edge of the platform for him, since the irori fire is rarely lit then. For most callers refreshments needing little or no preparation are brought out. The basic token of hospitality is tea and a sweet (chagashi), the latter often being dried persimmons or dried squid. For out-of-the-ordinary visitors, sake may be served instead of tea.

When householders of the community gather on business, the host provides only a site for their meeting. More frequently these days, however, both meetings of householders and of sodalities take place in a public building to avoid this burden on a private household. When a householder takes his turn on a rotating roster as host (yado) to an association, he follows the precedents of the group in planning his hospitality. Since ordinarily the group shares expenses equally, no one wants to be regaled extravagantly. In most cases, refreshments are only sake and an appetizer.

As a rule, weddings are the most outstanding family and household events which require some form of exceptional hospitality provided wholly by the host. Other prominent

TABLE 4

FORMS OF HOSPITALITY IN MATSUNAGI

	Type of Hospitality	Occasion		Kind of Guests
Scheduled	Formal banquet (gochiso); large-scale	Irregularly at times of household and family crises	Invited	Large number of house-hold representatives; all relatives (including shin-rui), as well as undif-ferentiated coresident households
	Special-dish feast (chigatta mono); medium to small-scale	Periodically or irregu-larly, including: 1. Household and family crises 2. Cooperative work calls 3. Kumi-rotating host responsi-bility		Many or few household representatives; related (including shinrui) house-holds on occasions 1 and 2, non-relative coresi-dents on occasions 2 and 3 (see middle column)
	Drinking party (o-sake); medium to small-scale	Occasions 1 and 2, above		Moderate number or few household representa-tives; largely shinrui and coresident non-relatives
Unscheduled	Tea (o-cha); very small-scale	Chance or indefinite visits or calls	Uninvited	Mostly individuals, as such, or small groups of companions, some unrelated coresidents, but most from outside the buraku

occasions include funerals, important birthday celebrations, visits of kinsmen at New Year's, and the presentation of a new child to its kin. But, in fact, for many of these events only one or two out-of-the-ordinary dishes need be prepared. Weddings aside, most people are inclined to minimize their outlay, especially when relatives are guests. When something as unusual as a formal feast (gochiso) is given, it generally marks an event of extraordinary economic or ceremonial significance.

No one is prosperous enough to bear the expense of a formal feast as regularly as folk custom demands, so community opinion condones simplification. Feasting in Matsu-nagi is obviously on a more modest scale than in the comparable community of Higashi-mura. Where in Higashimura people would give a gochiso, in Matsunagi a simple drink-ing party usually suffices. But parties may be as simple or as painstakingly and expen-sively prepared as the host feels requisite, and in size may range from five or six guests to over a hundred. The hospitality of a gochiso, most of all, may be reckoned a specialized and elaborated form of gift-giving. Invited guests are expected to bring some sort of present to the host, a small sum of money in a white paper wrapper, or a bottle of sake. When a householder is the sole host, he obligates his guests directly to him much as he does in gift-giving, but when an affair is sponsored by several, credit does not accrue to anyone in particular.

A classic gochiso is marked by formality of seating arrangements, high quality of utensils used, and the large variety of foods served, truly the apogee of local culinary efforts.[22] Such a feast requires the assistance of relatives and neighbors for as much as two days in advance. Early guests lounge in the front parlors and are served gohan and relish to stave off hunger until the banquet proper can begin. It is expected that guests will be slow in arriving, but when most are present, the host prevails on each, who displays much diffidence, to take his seat. In the main, age is given precedence in seating.

A bolster and a short-legged lacquer tray to hold dishes are at each place. The dishes and trays are the very best dining equipment the household possesses. Four or five containers, generally of lacquered wood, rest on each tray. One of them is a covered dish for fish broth, and beside it is a small dish of burdock slivers and another plate with soured rice (sushi) wrapped in seaweed, slices of raw fish (sashimi), and a whole baked fish. Sometimes, as a special treat, there are store-bought pastries with a sweetened cream filler, mochi or dango cakes, and sweet potato and giant radish cut in decorative shapes. All this food is cold when served. On the tray nearest the diner, are a pair of chopsticks and a sake cup turned over. A small plate rests on the floor mats to the right of the tray; this is for appetizers, which are usually nothing more than shredded radish and boiled soybeans. Large bowls of these appetizers are passed around the company during the drinking.

When all are seated, the host assumes his place in the middle of the room. He takes up his cup, into which the person serving, usually an adolescent daughter, pours the first drink. The host drinks this initial cup as a signal that the affair has begun. One or two women commence serving sake to the lines of guests, beginning with the most honored. Each guest murmurs a formal word of thanks to the host and turns, inviting his neighbor to have a cup also.

General drinking breaks out at this point, and servers are kept busy rushing about the square of guests with their large jugs of sake. Soon, in the general conviviality, everyone begins to hand cups back and forth, exchanging drinks, a common Japanese gesture of friendship. Except for a plateful or two of appetizer and the cold soup, food on the tray is almost untouched. It will be wrapped in newspaper at the end of the feast and carried home to lesser household members, who may not attend.

At a feast, say, following some major construction, the carpenter, who as the most honored guest is seated in the most prominent place, before the tokonoma,[23] is expected to lead off the singing. Consequently a good voice and a wide repertoire are important in his line of work. When the festivity is at its climax, someone feeling very gay may come to the middle of the room to dance the pantomime of catching mudfish in a flooded paddy, snatching up a tray as his make-believe net. Many, if not most, of the men's songs have sexual implications, and some may be downright salacious. Even children, who are permitted to listen quietly from the kitchen, act as though they comprehend and are amused by what they hear. Those men who stop after three or four cups of liquor retire to the kitchen to sit at the hearth and drink tea, but the young and the powerful drinkers do not depart until the small hours of morning.

Popular Social Amusements

In social singing men with good, durable voices are singled out for admiration by their fellows. Non-singers make no pretense of learning the old songs well, but skilled singers memorize a great many, for they know they may be called on to perform on any social occasion where there is drinking. All songs are sung to a few familiar tunes, commonest of which are Yasukibushi and Iso-ondo. The words also are usually old and popular rather than impromptu. Rhythm is maintained by clapping hands in unison or by beating a barrel drum. The singing lead may be snatched at will by anyone who has a favorite song he wants to sing, the rest joining in a chorus of nonsense syllables that separate verses. Most of the skill in folk singing lies in controlling the glottis and diaphragm rather than the tongue and lips, to produce a falsetto effect. As man gets older, he avoids the strain of singing, in part because there is a fairly positive correlation between heavy drinking and this skill.

Heavy consumption of alcoholic beverages is an important feature of sociability in Matsunagi, where the climate is cold and life is comparatively hard.[24] Drinking is freely admitted to be the primary local recreation. Three principal types of beverages are consumed: these are (1) true sake, or fermented rice wine; (2) shochu, a poorer grade of distilled rice wine; and (3) doburoku, a mash-fermented drink. Much of these intoxicants is supplied by illegal producers, primarily Koreans living in Ikura, who make cheap liquor of potatoes rather than rice or barley. Indeed, Matsunagi folk prefer the illicit product, which is stronger than licensed spirits. Foreign beverages, like beer and whiskey, are not popular since they are expensive and hard to come by except in town. Drunkenness is quite common at men's parties, but it does not often result in unpleasantness or quarreling, for almost any sort of foolish behavior under the influence of alcohol can be overlooked.

Drinking nearly always brings individuals or households into closer communal association. Alcohol dispels the tensions and inhibitions that normally surround interpersonal relationships. Songs of a sexual nature can be sung only when liquor has dulled one's sense of propriety. Women, properly speaking, should never drink, but several in the buraku are reputed to do so more or less regularly. Women and children are often given a sweet, thick liquid of fermented rice and sugar instead of strong spirits. Young men, three or four years out of middle school, are expected to attend parties, learning to drink as they learn to sing drinking songs. Though in some households men drink a little at each evening meal, the only liquor kept in most kitchens is a large bottle of shochu for the reception of casual guests. Also, on a tobacco delivery day, men may conclude their business by having a drink with friends and neighbors at one of the road-stalls set up for the public near the tobacco warehouse. But it is rare for a man alone to stop in town for a drink, even after he has finished all his business.

Among the pleasures of life, tobacco is almost as important as drink. Most young men begin to smoke in their early twenties. An old grandmother's venerable years may permit her the liberty of smoking openly, but younger women do it openly with peril. The fear of ridicule keeps women from smoking, just as it keeps them from drinking.

Men carry a small-bowled pipe of brass or pewter with a bamboo stem, usually suspended from the belt in a case. This pipe holds only enough cut tobacco for one or two puffs, and so, once lit, is repeatedly lighted with embers knocked from the bowl instead of a match or a hearth coal. Cigarettes are used by younger men as well as by most women who indulge, but these are only of the very cheapest commercial brand. Even then, they cost more than store-bought cut tobacco. Consequently, domestic use of illicitly withheld tobacco is very common in this area. Smoking is the major accompaniment of conversation in the brief respites in daily work which, for this reason, are called "tobacco" (tabako).

Singing, drinking, and smoking are major local pastimes in which self-entertainment is the theme. While parties and other less formal social occasions which occur all through the year constitute the bulk of popular recreation, entertainment to which the folk can come as passive spectators is far more memorable. For instance, on one occasion since the war the more gifted thespians among the younger men offered a theatrical performance, one of the undistinguished Tokugawa period pieces which are so well received in rural Japan. Families gathered at the temple for this program, bringing their own food, while temple funds were used to buy sake for all.

But for more diversified amusements, it is usually necessary to go outside. In early winter, people are attracted by a mime, or kagura, in a nearby buraku. A troupe of kagura players, usually residents of a neighboring upland mura, is engaged by a committee on arrangements in the sponsoring community, who also designate and make ready one house as a mime theater. Matsunagi sponsored a kagura last in 1945. Many outside guests, even children, are in attendance when the curtain goes up at dusk. For most of the night they enjoy the spectacle of brilliantly costumed performers reenacting the story of the legendary conquest of Izumo. Spectators bring jugs of sake to provide warmth during the night, for the chilling December breezes blow unimpeded through the house. About midnight, there is an intermission, so that people can eat the lunches they have brought along. The second half of the kagura continues on nearly till dawn.

Outside spectators are obliged to give money gifts (o-hana) to the sponsors, the amount depending on one's financial position. A committee official writes the amount and the donor's name on a piece of paper, fastening it on a house lintel for all to see. In this way, rather than by paying admission, the expenses of any such public performance are shared by all who attend. But spectators do not return empty-handed. At one point in the drama, the god of riches, Daikoku, appears and bursts open a straw cylinder filled with pieces of mochi, which he casts, to the audience. All who catch them are said to be assured of good fortune during the ensuing year.

In spring and autumn each year, companies of itinerant players of the popular theater can be counted on to appear in the mura, probably under the aegis of some buraku in the oaza. Expecting to draw a large crowd from all over the mura, the sponsors may set up an outdoor stage in the courtyard of the oaza shrine, and thus show a profit in their community fund from the o-hana of many spectators. Such theatricals are probably fewer today than half a century ago, when traveling players made one-night stands here to present such classics as the Chushingura and the Taikoki.[25] But today's drama is performed on the same traditional native stage with a runway leading onto it. The stage is covered with a hand-drawn curtain bearing commercial advertisements. All of the properties set up for the actors are made by the seinendan of the host buraku. Those attending take along their evening meal to eat while waiting for the entertainment to begin at sunset.

The behavior of the audience is very similar to that at kagura, for about midnight there is an intermission which permits a late snack to be eaten. Nowadays some of the pieces given are in the modern vein, including portrayals of romantic love with such warmth that they bring low embarrassed laughter from the crowd. Most plays are still set in the Tokugawa era and range in emotional effect from bravado to deep pathos. The audience never seems to lose interest, even though the program continues until the early morning hours.

Other sorts of amusements offered in the vicinity include the opportunity of seeing or participating in the annual school field meet, or Bon dancing, either at the schoolyard or in some buraku close by. Then too, Matsunagi people seem to find cattle auctions or tobacco delivery days equally entertaining to watch. Older men, like to avail themselves of occasional presentations of dramatic singing in the style called Naniwabushi,[26] or matches of Japanese wrestling.

A cooperative group of men from a funeral <u>kumi</u> help bring in the crops of a household in mourning.

A group of cooperating neighbors and relatives help raise the frame of a new tobacco curing shed.

A <u>kumi</u> of neighbor households <u>assists</u> professional roof-thatchers (at top) in repairing a house roof.

One member of an informal threshing kumi threshes his winter grain with the help of kumi neighbors.

Members of a mochi cooperative group, in rotating order, pound the white mochi in the wooden mortar in front of them.

While the menfolk pound the dough, the women · work the mochi into cakes to be stored for future use.

Since the war, there has been a growing interest in the American style of popular music among young people. This interest was shown in 1951, for example, in a variety show sponsored by the Young People's Society of the mura, in which a hired band played Japanese versions of the fox-trot and other jazz-style musical forms. But singing modern, popular songs does not require the peculiar skill that is needed for native style singing, and therefore has achieved no social standing in the buraku. Once a year, another variety program, partly native and partly western in content, is presented by elementary and middle school students; Matsunagi people usually attend this in family groups, all being anxious to see their children demonstrate accomplishments in singing, dancing, or recitation.

Among the amusements available in the town and city, moving pictures is a form that is known to all active ages in Matsunagi, but with the exception of those who attend school in Niimi or Takahashi, few have many opportunities to see them. Brothels, dance halls, and bars in town have very little appeal both because they are too expensive and because they are not considered very respectable. Some young men may go to square dances given by the Young People's Society, but none would think of engaging in social dancing in town, even should it be sponsored by such a reputable institution as the upper school there. In the spring, there are agricultural fairs, displays of crops and new machinery in Okayama. Some may visit the city to shop at a department store, or take the children to see a live elephant at the children's fair in the park.

During slack seasons, especially the holiday season in March, children and an escorting adult or two may go on picnics into the forest. In April, on the rest day called "metal taboo," people plan pleasure trips to Okayama, or to such points of interest as a limestone cave, a celebrated mountain-top temple, or a new dam rising on an interior river. Various famous shrines within a day's travel of Matsunagi may also attract excursionists.

In leisure hours at home, adults, especially mature, older men, play such native games as Japanese chess and a simplified version of the national game of go. Younger people play a sort of whist bridge, and from time to time may even put small wagers on the hands. But there is no regular gambling in or around the buraku. Though school girls sometimes play cards with each other, women never seem to have time for games.

Children have an indoor card game, which consists of matching pictures, like the American game of Old Maid. Outdoors, where most play time is spent, they engage in patchi, casting pasteboard cards at the ground in an attempt to overturn other cards lying there. School girls spend their time in jumping rope, bouncing balls, throwing bean bags, and playing a kind of jumping game that uses a taut elastic band instead of a rope. Most of these are done to the rhythm of familiar children's songs. School boys amuse themselves walking on bamboo stilts, catching birds in home-made snares, and fishing with line in a stream; they are equally fond of ping-pong and baseball. Though play equipment is scarce, there are a few bats, balls, and even gloves among the school boy population. They find time for baseball when they take cattle to pasture in Ikurakoge, and have even formed a team to play other buraku. An older boy or two owns skis, which he may find time to use in the skiing grounds of the central mountain range. The few other children who have them use home-made ones of bamboo. As a matter of fact, most toys and game equipment are made domestically.

Interpersonal Relations and Social Control

In the routine personal relations of buraku life, most norms of Japanese conversational etiquette are observed. Each day one greets his fellows once in the morning and again toward evening with a different stereotyped formula expressing the time of day, punctuating his salutation with a slight bobbing of the head.   At other times, a passerby may say to someone toiling in the fields, "I sympathize with you," or "It is very warm for you, isn't it?"   Children greet all adults with "I'm back," to which the spontaneous response is "Welcome back."   When encountering someone of slight acquaintance or of much superior rank, a somewhat more elegant salutation is used and the conversation limited to a few pleasantries on the weather.   Formal greetings exchanged indoors, particularly on the arrival of guests for a party, and the correctly formal manner in which a guest greets the company already assembled, are in marked contrast to the easy give and take thereafter. Since most people are acquainted with all those present, no one ever bothers to introduce a stranger, and after a few drinks any initial shyness is quickly forgotten.

In speaking to or about one's buraku fellows, the commonest designation is the house-name (yago), of which each household has its own unique form.[27]   Though legal surnames have supplanted yago for identification in official and public matters, yago still constitute an important part of popular usage in the community, and are generally combined with a kinship term.   Thus, an old man of the household named "before the shrine" (miyanomae) is called "grandfather of [the house] before the shrine" (miyanomae ojiisan).   This is not as formal, but equally as polite as a modern surname.   As residents of the same community, people may also use relationship terms alone for each other, much as they might for blood relatives, e.g., "older sister," "aunt," or "uncle."

In ordinary conversation, joking between equals is considered proper, provided it stops short of public humiliation.   Young men in particular joke with each other about some peripheral skill, such as singing, and about sexual matters, but it would be an indelicate offense to make sport of someone's ability as a farmer, his clothing, or his household's property.   Another joking taboo is that the old must not be teased.   No one, though, minds deriding himself or his group a little, perhaps with a jibe about how homely women are as compared to men.   Sexual jokes are often heard at drinking parties but they are most in order at a wedding.   The groom is the butt of much good-natured chaffing, largely from the older men.   Bantering between the sexes, except among siblings, is not regarded with favor.   Sex play is likewise suppressed, though a man in his cups will be forgiven if he approaches someone else's wife in a spirit of clowning.

Interpersonal contacts during the course of each day are numerous, and, at least on the surface, usually harmonious.   There is little thought of avoiding another just because of some earlier unpleasantness or friction.[28]   When there are quarrels between individuals though, they usually turn into quarrels between households.   A quarrel begins with an incident, comes to a climax in a scene of open brawling, and then subsides into weakening undercurrents of resentment, after the tension has been broken by this face-to-face outburst.

There is a high correlation between public disfavor of an individual and the degree to which he has violated approved patterns of behavior.   Theft and adultery produce the most serious social disturbances, but profligacy, indolence, extreme self-interest, and idle gossip also contribute a goodly share.

To illustrate, a man who had been absent for some years as a prisoner-of-war learned after his return that his wife had had an affair with another local man who had considerable reputation for this sort of behavior.   The husband confronted his wife's paramour and blows were exchanged; this incident resolved the quarrel and no grudges were borne on either side.   The wife, however, was forced to withdraw from public affairs as much as possible because of extreme embarrassment at general knowledge of her indiscretion.   In another case, a household refused to return payment received for a pig sold to one man but, before delivery, resold to another at a higher price.   The original buyer called to get his money or the pig, and there were blows, both sides claiming to have been wilfully assaulted. But the furor soon died out of its own accord.

More serious troubles have also occurred in Matsunagi. More than two decades ago, a buraku resident killed his nephew in a quarrel over inheritance rights, which the nephew tried to repossess after selling them to the uncle. The murderer and his brother, also living in the community today, were exposed through indiscreet talk of the former's wife. The murderer, after spending several years in prison, returned to the buraku, where he has been accepted without serious prejudice.

Suspicion of thievery is pointed at one or two households, but, should there be proof, it is unlikely that any course other than requesting the return of the stolen goods would be taken. Other social tensions are attributable to the ruthless and selfish domination of one or two women over their households, which draws general disapproval. Though one has the impression that the young adults of today are far more docile than their elders, the level of social friction beneath the surface in Matsunagi is still high, particularly as compared with the Okayama coastal plain.[29]

Friction in the community, by and large, is controlled by communal, i.e., extra-legal, means. Whatever may be said about the prevalence of social disturbances, it is always true that the community as a whole wants to keep disharmony to a minimum. To do this, there must be agreed points at which the group takes concerted action, as well as a consistent code of behavior when faced by a potential threat to public peace and private prerogatives. Events as innocuous as a dog killing a neighbor's rabbit, or someone's untended cow eating another's growing sweet corn, of course irritate and strain community harmony. But, while he may mention the loss to a third party, the damaged householder never alludes to it directly, or, by intention, indirectly to the owner of the animal. But should the innocent transgressor learn of his offense, he will doubtless go at once to apologize and offer compensation. And like as not, no amends will be needed, other than this gesture of good faith. Face-to-face with an embarrassing or otherwise trying situation, the person who, as the Japanese say, "knows etiquette" will accept it with good grace, striving not to betray his distress. A man who subjects his fellows to such embarrassment has probably done so before and therefore surprises no one; he is tolerated but never respected.

When there is a question as to whether or not an offender is responsible for his acts, the community tends to be lenient. A young man below average in mentality has a long record of stealing. Buraku people are likely not to report his thefts if their goods are returned, because of his apparent kleptomania and the possibility that further imprisonment for him would be permanent. Again, the quality of "human feeling" (ninjo) comes into play where there is good reason to believe that the culprit is not competent to judge his acts. It is fear of the consequences of notoriety, not so much to the thief's household but to the life of the buraku itself that is most effective in covering up theft.

Gossip is a weapon of social control. But idle talk, the habit of talking about the private affairs of others to outsiders especially, is a persistent cause of friction also. Most people do not willingly talk about their own neighbors and fellow residents except to stop idle gossip. A gossip who violates this rule is usually ridiculed behind his back, but soon this loss of community status reaches his ears by the same grapevine, very often chastening him into mending his ways.

Even very personal matters are not concealed from this efficient system of local gossip; adultery and seduction are public knowledge not long after they happen, but provoke amusement and ridicule rather than outrage. Ridicule, indeed, goes so far as to maintain the proper respect relationship with both local persons and outsiders of higher rank; a buraku farmer avoids breaking the code of behavior toward superior statuses in the society in order to avoid being laughed at.

When disciplinary gossip and ridicule fail to stop an offender, sterner measures must be tried. Isolation or ostracism are directed against inveterate offenders, and ultimately against their households as well. In one case a man with a long past of heavy drinking, gambling, and brawling, found it convenient, after his original house fell apart from disrepair, to move to a vacant satellite homestead, where he is largely ignored. A decade or so ago, another household of this type which had caused a series of irritations in one jokai, finally capped the climax in disregarding a compulsory rest day in the spring by raising a new barn. A further injury to conventions occurred when the householder called only his intimates to assist him, instead of inviting all the jokai as is customary. The jokai met and determined to cast this household from its ranks. Fortunately for him, the offender had such strong ties in the other jokai that he was readily admitted to it.

If at all possible, the community refrains from severing ties or exposing wrongdoing, because private relationships with the malefactor's household would also be profoundly affected or broken. Resistance to communal action is generally futile. For, as in Hearn's able observation, " . . . only a very rash man will invoke the new law against the communal judgment, for that action in itself would be condemned as a gross breach of custom."[30]

On the other hand, external agents such as the mura constabulary are not highly regarded as mediators of buraku conflict. First of all, a constable is an outsider, not even a permanent resident of the mura. Secondly, he represents law, which buraku folk do not understand well and distrust. Therefore, even when an outsider who has suffered wrongs through someone in the buraku calls in the constable, the latter usually has no objection if the affair is settled quietly without recourse to law. Though they fear the inequities of the law, the people of Matsunagi trust the judgment of their group to provide justice without undue damage to the wrongdoer's household and its social relations.

Notes

1. See Chart 5, which is a diagrammatic representation of the administrative structure of Matsunagi.

2. The election of jokai officials is in March, which every fourth year comes just before the mura elections for mayor and councillors.

3. This type of association was imposed on rural Japan by the military dictator Hideyoshi toward the end of the 16th century. About 1928, when Matsunagi split in two divisions, the present system of goningumi is thought to have been set up. Since the end of the war, one of the three original goningumi in Mae has split in two parts as a result of an increase in the number of households in its area. Ushiro, being smaller and more close-knit, has only weakly developed goningumi, which are not regularly identified by name like those in Mae.

4. Representative of the latter events are "rain-making" rites (amagoi) in drought years and the kagura mimes, or epic play, which a buraku might sponsor every few years. Unfortunately, limitations of space permit only a bare mention of these important community festivals.

5. Embree, op. cit., p. 79

6. Of nine such groups, only three are active enough to resemble the classic feudal pattern of obligations between a stem house and its branches. These groups are illustrated in Figure 2.

7. Ten sets of markedly interdependent households, which are considered shinrui, have been selected for demonstration (see Figure 2), the criteria being frequent exchange of equipment, goods, and labor. These household groups are numbered on the map figure as follows:

a. 3-5-6-7-8   f. 13-18
b. 14-17   g. 23-25
c. 15-16-17   h. 19-20-24-27
d. 12-13-15   i. 31-32-33
e. 17-19   j. 34-35-36

Note that these groups are not all mutually exclusive.

8. In Chugoku itself this kind of kinship appears to be rare. One of the best summary statements of distribution of types of community social organization in rural Japan is Seiichi Izumi and Tadao Urau, "Regionalism in Japanese Society," Nippon Chiri Shintaikei (New Geographical Encyclopedia of Japan), No. 2 (Sociology and Economics), 1952, pp. 37-73 (in Japanese); see especially pp. 44, 71-73. The authors ascribe this particular kind of kinship to much of northern Honshu and characterize Chugoku social organization as composed of associations of equals lacking a kinship orientation.

9. The Japanese word shinrui is used in our analysis to differentiate kinship by residence from consanguineal and affinal kinship; Matsunagi people, however, make no such linguistic distinction.

10. A very common practice is to call on some person of a related household to serve in this capacity, which avoids creating an entirely new tie. But it does not avoid the usual amenities due between benefactor and recipient of benefits.

11. They closely correspond to the three traditional neighborhoods of Mae, one of which is combined with the adjacent eastern area of Ushiro (see Figure 1). The final neighborhood and play area is located in the western part of Ushiro.

12. Kumi (literally: "group") is often translated "cooperative" or "association." It may refer to goningumi, buraku, or any of a large number of associations of households, smaller and more specialized than a buraku. "Voluntary" here carries the sense of spontaneous; for similar usage, see R. E. Lowie, Social Organization (New York, 1948), p. 12.

13. Yanagida observes that among mountain villages the practice of apportioning common land for fuel is rather widespread, though the manner of distributing plots is not usually left to chance as in Matsunagi. Timber, green fertilizer, and other forest products may be shared in the same way. See Yanagida, Sanson Seikatsu no Kenkyu, pp. 133-134.

14. The kumi in Mae was created in 1935, and that in Ushiro in 1945.

15. Since the war, six of the original seventeen households owning communal machines in Mae have begun to use their own private machines, thus reducing the number of work kumi in that jokai from four to three.

16. Until the Tokugawa regime rationalized the Japanese social system, pariahs of this sort seem to have been combined with the basest group of all, the eta. Though Chugoku is a center of pariah settlement (in the more populous areas, depressed groups live in ghettoes adjacent to ordinary settlements), very few are found in the vicinity of Kusama. More complete information on these pariahs is available in English in S. Ninomiya, "An Inquiry Concerning the Origin, Development and Present Situation of the Eta in Relation to the History of Social Classes in Japan," Transactions of the Asiatic Society of Japan, X (1933).

17. In selecting a mate, avoidance of one with a family background of leprosy, as well as a pariah origin, is of paramount importance.

18. Buraku wage-earners may be assigned to the following categories: lumberjack, sawyer, charcoal-burner, carpenter, cooper, geta-maker, laborer (farm and factory), peddler, Buddhist priest, school teacher, cooperative executive, yakuba clerk, postmaster, and postal carrier.

19. Factory labor, too, does not fit into the local economic and occupational picture, and so it is difficult to rate. One such worker is seasonally employed at the rape seed oil factory in the mura, while a few others work away in urban factories all the year around. These are known as dekasegi, those who maintain legal residence in the buraku but move to the cities to work and live.

20. This term is used in the sense of an association of individuals brought together "irrespective of whether they belong to the same family, clan, or territorial group. . ." Lowie, op. cit., p. 309.

21. In Matsunagi, and throughout Kusama, the fujin-kai raises funds by handling the collection of electric bills for the public power company.

22. See Embree, op. cit., pp. 99-104, for a more complete description of this type of social affair.

23. The same position always goes to the leading craftsman, e.g., the senior roof-thatcher at a party celebrating the completion of roof repairs.

24. Nishikiori in his study of a village in the northern prefecture of Yamagata observes: "The custom of drinking is very prevalent not only in this village, but also in Tohoku districts at large [sic]. It is considered as indispensable to a region where it is cold." Op. cit., p. 50.

25. The former is the famous "Tale of the Forty-Seven Ronin," and the latter depicts the life of the 16th century dictator of Japan, Hideyoshi, a popular national hero.

26. All of the traditional theatrical forms presented in the mura are popular rather than aristocratic in origin. Naniwabushi is a style of narrative singing dealing with the lives of the common people in the Tokugawa period.

27. Most of these yago are derived from the relative location of a homestead to the heart of the main buraku settlement, or from the name of the district (aza) in which it is situated. Formerly, before the ordinary peasants adopted surnames in early Meiji times, the official and popular practice was to use yago for identification just as surnames are used today.

28. This feature of behavior seems to be representative of a cultural theme enunciated by Embree: "The pattern of avoidance of face-to-face relations of embarrassment." See "The People," Japan (Ithaca, N.Y., 1951), p. 26.

29. The author experienced a much milder sort of temperament in Niike, a community in the lowland being studied by University of Michigan researchers. This impression was also borne out by comments of Okayama Japanese.

30. L. Hearn, Japan: An Attempt at Interpretation (New York, 1904), p. 117.

Chapter V

EXTERNAL RELATIONS IN THE CULTURAL MILIEU

Matsunagi is about as large and as homogeneous as a socially isolated and culturally independent tribal group; yet Matsunagi patently exists on a higher cultural level than a small tribal unit, largely because of its external connections. It is almost axiomatic that village society in Japan, and particularly a natural community like Matsunagi, cannot be fully comprehended without some knowledge of additional factors and active influences conditioned by the cultural traditions of the nation. Matsunagi's native folk qualities are tempered by the broader relations of trade, travel, sojourning, and communication.

When reduced to those elements that are firmly a part of community life, the folk mold of Matsunagi seems to be almost unaltered by outside forces. In spite of numerous and varied modern accretions, the buraku's socio-cultural configuration, situated in the Japanese cultural milieu, basically agrees with Kroeber's definition of a folk culture:

> A characteristic folk culture . . . belongs to a small, isolated, close-knit society, in which person-to-person relations are prevalent, kinship is a dominant factor, and organization, both societal and cultural, is therefore largely on a basis of kinship. . . . By contrast, political institutions are weakly developed. . . . Folk cultures afford their individual members full participation in their functioning . . . . The relatively small range of their culture content, the close-knitness of the participation in it, the very limitation of scope, all make for a sharpness of pattern in the culture . . . . Narrowness, depth, and intensity are the qualities of folk cultures.[1]

The physical, total cultural, and political contexts that Matsunagi occupies are not all of equal importance. Broadly speaking, these contexts are: the nation and the state; the general region or an area somewhat larger than the prefecture; the Atetsu area and its environs; and the mura. Matsunagi is bound to the nation by ties of ethnic and political allegiance; to more restricted parts through kinship, direct contacts of trade, travel, and government. Let us define the cultural setting of Matsunagi and consider the nature of its external contacts.

The Buraku and the Nation

The Matsunagi folk are most conscious of the external forces at work in their own community in their relations with the state through local government, the schools, and commercial and production organizations (e.g., the Agricultural Cooperative, the Animal Husbandry Cooperative, the Tobacco Monopoly), which operate at buraku level. National affairs, while important, are strictly secondary to regional and local matters.

In the late thirties, the buraku erected a wooden flagpole near the center of the main settlement specifically to fly the national flag on holidays. When war came, households with men in service sent someone to the oaza shrine most mornings at sunrise to offer prayers for their safe return and the victory of the nation. The women of the Women's Association were organized to support the home front, to help the families of soldiers, to receive the ashes of military dead, to visit hospitals, etc. In these and other less well-remembered ways the people showed their patriotism.

During wartime their sensitivity to the nation was of course at its peak, but now it has declined so that Matsunagi people have a strong feeling of revulsion toward the wartime political regime and the militaristic policies that led Japan into World War II. Supression of prewar national holidays, fetes such as Empire Foundation Day or the death day of the Emperor Meiji, has meant little to the ceremonial life of the buraku. Nor have the new national holidays instituted since the war made any more impression on the community. Still, the people are fully aware of their national citizenship and of their relationship to the state and nation.

Probably the strongest emotion the Japanese nation felt at the close of the war was despair. This sense of defeat filtered down to the level of the buraku as well. Returning soldiers came home to very austere receptions; neighbors and relatives went out to greet the returnee along his road into the buraku, but his household could not celebrate his return with the customary drinking party because the desperate shortages of those days denied them even the makings of the rudest home-brew. Yet, graves of the war dead have been marked much more elaborately than ordinary graves, and memorial services in the mura are well attended by those who lost sons in the war. The wartime is little discussed in conversation even now, because, as one man put it, the embarrassment of defeat is the burden every Japanese bears. Not all buraku people are so acutely aware of belonging to the nation and not many can verbalize what they feel, but most of them sense a need to erase this national failure and loss of face, part of which is accomplished by not reminding themselves of their nation's inadequacy.

Surprisingly many of the young and more substantial citizens keep up with national and other external affairs. Politics—national, prefectural, and local—are continually of great interest. Buraku people consider themselves affiliated with one national political party or another when they vote in elections of prefectural or national significance. Prefectural politics are somewhat better understood and the qualifications of candidates, ranging up to governor, are known and discussed. Much of this interest, though, seems to have appeared since the war, after a system of direct election was instituted.

Mura Government and Politics

The mura is the arena for the bulk of the buraku's external relations and is the locus of its chief sources of economic assistance, such as the Agricultural Cooperative and the prefectural Veterinary Station. The mura has these functions vis-à-vis the buraku because it is the immediate unit of government and politics. Its governmental and political functions deserve separate attention.

The yakuba, or village office, is the heart of the political mura. Its personnel and administrative committees serve under and are supervised by the mura mayor, who also combines in himself the administrative authority of such mutual associations as the Health Cooperative and the Forestry Cooperative. The mayor must answer to an elected village council but if, as in Kusama, the chief executive is a strong leader, the council by and large serves as his tool.[2] Administrative mechanisms of the buraku itself are extra-legal, devised for liaison with the yakuba administration, in matters either originating in the yakuba itself or coming through from the prefectural or national governments. At the mura level, selection of administrative officials is accomplished in a vigorous election campaign every four years.

Mura politics are not waged in terms of parties but in terms of personalities and, more importantly, of old versus new Westernized ways of thinking. Much of the political conflict resolves into differences between those who are worldly and educated, and those of little outside experience and little sympathy with changes in the social system. Enthusiasm for the new is lodged in general with the younger men, but in both camps the leaders belong to households of considerable economic means. A resident of a buraku like Matsunagi

running for office is usually assured of the full support of his community. He is further
assured of the votes of all his circle of relatives throughout the mura. Indeed, the women,
who were enfranchised in 1946, and other voters in an average household usually follow
the lead of the household head in casting their ballots. No one is supposed to purposefully
influence another's vote, but buraku attitudes toward candidates inevitably become alike
through the exchange of opinions. Despite the normal disagreements and self-interest that
are found in the buraku at all times, the community shows remarkable solidarity behind its
own candidate, all differences for the moment being forgotten.

The campaign manager may well be a close relative of the candidate. Even those who
are not particularly warm toward him otherwise would not risk public censure by refusing
to cooperate in the campaign. Campaign helpers are sent out to canvass other buraku
where they have relatives. There they meet discreetly with sympathetic neighbors of these
relatives to discuss the election and the candidate.

A man does not declare himself a candidate for some high mura office unless he has
first explored the grassroots in each buraku to estimate what his chances are. An effective candidate for mayor represents a group of important leaders from all over the mura;
these support his candidacy in their respective localities, working as the candidate himself
does through relatives and close friends. In each buraku where he has strength some man
agrees to serve as his contact, to keep a finger on the political pulse and report fluctua-
tions to headquarters. Campaign funds normally are supplied by the candidate himself,
but in fact contributions are also raised in money or in farm products from among the
households of his buraku.[3]

The more formal aspects of a campaign, such as political speeches and posters, are
of little importance in mura politics, though they are used extensively in prefectural campaigns. Very few persons, however, are interested enough in politics outside the mura to
attend the electioneering meetings held at the school during a prefectural campaign.

External Kin Relations

Though in many areas of Japan there is a clear feeling of oneness with a well-defined
group of kinsmen, this is not typical of Matsunagi.[4] Matsunagi people speak of "relatives"
but never as if this were a group with definite limits. Kin ties bind together some co-
resident households and other widely scattered households. Many, if not most, of the latter are linked through individuals, for example, those brought into one's own household
through marriage or adoption. These constitute the kindred.[5] Such relatives, however far
the concept is extended, may all be called shinseki.[6]

An important reason for tracing actual kinship is to provide outside links, within or
beyond the mura limits, since in the buraku relatives and non-relatives are often so am-
biguously merged that it is difficult to distinguish them. Much of the outside world as the
buraku know it is organized in terms of a circle of kin. One rarely leaves the buraku for
more than the daylight hours unless he has a relative to accommodate him at his destination. When there is a performance by a traveling theatrical troupe or a performance of
the kagura in another buraku within walking distance, a Matsunagi man may want to attend
very badly, but unless he has relatives among the group of households sponsoring the entertainment, it would be a breach of good manners to go. When a householder is looking
for a wife for his son, he may request relatives in other buraku to look around for him.
Usually, though, there is very little intercourse with outside relatives except at holidays
or when one has some business. During such holidays as the Bon festival and New Year's
as well as times of non-cyclic family celebrations, visits are exchanged with the more intimate outside kinsmen almost as commonly as with other relatives living right in the

buraku. Whenever possible, some working adult may be spared to help an outside relative harvest his i reed crop or pick his tea bushes, occasions which place brief but heavy burdens upon a household's manpower; but there is not a great deal of this exchange, chiefly because of the physical difficulty of commuting.

In relationships outside the buraku, in fact, consanguinity and affinity come into their own as a network supporting many of the vital external contacts on which the economic welfare of the community depends. Emigrant relatives, often widely scattered through Chugoku, may enable a householder to have extensive connections that can be used in buying and selling.

But the greater part of this outside network is a result of buraku exogamy. Though it is optional, there are recognized advantages in choosing a mate from some place other than one's own buraku. Often there is no one of suitable age or background locally at the time a household wants to arrange marriage for one of its children. Of 113 marriages[7] of lineal heirs ranging from early Meiji to the present, only a little over 10 percent were contracted within the buraku. Until the second decade of this century, most marriage connections were with households no further away than the limits of the oaza of Matsunagi, primarily the southeastern buraku of the mura. But more recently there has been an increase in number of ties with the other oaza, Tarumi and Tsuchihashi.[8] Not much change is noticeable in marriage outside the mura, except that since 1920 there has been a drift toward alliances with places beyond the general Atetsu area, even well away from this prefecture. Most distant out-marriages are of men who go away to towns to work and settle. As far back as there is record, marriage relations with the three mura immediately to the east of Kusama, Toyonaga, Nakatsui and Nakai, have been particularly attractive, for the economy and physiography of these areas are similar to those of Kusama. In recent times, the marriage area has come to include nearly all the other mura on the peripheries of Kusama, whether in Atetsu or not.[9]

External Commercial Relations

Like those of kinship, the relations of trade radiating out from the buraku have no fixed terminus, but roughly the scene of most of these contacts can be defined by the boundaries of the western villages of Okayama prefecture.[10] These ties are directly instrumental in sustaining life and keeping the people appraised of this limited world, as well as of others so distant that the provincial mind barely conceives of their existence.

An informal sort of trade between the people and itinerant merchants who regularly or occasionally visit the buraku is presumably quite old here. Every morning a few peddlers leave the up-train at Ikura, dispersing into the back country on either side of the river to peddle their wares, or, equally important, to buy up the local produce for town or city markets. On very many days out of the year, Matsunagi is visited by one or more of these, who come along the narrow footpaths from buraku to buraku, some calling at every house they pass, others dropping in only where they have established contact and are well known. In the warmer seasons and during slack periods between harvests, a farmer often takes to the trading circuit with a few things to sell, perhaps clothing, which is a readily salable item in this upland.

The casual peddler has few contacts in the buraku he visits; often he is a total stranger. He carries his goods in a large bundle-kerchief (furoshiki) on his back, spreading them out for display on the floor of a kitchen or in a dooryard, wherever there is room and someone will spare him a moment. Many peddlers give their full time to this work, usually specializing in a particular line of goods and limiting their trade to familiar households only; such a relationship is called togui. For example, a resident of a nearby buraku

deals in cosmetics only; he makes the rounds of a definite area, comprising the buraku of
Kusama and of adjacent Toyonaga which are within a day's walking distance of his home.
But he excludes his own buraku from this circuit because no one cares to deal on a commercial basis with neighbors. It may be that a peddler comes from farther away, even as
far as Okayama, returning to the city at dusk, or when he has sold his wares or obtained
a full pack of local produce. No large bulk of goods can be handled by such traders, but
they can turn a quick profit by buying up the first of each crop and rushing it to urban
markets for the highest prices.

TABLE 5

IMPORTANT SHOPPING CENTERS AND THEIR
PRINCIPAL GOODS AND SERVICES

Place	Principal Goods and Services
NIIMI.............	Books and magazines, cloth, clothing, dental services, dishes, dry-cleaning, electrical supplies, liquid fuel, higher education, hardware, manufactured footgear, meat, movies, pastry, photography, radios and radio repair, reed mats, specialist doctors and clinics, stationery supplies, toys
ISHIGA	General metal-working
KADOMATSU.......	Heavy wrapping paper, paper for house panels
YUKAWA	General medical care and hospitalization, grain milling, machinery repair, rice liquor, salt and brine
OBARA............	Candy and chewing gum, cattle market, fish, fried bean-curd, fruit, grain milling, rubber work shoes, rationed staples, rice paper, soap, soy sauce, seamstress, trepang, tooth powder, veterinary services
HOMMURA.........	Basic education, chemical fertilizers, farm implements, haircuts, insecticides, postal service, rape-seed pressing, rubber work shoes, seeds, sugar, telegraph, telephone, theatrical entertainment, truck cartage.
IKURA	Beauty care and hairdressing, rail transportation
TANIAI...........	Newspapers
TAKAHASHI	Farm machines, books and magazines, cloth, clothing, dental service, furniture, higher education, manufactured footgear, meat, optical service, photography, reed mats, sewing machines, specialist doctors, stationery supplies
KURASHIKI	General market for farm produce
TAMASHIMA.......	Ship transportation to Shikoku
OKAYAMA.........	Advanced medical care, agricultural exhibitions, cloth, clothing (particularly expensive items for girl's trousseau), farm machinery, furniture, movies, theatricals, various sorts of expositions

These peddlers come to Matsunagi from the interior zone, from the direction of Yuka-wa, from the upland heart of the mura, and from places along the Takahashi drainage from Niimi to the Inland Sea. Peddlers selling articles with a high demand such as cheap cloth-ing and, in summer, the ice-stick confection called "ice-candy," are less numerous than those who appear regularly. In Matsunagi, too, part-time peddling regularly supplements the income of three households and several more have engaged in it at one time or an-other. In a few exceptional cases, regional wares, including baskets from the Sanindo and patent medicines from the Nara area, are brought to Matsunagi by people from these re-gions.

Those who come to buy the buraku's products often operate through an involved system of interdependencies, whereby one group of itinerant merchants does nothing but ride back and forth between the coastal plain and Niimi selling such things as candy to other peddlers on the train. These in turn use such goods to sell or barter in the countryside.

During the first few years after the war, a constant stream of people appeared in buraku dooryards wanting to buy or barter in the black market for controlled or rationed goods. Without exception, it seems, the householders accepted this sort of trade and many were able to reap large profits from the demand for their farm products. Vegeta-bles of all sorts, even staples of the mugi group, soybeans, rape-seed oil, in fact almost all things grown could be sold to these city people, who had little food of their own. Black market selling of tobacco which had been withheld from delivery to the government's trad-ing agency brought in a great deal of cash. After 1949, people say, this trade became in-significant. In some other things, however, there is still a steady commerce, for exam-ple, rationed sugar. More often today, buraku people are buyers rather than sellers of black market goods, particularly of liquid fuel and rice. Matsunagi folk are not able to satisfy their needs in rice within the buraku, so they must make the trip, usually under cover of darkness, to some nearby rice-growing place such as Yukawa or the low-lying mura to the north or southeast, where there are surpluses. The importance of black mar-ket dealing to the buraku economy is that it provided a large cash surplus, more than enough to supply wants in clothing and other manufactured items. This surplus has been used to buy new machines and related farm equipment as well as to erect a variety of new buildings. The decline of the black market in the past two or three years has been accom-panied by a slight drop in real income, a factor that contributes to the people's uneasiness over the future.

When supplies were low, farm products could be sold in driblets at high prices, but now that the economic advantages of the farmer have disappeared, most goods must be traded in bulk or even in cooperation with other households to a professional wholesaler. Cash crops such as konnyaku recently have been sold jointly through private arrangement with a dealer by the group of producers. When only one or two households grow important quantities of a cash crop, the producer arranges to sell his crop to a dealer independently. Most cash crops can be and often are sold through the Agricultural Cooperative, one of whose major functions is to mediate for its members in trading their produce. Chili pep-pers, for instance, are disposed of in this way, and so is rape seed. Crops that are still subject to controls must be sold through the cooperative, which acts as a semi-official agent of government. Though rice is unwillingly surrendered, mugi is readily, and even gladly, sold at the government price because a farmer generally has so much more than his household needs. Tobacco must be sold at official, regulated markets and cattle are preferably sold in this way, too.

Nearly all transactions involving local products take place in the precincts of the buraku, or no farther away than the mura boundaries. With lumber, cork bark, or any other forest product, the sale is consummated in the owner's house. A local man then removes them from the forest and brings the materials as far as the edge of the buraku, where the jobber's truck comes to take them away. Farmers never attempt to sell what they grow directly to consumers, except occasionally as a favor to a neighbor or relative; it is always done through an intermediate agent.

Buraku people resort more to barter than to money exchange among themselves, giving assistance, for instance, at the harvest for a fuel wood supply, or exchanging a day's work in the fields for a new pair of wooden buckets. Such barter is casually arranged without benefit of a third party and is very much like gift-giving, a needed article offered and a response on which neither side drives a hard bargain. Though in Matsunagi only a few households with otherwise unproductive oldsters make enough to sell, things made by local hand industry, such as straw mats, sandals, or packsacks, if sold at all, generally go directly to consumers residing nearby.

To obtain these manufactured and processed goods which have become so necessary to life today, the average household cannot rely solely on itinerant peddlers, for their coming is never certain and their wares rarely provide a wide selection. Things of daily need, such as soy sauce, trepang for seasoning, soap and matches, cannot normally be procured from peddlers, who carry a special rather than a general line of goods. A ten-minute walk from Matsunagi, however, brings one to any of the four general stores of Obara. These stores and others in Yukawa and Hommura define the most intensive zone of external contact; the professional services of the veterinaries, the seamstresses, the post-office, the schools, the doctor and his clinic in these same buraku help to substantiate this definition. These places are visited more frequently than any commercial centers of the whole trading area.

The main trading towns, Niimi and Takahashi, which demarcate the next wider zone of contact, are considered even more important; they offer a truly varied series of goods and services, from fountain pens to dynamite, from the latest motion picture to a tooth extraction. Between these towns and beyond them to the south, in the cities of Kurashiki and Okayama, are other merchant establishments where buraku people buy less often. But, when they do, their purchases are unusual and important; for example, a centrifugal pump at Ishiga or a pair of leather shoes in Okayama. Actually, though, shopping is by no means restricted solely to the places shown in the accompanying illustration (see Map V).

Most shopping in a place close at hand such as Obara is done by an adult male or the half-grown children of the household; women are generally too busy. One does not undertake an excursion to the trading town casually, for the trip there and back takes about four hours. Men make these jaunts only on business; yet there is no harm done, some feel, in enjoying a small pleasure, probably a movie or a drink or two of sake after the main mission is accomplished.

Travel and Vocational Relations with the Outside

The primary area of travel is very much the same as that circumscribing trade relations. Apart from brief sallies on business, people are moved to travel for pleasure, for piety and worship, or for education and work. A genuine journey means at least one night away from home. Normally, one does not travel about in the uplands of Atetsu unless he can stay with relatives. But as distances increase, relatives are fewer, so that travel becomes more expensive and therefore less frequent. Fortunate is the household with a second son or a daughter living in Okayama; their visits to the city are naturally frequent.

The metropolis, Okayama, is a magnet that attracts all, but only a few reach it on more than a handful of occasions in a lifetime. The leisure period of the spring offers the best opportunity to get there, and around this season the city beckons most enticingly

MAP V

THE TRADING AREA OF MATSUNAGI*

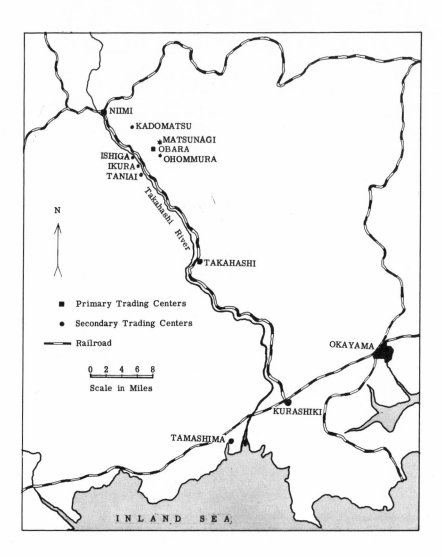

*The commercial importance to Matsunagi of each place on this map is shown in Table 5.

with exhibitions of farm equipment, fairs for children in the great public park, and new goods for spring in the department store. A farmer is lucky to get there once a year. His mother may very well never have gone, and his wife only once or twice. Family groups do not often travel together, but women can and do make trips to famous shrines or temples, to the homes of relatives, or even to town with a neighbor to see a movie.

The country folk prefer to see places important in Japanese history, particularly the shrines and temples of Chugoku and Shikoku, the most popular of which is the great Inari shrine at Takamatsu in the coastal plain. The shrine of Kompira in Shikoku and the Grand Shrine of Izumo on the Sea of Japan coast[11] are known only slightly less well. Most often the religious aspects of such journeys are only nominal and perfunctory.

Extended sojourns away from the buraku to attend school and for employment result in more familiarity with the outside than is possible on short trips. Young people have for many years gone out to the towns or cities to work for wages, in shipyards on the Inland Sea, in textile mills in the coastal plain, as apprentices to learn a trade in town; before the war more worked outside than now. They tend to go at least as far away as the coastal lowlands, where factory jobs are numerous, rather than commute to work at such local industries as limestone quarries in Ikura or a cement plant near Niimi. Students live away from home while attending advanced schools in Takahashi, Niimi, Okayama, or even Tokyo. Those who spend a few years outside return to the buraku with a much wider range of interests and far more worldliness than the stay-at-homes. For most individuals the first important experience of the outside is an excursion made upon graduation from school, but it was the wartime that exposed the young men to the greatest broadening influences any generation had ever known. In this generation no fewer than twenty men served in the armed forces and all but a few were sent abroad, as far as China, the Philippines, and Borneo.[12]

Communication with the Outside

Various means of communication keep the buraku resident informed about the outside world, even when he does not venture beyond the confines of his mura. He reads a daily newspaper if he has time.[13] But, except for young adults, few farmers are disposed even to this much regular reading. Today only thirteen households receive daily newspapers, a substantial decline from the wartime peak. In the past three years, several households have given up their subscriptions because newspapers began arriving a day late. Many have turned to radio as their only means of getting outside news. Actually, most households have owned radios only since the war period.

The younger men and the better educated young women are no less well informed than the average resident of a town such as Takahashi or Niimi, though perhaps they do not measure up to the standards of the city. Still, these young people are a relatively small group out of the population of the buraku. This population, though unquestionably aware of the outside world, still has a narrow range of information and interests. The people are interested in national economic affairs as they affect the buraku, and in war or unrest in the Far East, e.g., the Korean conflict, for its probable consequences for themselves as Japanese. The young, who are reasonably literate, may turn to novels for amusement while alone tending the electric grain mill or in a free moment just before bedtime, but the average person has little experience with books. Except for one household of high educational standing with a large private library, few own any books.

Finally, the means of private communication also serve to keep the people informed of the outside. Although the buraku has had postal service since early Meiji, Kusama had no post-office of its own until 1945. Of late, telegraphic, and especially telephonic, services

have been used increasingly.[14] But the average household has occasion to send or receive a telegram only to bear news of the death of a close relative. Because sharing
scarce facilities is a necessary courtesy, any local telephone is tacitly recognized to be a
public telephone. The average daily mail delivery to the entire buraku is less than twenty
pieces, largely postcards. Outgoing mail is even less voluminous. The more prominent
households receive more mail because, in addition to their numerous magazines, they receive a large amount of mail originating outside the mura. But, unless there is some
specific business, people rarely bother to write.

Buraku Traditionalism Faced by the Modern World

Far-ranging affairs of politics and commerce often serve to unite the community in
common activities, such as electing its own candidate or getting a good price for its crop
of konnyaku. But most external relations, like internal ones, involve households instead of
larger units; for instance, outside kin relations are viewed as ties between households, and
so the external network of kin, consanguineal and affinal, supports the activities of all
members of a household, not just one individual through whom the connection is joined.
Buying and selling, too, are conducted primarily by household units, and it is usually in
the interest of his household that one leaves the buraku for longer periods to take advanced
education or a factory job, both of which bolster the household's community standing and
economic stability.

It is difficult to deduce from available evidence how long contacts with the outside have
been as plentiful as they are now; very probably there was a spectacular rise soon after
the railroad and motor roads penetrated Kusama some twenty-five years ago. The simple
trading system of the peddler, for instance, is undoubtedly much older than that, but its
impact was never great enough to impair the folk quality of buraku life. On the whole, the
impression is strong that the absorption of elements from the cultural milieu, though it has
effected considerable tangible change in the technological and economic areas of the culture
and has weakened most buraku unifiers, has left largely intact the underlying traditional
social features.

Notes

1. A. L. Kroeber, Anthropology (New York, 1948), pp. 281, 282.

2. Before the postwar political reforms, the mayor was named from the ranks of these
   councillors by a vote of their group; only the councillors themselves were directly
   elected by the people.

3. The candidate is limited by law in the amount of money he may spend on the campaign,
   but there apparently is no limitation on contributions in kind.

4. In Chugoku, the common term for a finite group of kin is kabu-uchi; this word is applied to groups of relatives linked through lineal and collateral descendants of a central lineage. Such groups are most often resident in one community rather than scattered in several. Japanese sociologists call this social group of kin, dozoku, and this
   is understood more specifically to consist of one or more branch households issuing
   from a stem (central lineage) household. Cf. Yanagida, op. cit., p. 190, and Minzokugaku Jiten, pp. 399-400, wherein these points are substantiated.

5. "Kindred" here, in conformity with Murdock's exposition (op. cit., pp. 45-46) refers
   to a bilateral group of kin.

6. There are other regional terms to designate kinsmen used, all of which seem to be approximately synonymous. As we use it, shinseki is a broader term than shinrui, which implies only kinship by co-residence (see Chap. IV, pp. 180-181).

7. The smallness of the sample and general incompleteness of the older data does not permit a more detailed statement of change in spatial distribution of marriage ties.

8. Similarly, Izumi has found a pattern shift away from local endogamy on the buraku, oaza, and mura levels between 1890 and 1949, in his village study made in Nara prefecture, in the heart of the peninsula east of Osaka. See S. Izumi, Aru Sanson no Monogurafu (Monograph on a Mountain Village) (Tokyo, 1951), p. 44.

9. Probably the earliest marriage ties outside the general Kusama area were with places along the Takahashi river as far as Tamashima on the Inland Sea; in the current generation, the wife of one buraku resident is a native of Kagoshima in the far southwest of Japan.

10. The coincidence of this trade area with the old province of Bitchu is amazingly close.

11. The Takamatsu shrine is dedicated to the deity of rice, Inari, being especially popular with the rice farmers in the plain about it. Kompira shrine was founded by a Buddhist teacher, but after the separation of Buddhism from State Shinto in Meiji times, it remained a Shinto sanctuary. The Izumo shrine is the cult center of a pantheon of national deities, which seems to be deeply tinged with Korean influences. In national importance it is second only to the shrine of the Sun Goddess, Amaterasu, at Ise.

12. In the oldest generation, the most traveled person is an old man who went as far as China and the Philippines in his youth. Among the younger men, one boasts the fabulous experience of spending a year at Tashkent in Russia as a prisoner-of-war before being repatriated.

13. All daily newspapers are published in Okayama, as are most of the weeklies or other periodicals, largely agricultural, that reach the buraku by subscription; the latter, however, are read only by the more educated and progressive farmers. Popular magazines in great variety are also known, but most of these are intended for children and housewives.

14. A telephone was installed in the mura police station as early as 1915, but not until the end of the war was there much expansion of this service. Now the Agricultural Cooperative, the yakuba, and the prefectural Veterinary Station are equipped with their own phones.

At a drinking party the senior men of the buraku are seated in places of honor and bottles of shochu stand before them.

At Bon time these men, carrying fans, dance the traditional Bon steps to the song of the caller, who holds a raised umbrella.

At the Fall Festival young men of the buraku bear their god-palanquin about the courtyard of the oaza shrine.

Chapter VI

HOUSEHOLD PRECEDENCE IN RELATIONS OF KIN,

COMMUNITY, AND INDIVIDUALS

In buraku life, the social aggregate called "household" is the pivotal institution both to the kindred and to the community. The individual reacts to his kindred and to his community through the medium of the household. His immediate world of social relations is organized in patterns of kinship bonds and residence associations. But these two kinds of connections are not always different in form and purpose.

As Murdock has written, kinship is "a structured system of relationships, in which individuals are bound one to another by complex interlocking and ramifying ties. [But] particular kinship bonds, isolated from others, may and often do serve to unite individuals into social groups. . . ."[1] In our buraku descent affiliates an individual with a large circle of kinsmen; this "kindred" is a bilateral descent group, though it has no definite extension, organization, or sense of unity to compare, say, with the exogamous clan of China.[2] Usually, it is useful to maintain relations with outside relatives for a generation or two after a new marriage bond has been established. Connections with collaterals of one's lineage who have gone out to other places to settle are more durable. More distant relatives, linked through these relatives, are recognized, but little is done to activate these relationships. Some of these kinsmen, including maternal grandparents, parental siblings, or spouses of own brothers and sisters, are called "near" relatives. But, again, people are not sure just what degree of relation should be called "near" nor are behavior patterns toward each type of "near" kin clearly differentiated.

What we call "kindred" is a practical synthesis of the kindreds, or circles of kin, of all individuals belonging to the best integrated kin group of buraku society, the unilocal family. Actually, relatively few of the bonds which make up one's kindred aggregation are exclusively of individual to individual. Most ties are observed to be fundamentally between households. Indeed, outside the co-resident family group, the sense of kinship connection is very largely conceived to be a relationship of one's own household to another household or to a group of households. One uses "kinsmen" for all inhabitants of these households, rather than words denoting explicit relationships to the separate individuals.

If there is occasion to refer to an individual of a related household specifically, whether or not the exact relationship is known, a kin term signifying his role in his own household is used. Special factors may produce inconsistencies. A close affinal relative, for instance, a daughter's husband, may be called "uncle" (ojisan) and the daughter "aunt" (obasan), not the usual "husband" (muko) and "daughter" (musume), when there are young children in the household, because adults try to use terms that seem most natural to the young. However, other members of a son-in-law's household are likely to be identified by household-role terms. Although practices are not highly predictable because there are so many optional ways to speak of a kinsman, his association with a household group is usually terminologically recognized in some way. Exact genealogical relationships, when they are traceable, are pretty much matters of academic interest.

Most relationships between households are contracted through the exogamous marriage of an individual. Marriage affiliates household A with household B, and through B perhaps with household C, or even others. But some ties are produced by establishment of new households, either in the buraku or at more distant places. The spatial distance between kinsmen does not govern the "nearness" of the connection, but it does have a practical effect on the fulfillment of kin obligations. Most of the "near" kinsmen, however far away they live, are obligated to participate in events vital to the lineage: the birth ritual for a child, critical anniversaries of a household head, or a funeral. Then, too, if physically possible, there may be exchange of economic assistance between closely related households. Less closely related households may conceivably join in family ceremonial activities, but are unlikely to give direct economic aid. As kinsmen, their assistance chiefly consists of providing lodging when one travels outside the buraku, or in helping to seek a mate for a son or daughter.

Family and household in Matsunagi are much the same social unit. It makes little difference whether we think of kin connections as joining families or households, for a member of a related household who is not one of its family lineage, for example, an apprentice living most of the year with his master, may be indiscriminately classed with the kin. Kinship of the descent type does not account for a large area of buraku social relations popularly conceded to have to do with kinsmen. Kinship by descent forms a proliferating network that extends the attitudes and trappings of kinship beyond the minimal residence group, and is the principal route for liaison of this group in its area of contacts outside the community. But, internally, descent is far less important in holding related groups together than the factor of common residence.

As Kroeber has said of preliterate peoples, "They strongly want close and constant association with their kin."[3] And Titiev adds, there is "ample support for the contention that co-residence may be more essential than consanguinity in the classification of relatives, and it may be readily shown that in numerous primitive societies ties of kinship are actually established by virtue of common residence rather than by common descent."[4] Embree extends this proposition to the Japanese community: "Frequently, the local group of relationships and those of kinship overlap. . . . At any rate, the local group constitutes an important part of the social relations in preliterate and folk communities."[5]

In Matsunagi too, common residence yields, as Murdock says, "standardized relationships like those of kinship . . . which facilitate social intercourse, and many [interpersonal relationships] are aggregated into clusters around common interests, forming groups. . . which help to bind the families of the community to one another."[6] Here, however, this takes the form of associations of households not otherwise related, instead of relationships among particular persons. In fact, it is precisely on the household that kinship and associational relations are focused and where they imperceptibly merge. When they coincide we call the product shinrui (literally: "relatives").

Shinrui (see Chapter IV) ties may be built on some sort of service, characteristically the reciprocal relationship between a go-between and the couple whose marriage he arranges. They most closely resemble those within the descent group, because it is a bond through individuals with another household, which develops at times and in form stipulated by custom. But more important are shinrui connections created by the ever-present necessity of people working and relaxing together when their households exist side by side.

The custom in Matsunagi of calling one's co-residents and neighbors "relatives" is not duplicated in other ethnographic materials from Japan.[7] For instance, Embree does not report this fact for Japan proper, although he does state that among Japanese immigrants to Hawaii, unrelated people from the same place in the mother country (tokorono-mono) act like kinsmen.[8] This supports our conclusion that certain sectors of Japanese kinship may be about the same as extreme neighborliness.

In Matsunagi, neighborhoods are indeterminate clusters of households, which are the focus of most of the patterned social activities of the community. The importance of such groups of neighbors in community life is suggested by the high rate of coincidence of various sorts of kumi aggregations on a limited territorial group of households (See Figure 3, for an illustration of the kumi relations of two typical buraku households). However, the larger the group, the fewer ties any one household has with the rest. But at a threshold size, often smaller but never larger than a goningumi, neighbors usually become so close that they consider themselves shinrui. This is confirmed in the kin-like behavior among households so related. Like households bound by descent ties, no two related households need have identical shinrui connections, since the location of each household puts it with a slightly different set of neighbors. Thus, even though all are in the same neighborhood, households A and B, and B and C, may be shinrui respectively to each other, but households A and C need not be.

Though there is no direct evidence, social relations between buraku households may have changed from a basis of descent kinship to one of common residence. The absence of strong stem-branch groups of households may be attributed to a scarcity of arable land and high population density, which made division of land among branch households difficult. Another factor may have been the expansion of the marriage area, which would make local kinsmen fewer and distant kinsmen less accessible. As transportation facilities developed and industrial cities grew, more buraku people were able to migrate further and further away, so that the generally less prosperous branch households were encouraged to leave the community. The kindred, in becoming more scattered, were less regularly united by ceremonial obligations. Special households, such as those with a record of leprosy or particularly well-to-do ones, however, are inclined to cling more to their circle of kin, even though they all live in other places.[9]

The most characteristic social feature of community co-residence is organized association of households, or kumi.[10] When we come to consider developments among kumi themselves, it appears that associations have been shrinking in size as their functions have dwindled. For example, the passing of many religious functions which used to bring many households together removed the need for large kumi organizations that sponsored them.

Large-scale economic activities by kumi have undergone a similar fate. The fact that the temple parish no longer joins cooperatively to repair community religious structures is to be expected, in view not only of weakened religious feeling but, also, of the deteriorating sense of buraku unity in general. Moreover, in building, it is said, the assistance of whole units such as the buraku or a jokai is requested much less often than formerly. Other instances of householders neglecting prescribed patterns of work assistance, to rely instead on their own manpower, are on the increase. Even the rather recently organized kumi which own threshing machinery are being liquidated by the purchase of private machines. The reciprocity of hospitality and gift-giving is diminished. Thus, reciprocal obligations are minimized because a large framework of reciprocal relations is no longer felt to be economically and socially necessary.

Seemingly it is a paradox that this "weakening of the integration of the buraku," of which Embree, too, writes,[11] should bring no concomitant de-emphasis on close shinrui relations among neighbors. This phenomenon, the author feels, is really a tendency to reduce the scope of community relations, and does not strengthen shinrui relations themselves.

As the size of communal associations has declined, the household unit, by remaining a constant, has come to stand out as the key to buraku social organization. The internal structure of the household, though patterned on family organization, is a residence grouping, in principle the same as any communal association. Whereas community and kumi aggregations have lost ground, the household has surrendered none of its importance at all. Even among reform-minded young people of the community, the household system is considered a necessary part of Japanese society not likely to be replaced.

224

Figure 3

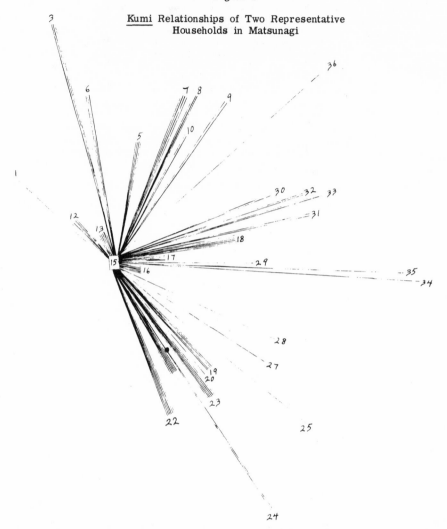

Kumi Relationships of Two Representative
Households in Matsunagi

The diagrams illustrate the intensity of social relationships of two selected households with co-resident buraku households. The selected examples are especially apt because they are long-established and have a full complement of typical community relations, yet they have little in common with each other, primarily because they are situated in quite distinct parts of the buraku. Each line radiating out from the sample household (indicated by a boxed number) represents a kumi relationship with the household to which it extends (shown by key number). The number of these lines, not their length, suggests the relative strength of relationships with the datum household.

Figure 3—Continued

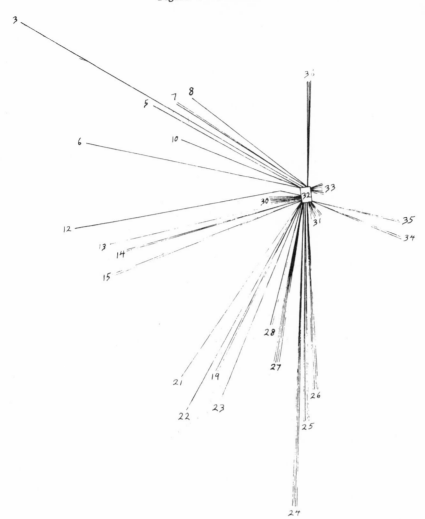

From the evidence in these diagrams it seems reasonable to conclude that there is a clear tendency for a household to have more identifiable ties with its immediate neighbors, than with any other co-residents; and to have more ties with members of the same neighborhood or the same _jokai_ than with those of other parts of the community.

Kinds of _kumi_ relationships are not differentiated in this illustration, but each radiating line stands for a relationship that is more fully defined in Chart 7, Chapter IV. Households are mapped by key number in Figure 1, Chapter IV.

From an economic point of view the household is the principal property-owning organization in the community, in that it controls wealth-creating pieces of land and, at least preferably, owns the tools and machines with which it works this land and processes crops. Though these properties nominally belong to the household head, he is not at liberty to use them contrary to the wishes of the other mature members of his household.

Communal property exists under special conditions where the resources of one household are not great enough to permit development and use, for example, of common pastures and irrigation ponds. But in the end, most communal ownership is only an interim arrangement, which breaks down into private (household) ownership as each of the associated households become financially able to support resources of its own. Communal funds such as jokai monies kept by its treasurer, or temple funds husbanded by its trustees, have no real economic significance at all. Income from something like the sale of timber from temple forests generally is applied to an immediate expense, often a group party.

The existence of a dependable labor force is a major cause of the household's dominant economic position in the community, and supplements the household's control over productive resources in land, tools, machines, and, increasingly of late, money. While to be sure there are numerous other work groupings, none approaches the household in the diversity, constancy, and selflessness of its internal cooperation.

In communal cooperation individual skills call for assignment to certain tasks but most of the work force is pooled, so that older men, and even women, often do about the same jobs as young men. Though one man may appear to be in charge, his position, unlike that of the household head, carries no real authority over his peers. Under ordinary conditions of cooperation, the status of each worker is an example of egalitarianism among households.

To preserve the integrity of a household's property, individual competency in general must be ignored, so that the first son can inherit. But even the extinction of a family lineage need not mean the disappearance of a household; for a new line of owners may replace the old, without changing homestead, buildings, land, or house name.

Income and outgo, whether measured in goods or cash, pertain almost wholly to the household budget. Taxes, too, are levied against the household; even the new income tax is frequently paid collectively by the household head rather than by each breadwinner. The tacit acceptance of this practice by the government especially illustrates the many ways in which the preferential status of the household is officially supported.

To meet routine and extraordinary expenses, each working member of the household is expected to contribute his labor and wages to a common pool and to draw from these funds for his personal needs with the consent of the group. Of course, this duty and privilege are less keenly felt if the individual expects eventually to settle elsewhere or marry out. Since the use of money has expanded, and with it the opportunity for wage-earning, every household desires a wage-earner or two. This means that the interests of the household, more than those of the individual, are served when someone works for pay. Things needed in routine living, including food, clothing, and implements, are paid for collectively, except for personal items such as cigarettes or haircuts. Or again, investments such as life insurance policies, most of which are carried on the young, are registered in the name of the household head and are not intended to endure beyond the insured's connection with the household. Gifts are very largely household gestures, even when the obligation is incurred by one member rather than the entire group.

Inasmuch as every individual is almost wholly dependent for his livelihood on some household, he is obliged to subordinate his personal motives and aspirations to the welfare

of this group during most of his life. Only in childhood and early youth does he have considerable freedom to associate with fellows of his age level as he chooses and to spend
time at his own devices.[12] This freedom disappears when he marries or at least when he
takes up adult responsibilities in his household. Until assuming mature responsibilities,
his interests mostly turn toward other community residents of the same age and sex.

Most formal associations of individuals are of recent vintage and have been instigated
by the state. Though today there are several active local sodalities, such as the children's jiyu happyo-kai, the seinendan, the fujin-kai, and the P.T.A., covering a wide
range of ages, the facts in Matsunagi agree with Embree that "associations not based on
kin and neighborhood groups are not very highly developed in rural Japan."[13]

It seems fair to say that in some of these sodalities, membership is actually a function of the household. For instance, as a rule only one woman at a time participates actively in the fujin-kai, which amounts to being a representative of her household rather
than acting as an individual. Belonging to the P.T.A. is also a household matter, for
only one parent of a household is active in it at one time. And no household allows more
than one of its men at a time to serve in the shobodan. In the cultural background of individual behavior, consequently, the preponderant values are of the group, not the individual.[14] The average person does not sense Benedict's "dilemma of virtue"[15] as between
loyalty to household and to age group.

A number of young men say they would take advantage of higher technical training in
agriculture, in veterinary science, and even in commercial skills if they could. But, for
most of them, higher education seems substantially worthwhile only if it makes them better farmers. For it must be remembered that in Matsunagi the basic objectives in continuing education are those of the household. Although nowadays young people are particularly interested in going on to higher schools, they can resign themselves to a minimum
of schooling without more than passing regret. Still, it is in youth especially that conflicts may arise between the hopes of the individual and the purposes of his household.
The selection of a mate is one such instance. A modern young person may resist the decision of his household to marry, but in the end hardly anyone fails to conform. Today,
the conflict at these critical points of life is probably greater than before, though not
strong enough to disrupt the accustomed balance of values.

What the future holds in this potential struggle between the motivations of the household and the individual is not clear, though something of the individualism of Western culture has indeed been emerging in buraku life since the war. Despite the fact that buraku
people insist on the need for the "household system" in their society, Westernization and
its consequent economic changes cannot but make some difference in the individual's feeling of duty to his household group. But at the present time in the relations of kinship, of
community, and of individuals per se, the household is the key to understanding how these
major social factors fit together dynamically. In a word, this is common ground for all
three.

Notes

1. Murdock, op. cit., p. 92.

2. Cf. Hsien-chu Hu, The Common Descent Group in China and Its Functions (Viking
   Fund Publications in Anthropology, No. 10) (New York, 1948).

3. Kroeber, op. cit., p. 353.

4. M. Titiev, "The Influence of Common Residence on the Unilateral Classification of Kindred," American Anthropologist, XLV (1943), 515.

5. Embree, "New and Local Kin Groups Among the Japanese Farmers of Kona, Hawaii," ibid., XLI (1939), 400.

6. Murdock, op. cit., p. 82.

7. The author has been unable to find any material in either Japanese or English to verify a wide distribution of this particular phenomenon in Japan. But there is at least one interestingly close parallel in T. Furushima, Sanson no Kozo (The Organization of a Mountain Village) (Tokyo, 1949), pp. 181-182. He reports, of a buraku on the slope of Mt. Fuji near Tokyo, a group of three neighbors, each two households being called ichirinka by the third. Functionally, people who acknowledge each other as ichirinka join to support one political candidate, help each other at weddings, and exchange formal calls (like relatives) at Bon and New Year. Ichirinka are the closest local ties one has and have the same standing as stem or branch houses, or local affinal relatives.

8. He says, "They are closer than kumi [buraku] people, just as relatives are closer than buraku people [in Japan]. The closer to one's home village a man lived, the closer friend he is and a man from the same village is practically a brother." Acculturation Among the Japanese of Kona, Hawaii (Menasha, Wis., 1941), p. 102.

9. Embree remarks on this too: "Rich men tend to become isolated from the buraku and to lose some of the social values accruing from democratic co-operation and exchange in the things of everyday life." Suye Mura, pp. 307-308.

10. Embree seems to agree but presents this in terms of "neighborhood cooperation." Acculturation . . . of Kona, Hawaii, p. 88.

11. Ibid., p. 308.

12. The author must disagree with Embree's assertion that the "same-age" tie is a relationship that remains strong throughout life. Op. cit., p. 190.

13. Acculturation . . . of Kona, Hawaii, p. 88.

14. As Beardsley has written, "The Japanese villagers emphasize the household over the individual, the consanguine over the conjugal family, and ascribed status over achieved status." R. K. Beardsley, "The Household in the Status System of Japanese Villages," Center for Japanese Studies, Occasional Papers, No. 1 (1951), p. 70.

15. See R. Benedict, The Chrysanthemum and the Sword (Boston, 1946), Chapter 10.

Chapter VII

SUMMARY AND CONCLUSIONS

This study focuses on a single Japanese socio-cultural entity—the community of Matsunagi—and examines it by means of objective description and empirical analysis. To orient the reader in some practical way to the Japanese context, Matsunagi is described as a "mountain community," in contrast to the other conventional classifications of communities, which are "farming" and "fishing."[1] With enough comparative material, it would be possible to specify more precisely the position of Matsunagi in this frame of reference. But even were it possible to draw clean distinctions between these three categories, there would still be the recognized qualification that this division is based primarily on economic factors. In addition to the economic factors used as criteria for this frame of reference, the researcher would likely have to deal with a residue of data requiring his own judgment to reach a conclusive evaluation.

Locale is another criterion for classifying the community. Matsunagi is in the Chugoku region and its cultural sub-areas of Bitchu and Izumo. In particular, the imprint of this regional setting is apparent in material things like tools, carrying baskets, and the simple folk machines of the farm. But such material things are tenuous evidence for assuming a whole regional configuration, since so little is known of their total distributions and their origins. A somewhat better systematized basis is religious tradition and lore; a large number of god-cults, including that of Matsunagi's own tutelary deity, are oriented to regional gods in one or another of their variant forms. Many of these are derived from the mythological tradition of the Izumo district. Another strong link with Izumo is the popular kagura drama, which depicts the legendary founding of the Izumo pantheon. However, these are but isolated elements of tradition, unintegrated to an accepted whole pattern. Cultural regionalism in Matsunagi is probably of more than incidental importance, but its proper interpretation must await much more field research. A more definitive cultural classification of Matsunagi is difficult because of the scarcity of comparative knowledge.

In what way does Matsunagi merit the name "community"? Why not use some social aggregate other than the buraku in a community study? Several lines of evidence support the choice made here. The buraku has physical unity; it is the largest social entity with dwellings nucleated enough to permit constant face-to-face contacts. It also has some legal standing as a unit. But what is most important is that it is the maximum group with such physical cohesion that also is characterized by great social solidarity.[2] Matsunagi is one of the several "natural" communities of a similar order, in terms of size, which comprise Kusama village.[3] Moreover, it has greater psychological unity, a more firmly entrenched esprit de corps, than any other unit of comparable size. Though we lack the historical perspective we have for larger areas (Okayama, Bitchu, Atetsu, or even Kusama, named in descending order of size), even our meager store of lore and inferential data from the past permit us to establish that the buraku, in much its present form, is mature and durable.

Social organization has received the bulk of attention in this study. The results have implications that ultimately go beyond the range of mountain communities to the main arena of Japanese society. The method of analysis applied is structural; it reveals that Matsunagi people not only are organized as a community but also form smaller, less generalized aggregates, varying in relative importance. This analytic method also penetrates the web of social relations to clarify the functions of such units with respect to each other and to the whole social structure.

229

This point, made repeatedly, should be grasped as perhaps the most salient feature of buraku social organization: groups, of various sizes, are the basic components of society. In contrast, individuals are not very important. Of these groups, the largest is the community whole; intermediate groups are numerous and varied, consisting both of community co-residents and kinsmen; and smallest is the household, which is the constituent unit of all the others.

Simply stated, the community social structure is shaped by two opposed tendencies, consolidation and division. The factors working toward consolidation are mainly religious, psychological, and political. The psychological factors have no direct expression in social structure, but one of them, the sense of being a "native son," is indirectly related to the cult of the tutelary god. Besides acting as a unit for the activities of this religious cult group, the community also comprises a Buddhist temple parish. Though political solidarity of the buraku has been reduced by a division into two jokai, still, these administrative units have socially and politically unifying functions, e.g., the giving of funeral assistance, and so each acts as a consolidating factor. Only sodalities of individuals, among social groups, cut across the society and are defined by age levels; their consolidating effect, however, is felt almost solely among the young and immature.

Second are factors of division which stem from groups of intermediate size and influence, such as goningumi (of a political nature) and voluntary kumi of households, ranging in size from a jokai group down to two or three participants. Kumi serve many special social and economic purposes, each group bringing into cooperation a restricted segment of buraku society, typically having contiguous residence; moreover, the different types of kumi are interlocking and highly coextensive, both among themselves and with goningumi too.

In this conflict of forces, the divisive factors tend to override the buraku unifiers. Therefore, community life tends to break down into neighborhood units. A neighborhood may be a physical cluster of homesteads, but always and necessarily it is a focus of social relations and lacks the definite boundaries that are characteristic of such groups as kumi and goningumi which help to define it.

In kinship, individual relationships have yielded to ties between household groups, so that it is proper to consider all members of one group related, in much the same generalized way, to all of another group. Kin relationships may also take the form of smaller and less stable foci of social relations than neighborhoods. The clear development of such kin groups in Matsunagi presents a phenomenon of social organization that has not been explicitly recognized or interpreted in previous field reports.

Such kin relations are called shinrui. They usually bind together a group of households which is circumscribed from the point of view of only one of them; as a rule, no two shinrui share exactly the same set of "relatives," though sets do overlap. The close relations of neighbors are conducive to the establishment of kin ties between households; certain kinds of gratuitous services, most often that of a marriage go-between, lead to such kinship, too. Finally, these ties fit the concept of kinship not only because such kinsmen are intimate and call each other "relative" but, in ritual and practical affairs, their behavior is essentially the same as between blood kin.

The elemental unit in Matsunagi is the household. It is the key social unit because in all social relations, extending to the buraku limits, the participants are households, and because individual relations lack a pattern except in connection with the household. Because it is the focal residence unit, the household achieves the greatest solidarity of any local group. Internally, as we have described this unit, it is a structure of complementary roles, each ascribed to one or more household residents. Though based on family ties and on descent lineage, its role relations are those of person to group instead of the familial ones of person to person. The reality of this concept of "household role" is demonstrated in the fact that resident members of the family, or even outsiders such as a distant blood kinsman or an unrelated craft apprentice, are generally assigned or reassigned roles in keeping with age and sex. Sometimes role allocation may ignore age to make the role structure appear more consistent to the children.

The foregoing evidence justifies two major conclusions:

1. The household is the primary unit of buraku social structure; furthermore, the usual participant in social life is the household group, for which the household head or some other member merely acts. In contrast, aggregations of individuals as such, i.e., sodalities, which are mostly created at government insistence, are weak except at young age levels when the individual is not yet fully incorporated into vital household functions. In belonging to sodalities, mature individuals in effect often represent their households. Except in relation to his household, the individual has no community standing. Even his kin relations comprise connections with a synthetic body of kindred, the sum of the personal kindreds of all members of the household. On the other hand, the family lacks the concreteness of the household in relation to community organization. It is more a pattern of social relations than a real social group.

2. Social relations in Matsunagi have a strong residence emphasis; descent is of secondary importance.[4] The household unit, as defined by its role construct, is based on residence. In the larger arena of social life, kumi are characteristically composed of contiguous households, and, regardless of function, tend to be coextensive, thus reinforcing territorial unity with social solidarity. Community social life is most intense in neighborhood foci, which in general are defined by the overlay of both political and voluntary associations. Sometimes associations are so concentrated that people seem unable to distinguish between them in the same neighborhood matrix.

Residence is particularly decisive in the case of in-buraku kin relations. Local groups of blood kin, i.e., a stem household with its offspring branch households, are few and weak, and buraku exogamy reduces local affinities to a minimum. Therefore, residence-oriented shinrui connections are most representative of local kinship. Even when a shinrui tie originates in a gratuitous benefaction, the benefactor, though he may not be a near neighbor as are other shinrui, is invariably a resident of the same community. Ties with such benefactors, however, are fewer and less generally useful than with close neighbors. As for descent relationships, their principal theater is the world external to the buraku. But both externally and internally, kinship is still a dominant factor in social relations. In Matsunagi, the importance of residence in forming kin relations suggests that residence may be a far more vital characteristic of Japanese society than anyone, even the Japanese themselves, have imagined.

Notes

1. For instance, Minzokugaku Jiten observes that ". . . to say mountain community ⌈sanson⌉ means, on the one hand, a community where people are engaged in hunting, forestry, and the production of firewood and charcoal, as well as in the cultivation of mountain field crops. On the other hand, it means an agricultural community which is qualified merely by its mountain location. However, in its agriculture certain mountain peculiarities, such as fire-field cultivation, can be recognized, and on a number of points special adjustments to the mountain terrain can be observed." Yanagida, op. cit., pp. 244-245. The reader is also referred to Embree, Suye Mura, as an illustration in · English of the "farming" way of life, and to E. Norbeck, Takashima, a Japanese Fishing Community (Salt Lake City, 1954), which exemplifies the "fishing" form of community.

2. Cf. the following definition: "The term 'community' connotes the maximal group of persons who normally reside together in face-to-face association."   Murdock and others, <u>Outline</u> <u>of</u> <u>Cultural</u> <u>Materials</u> (New Haven, 1950), p. 93.

3. The expression "natural community" (<u>shizen mura</u>) is used by Izumi in reference to a considerably larger social unit, but which he says is called <u>buraku</u>, in Nara prefecture. He describes it as having a long historical integrity and a former (feudal) political function, and it is the locus of most of the life activities of its residents.   Whereas the word "natural" may fit this larger and more dispersed grouping in Nara, in Kusama the term seems to be more suitable for a close-knit <u>buraku</u> such as Matsunagi.   See Izumi, <u>op</u>. <u>cit</u>., pp. 52-53.

4. A scheme of community classification that has some popularity among Japanese sociologists places all Japanese community societies along an axis between two extreme forms.   These extremes are the completely descent-organized society and the completely egalitarian communal (co-residence-organized) society.   Professor Fukutake, of Tokyo University, ascribes the former to communities of the harsh, marginal northern part of Honshu and the latter to the southwestern part of the island, which includes the Chugoku region.   See T. Fukutake, <u>Nihon</u> <u>Noson</u> no <u>Shakaiteki</u> Seikaku (The Social Characteristics of Japanese Farming Villages) (Tokyo, 1949), pp. 34-48; 69-115.